AUSTRIAN ECONOMICS: HISTORICAL AND PHILOSOPHICAL BACKGROUND

AUSTRIAN ECONOMICS

HISTORICAL AND PHILOSOPHICAL BACKGROUND

Edited by WOLFGANG GRASSL and BARRY SMITH

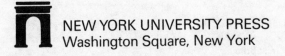
NEW YORK UNIVERSITY PRESS
Washington Square, New York

Published 1986 in the U.S.A. by NEW YORK UNIVERSITY PRESS

Washington Square, New York, N.Y. 10003

Library of Congress Cataloging-in-Publication Data
Main entry under title:

Austrian economics.
Includes bibliographies.
1. Austrian school of economists — Addresses, essays, lectures. 1. Grassl, Wolfgang.   II. Smith, Barry, Ph.D.
HB98.A97 1986   330.15'7   85-31054
ISBN 0-8147-3007-8

Printed and bound in Great Britain

CONTENTS

PREFACE: AUSTRIAN ECONOMICS FROM MENGER TO HAYEK

Barry Smith

The Austrian school of economics has its beginnings in the publication, in 1871, of Carl Menger's *Principles of Economics,* a brilliant demonstration of the possibility of an economics which would be at one and the same time truly theoretical ('exact') and also subjectivist. Thus the laws of the theory, laws of economic action and of economic value, are in every case related by Menger to individual utility, individual perception and individual decision in such a way as to embrace the recognition that all social phenomena are the result of human activity, all value the result of individual preference. An economy is not, from this subjectivist point of view, an autonomous formation with unintelligible properties of its own (it is not, for example, the circular flow that one finds represented in the standard textbooks). Rather, one can *understand* the workings of an economy. One can see, for example, how the value of goods at earlier stages in the productive process is in every case derived from the value to actual consumers of the products of the later stages.

The phrase 'Austrian school' was at first employed as a term of denigration by opponents of Menger's ideas, above all by the members of the German historical school. For in contrast to its more developed neighbours to the west, Austria at that time could look back on almost no important theoretical or scientific achievements of her own. Moreover, Austrian intellectual life was still permeated by an underlying philosophy of Aristotelianism and scholastic realism, a philosophy which must have seemed, from the perspective of a forward-looking and enlightened Germany, with its Kant and its Hegel, merely quaint and old-fashioned. Paradoxically, however, it was at least in part this Aristotelian background which enabled Menger to make theoretical advances of a sort which were ruled out by the narrow inductivism of his German contemporaries. For Aristotle had insisted that there are qualities, for example, of action or knowledge or of more complex social phenomena, which are knowable a priori. Such phenomena thereby satisfy laws which do not stand in need of being inductively established. Menger was thus drawn to seek out such laws in the economic sphere, setting in train a tradition of research which can now be seen to have contributed much to our understanding both of the nature of the economic sphere and of the limits of economic theory.

The first-generation members of the Austrian school, Böhm-Bawerk and Wieser, were both, like Menger, professors of economics in Vienna, the latter in particular carrying forward Aristotelian ideas of the sort utilised earlier by Menger. Austrian economics then took part in that renaissance of intellectual and cultural life which is so characteristic of *fin-de-siècle* Austria. One can point, for example, to the names of Schumpeter, Mises, Mayer, Schönfeld-Illy, Rosenstein-Rodan, as well as to Austro-Marxists such as Hilferding and Otto Bauer who were also influenced by the thinking of Menger. It was above all, however, the circle of thinkers around Ludwig von Mises who did most to establish the characteristic methods and insights of the Austrian school — particularly in relation to the now increasingly influential Austrian theory of the trade circle — and to spread the Austrian ideas beyond the borders of Austria herself. Mises' circle included not only economists such as Hayek, Haberler, Machlup and Morgenstern, but also philosophers such as Felix Kaufmann and Alfred Schütz. Its influence is seen, for example, in the work of Lionel Robbins, but also — and more radically — in the philosophically challenging extreme subjectivism of G.L.S. Shackle.

Austrian economics in the present day is represented above all by Friedrich von Hayek, by Ludwig Lachmann, and by Israel Kirzner. Lachmann has perhaps done more than any other thinker within the Austrian tradition to push back the limits of subjectivism, particularly in relation to the role that is played by individual expectations in economic theory. Kirzner, who has developed and refined many of the ideas of Mises and Hayek on the role of knowledge and error in economic action, has shown how it is possible to utilise Misesian ideas on entrepreneurship in a way which has powerful consequences for economic theory in general and for our understanding of competition and the market in particular.

Competition, in the Austrian view, is never 'perfect'. The plans and expectations of distinct market participants are never even approximately in harmony with one another. Yet there are manifest benefits of market competition, benefits of a sort which, as the early Austrians did much to demonstrate, would seem to be incapable of being simulated by, for example, a centrally planned economy. How, then, are such benefits to be understood? Classical economic theory has tackled this problem almost exclusively by examining the properties of the equilibrium state — a state which involves perfect harmony of all participants' plans — and by demonstrating mathematically why this state, for given — fixed — external conditions, is preferable to all others. Thus it has paid little attention to the problem of how the benefits of competition and of the market can be understood under the actually prevailing circumstances of endemic imperfection and of constantly changing external conditions. Austrian economists, in contrast, think not in terms of an ideal *state* of achieved equilibrium but rather in terms of a faltering *process* of always partial movement towards such an ideal state. Kirzner, in particular, has shown how it is the perception of disharmonies or of the mismatchings of plans on the part of individual entrepreneurs that serves as the motor giving rise to a tendency towards relatively greater harmony, and thereby to the realisation of economic opportunities hitherto unexploited. But now the entrepreneur's task, in a view of this sort, is not, as in the classical (Robbinsian) view, one of *calculation*, as if the means and ends of economic activity were already identified and all that remained would be to fit the one to the other in the most rational possible way. The entrepreneur rather *discovers* these very means and ends themselves — or indeed he brings them into being by a process of serendipity.

We said that Menger's recognition of the possibility of an exact or a priori theory in economics has contributed to our understanding both of the economic sphere and of the limits of economic theory. In fact, the consequences of Menger's work extend much further, showing us the way to a more adequate understanding of large-scale social formations in general, both within and without the economic sphere. It is above all Hayek who has done most to show how we can refine and deepen Menger's insights to the point where we can understand — albeit at a level of generality and of theoretical abstractness which rules out prediction and quantification — even the ways in which such social formations may represent the *unintended* consequences of individual actions, that is, the consequences of actions directed towards other, quite disparate, ends. Building on the work of Menger, Hayek has provided a theory of spontaneous orders in society which has implications for our understanding not only of economic formations but also of language, law, religion, politics, morals, and indeed for the subtle inner workings of scientific theory itself.

The present volume is a detailed treatment of the historical and philosophical background of the Menger tradition in nineteenth- and twentieth-century Austria. It puts forward an interrrelated collection of ideas and theories, from both philosophy and economics, in a way which will, it is hoped, contribute to future research both on the

Austrian background of the Austrian school and on the wider interplay between economic value theory on the one hand and general (philosophical) value theory on the other.

At the centre of the volume is the work on value and on philosophical method of the Brentano school, and the volume includes a unique study of the relations between the Austrian theory of values and the new economic approach to human behaviour propounded by Gary Becker and others in Chicago. It also includes considerable bibliographical material on general value theory which it is hoped will be of benefit both to philosophers and to economists with an interest in the field.

The seeds of the volume were planted at a symposium on 'Austrian Economics and Its Philosophical and Historical Background' which was held in Graz, Austria, from 27 to 31 July 1980. Of the participants in this symposium who are not represented here, the editors would like to thank in particular Professor Israel Kirzner, who is in many ways responsible for the fact that this volume exists at all, and, for his unfailing encouragement and guidance, Kenneth S. Templeton Jr. of the Liberty Fund, by which the Graz symposium was sponsored.

1 AUSTRIAN ECONOMICS AND AUSTRIAN PHILOSOPHY[1]

Barry Smith

1. Positivism and the Methodology of Economics

Contemporary neoclassical economics has increasingly adopted the methodology of the natural sciences. The fundamental postulates of economics are regarded by the proponents of neoclassicism as hypotheses whose scientific value is measured, exclusively or predominantly, by their assumed predictive success.[2] The workings of an economy are, it is accepted, highly complex, and may rest on interconnections and interdependencies not foreseeable by the economic theorist. But this is taken by the neoclassicist to imply that it would be mistaken to restrict the hypotheses of economic science to those displaying the character of intuitive validity: such hypotheses should rather include, precisely as in physics, bold — that is to say superficially counter-intuitive — conjectures, the specific propositions derivable from which are yet amenable to testing.

Unfortunately the positivistic methodology of hypothesis, deduction and testing is, when applied to the domain of economic formations and of social phenomena in general, confronted by obstacles not encountered in the domain of physical phenomena. The large-scale social structures which confront the economist when he makes the attempt to apply his theories to reality are, first of all, typically more complex and less determinately delineated than the more or less cleanly isolable segments of material reality which are at the disposal of the physicist in his laboratory.[3] But the crucial difference between the object-worlds of the economist and of the physicist consists in the fact that the individual economic agent who constitutes the most important element in the domain of economic theory exhibits one trait, consciousness, entirely absent from the realm of physics.[4]

It is of course possible for the positivist to advance hypotheses concerning what he thinks may be the theoretically relevant aspects of the conscious behaviour of the economic subject. It is possible, that is to say, for him to develop mathematically precise models of conscious economic action and to integrate these models into the structure of his theory. But unfortunately it is not only the systematic or rule-governed

1

aspects of economic action — aspects which have traditionally been grouped around the notion of the rationality of the economic agent — which are of relevance to the workings of an economy. Economic agents may also act irrationally (or, better, arationally). Economic agents may change their minds, may initiate or abandon projects for no apparent reason, and may, above all, act *creatively* — which is to say, in such a way as to depart from hitherto accepted systems of rules without descending into merely deviant behaviour. Economic agents may differ still more radically from the constituents of the object-world of physics also by virtue of the fact that they may more or less consciously or deliberately take account, in their actions, of the actions of the economic theorist himself. They may allow their actions to be guided by what they take to be the prevailing orthodoxy amongst economists, in ways which may serve, in cumulation, to subvert the fundamental premises of that orthodoxy.

The idea that counter-intuitive postulates relating to economic phenomena may come to be established as scientifically valid or invalid as a result of a process of empirical testing is, then, at least dubious. This is first of all because the necessary test conditions are incapable of being laid down: we should never know which hypothesis had been established as valid. But it is secondly, and more importantly, because the objects of economic science are distinct in their nature from the objects of the natural sciences.

2. Economics and the A Priori

The economics of the Austrian school has sought to offer a methodological alternative to economic positivism and empiricism, by taking as its starting point this heterogeneity of the objects of natural and social science: Austrian economics acknowledges in its fundamental axioms the methodological and ontological centrality of the economic agent. Now there is one sense in which this centrality is capable of being established empirically: the economic significance of human action, deliberation and choice (and of such complementary notions as gratuitous behaviour and forgetfulness) is repeatedly verified in observation. But the proponent of Austrian economics goes further in arguing that there is also a certain a priori or essentialistic aspect to this empirically established fact.[5] An isolated system of purported exchanges between automata, between entities entirely lacking in consciousness, would not and could not be an economy, however many

superficial similarities its operations might bea
undertaken between men. And this proposition i
we can have evident knowledge without the ne
possibility of, empirical investigation.

The proposition that an economy presuppose
degree of intuitive or evident validity which it sh
tions of mathematics. And because he takes s
involved in the empirical verification of economic propositions, the proponent of Austrian economics insists that this character of intuitive or
evident validity should mark all the basic postulates of his discipline.
Anyone, he argues, who has familiarity with economic phenomena (be
they actions, choices, money, prices, contracts or debts) will acknowledge, independently of empirical testing, the truth of certain
necessary propositions relating to these phenomena, and it is these propositions which must form the axioms of the science of economics.

Economics becomes, therefore, an entirely aprioristic discipline.
And should it follow as a consequence of this conception that certain
large claims of traditional economic science (for example the notion
that economic theory has a predictive capacity) have to be abandoned,
then the Austrian will take this in his stride. These claims would be held
to derive from an ill-thought-out analogy with physics.[6]

Menger's own formulation of the aprioristic dimension of Austrian
economics has distinctly Aristotelian overtones.[7] In a letter to Walras
of 1884, he wrote that economists

> do not simply study quantitive relationships but also the *nature*
> *(das Wesen)* of economic phenomena. How can we attain to the
> knowledge of the latter [e.g., the nature of *value, rent, profit,* the
> division of labour, bimetallism, etc.] by mathematical methods?[8]

The idea seems to be that *value, rent, profit,* etc., are intrinsically
intelligible natural kinds,[9] types or (to use an Aristotelian term) species;
and that necessary laws concerning these species, and specifically concerning their interrelations, can be grasped as evident by anyone who
makes it his business to understand the structure of the underlying
phenomena (the *instances* of the given species). These laws are not,
therefore, empirically established. But neither are they conjured out of
nothing. They presuppose a familiarity with the workings of the
economic sphere and a capacity to exploit this familiarity in a way
which can serve as the basis of a consistent and coherent theory. The
given laws are, then, a priori; but only in the precise sense that they can

ped as evident by virtue of the intrinsic intelligibility of the
lying phenomena. They are not, for example, innate to human
nsciousness; nor are they 'laws of thought'.[10]

Necessary laws concerning economic kinds are, for the Aristotelian,
no more problematic than necessary laws concerning natural kinds in
other spheres. A mere articulation of the words 'I promise to pay you
$1,000,000 tomorrow' uttered, for example, whilst asleep, would not
and could not be a promise. An underlying substratum of intentions
appropriate to a promise is, as a matter of necessity, indispensable. This
is an example of an a priori law concerning the social act of promising.
Other examples of such laws are familiar in the field of colours and
colour-relations (for example, that nothing can be both red and green all
over, or that blue and green are more similar than blue and scarlet).
They are familiar also in the field of mental acts and states (that
jealousy and hatred are distinct emotions which can, however, of their
nature, co-exist in a single consciousness; that an individual cannot
remember an event unless he has himself experienced that event). Each
one of these laws is necessary, and its necessity is evident — in a perfectly commonplace sense of the word 'evident' — to anyone who has
grasped the nature of the phenomena in question.

Yet however commonplace Menger's conception of the objects and
laws of economics may appear on this aprioristic, Aristotelian interpretation, it nevertheless stands in radical conflict with one
methodological principle which has come to prevail as orthodoxy
amongst philosophers and methodologists of science, a principle which
may be formulated as follows: scientific propositions are either contingent or necessary. Contingent propositions lack any character of evident validity; they are capable of being established as true (if at all) only
by empirical testing. Necessary propositions, on the other hand, which
are capable of being grasped as evident, are true purely in virtue of the
meanings of their constituent terms or of relations amongst the concepts
expressed.

It is a consequence of this principle, which forms the basis of contemporary positivism, that all necessary propositions are capable of being
established as true purely by armchair methods — by direct inspection
of the meanings they involve (supplemented, if necessary, by
mathematical calculation). Candidate necessary propositions which
do not stand up to this test — for example, many of the propositions of
traditional metaphysics — are either to be dismissed as nonsensical or,
alternatively, they are to be unmasked as contingent.

If, however, all necessary propositions are capable of being established as true simply by an inspection of meanings, then such propositions can tell us nothing about the world itself. This consequence is indeed accepted by the defenders of positivism, who point out that we do not cast aspersions upon the propositions of logic simply because they tell us nothing of the world. The positivists argue, indeed, that necessary propositions should as far as possible approximate to the condition of the logical tautology: a necessary proposition is properly to be accepted as being meaningful if and only if it is capable of being reduced to the status of a tautology by successive elimination of its defined terms.

The three traditional dichotomies of necessary/contingent, a priori/a posteriori, and analytic/synthetic prove, on this account, to be co-extensive. A proposition is necessarily true if and only if its truth is capable of being grasped as evident; a true proposition is capable of being grasped as evident if and only if it is true purely by virtue of relations amongst meanings, and therefore also if and only if it lacks cognitive value (makes no substantive contributions to our knowledge of the world).

The implications of this principle for the Aristotelian conception of economic laws are serious. If these laws are necessary, as Menger believed, then they must be true by definition. But from this it would follow that they could have no substantial contribution to make to our knowledge of the economic world. If, on the other hand, we wish to hold on to the idea that economic laws are not mere tautologies, that they picture independently existing configurations of economic reality, then we must reject the view that they are necessary and that they exhibit any character of intuitive or evident validity.

The first of these two alternatives has indeed been adopted by many post-war Austrian economists under the influence of the methodological writings of Ludwig von Mises.[11] The second alternative we have already seen reason to reject as dubious: it implies the methodology of economic positivism.

3. Hume and Kant

An impasse has been reached. But are we to accept it as inevitable? Before answering this question it will be instructive to investigate something of the background of the debate on analytic and a priori propositions. This will not only help to establish the origins of the positivist principle in eighteenth- and nineteenth-century philosophy, but will also point us in the direction of an alternative to Mises' conclusion that commitment to the conception of economic laws as necessary and evident carries with it a view of such laws as merely analytic.

The theory of natural kinds as entities given in reality and the associated doctrines of a priori knowledge were first expounded by Aristotle and by his followers in the scholastic period. It was from this source that Menger himself almost certainly derived at least some elements of his aprioristic methodology. Classical and medieval philosophers had still been able to take for granted the existence of a whole class of propositions about reality whose truth is evident yet which are not derivable logically from empirically established truths. Propositions expressing causal relations will constitute for us the most prominent category of such purported synthetic a priori truths.

It was only with the beginnings of modern philosophy that this assumption began gradually to be called into question; and only then did philosophers begin seriously to investigate the nature of the presuppositions on which it rests. Thus Locke, in his *Essay,* isolated a class of what he called 'trifling' propositions — propositions which are true of necessity, but which do not serve to increase our knowledge. These include identical propositions of the form '*A* is *A*' and propositions such as 'Lead is metal' predicating part of some complex idea by a name of the whole.[12] Trifling propositions serve simply to elucidate the meanings of words. But not all necessary propositions are trifling in Locke's view. He discriminates a further class of non-contingent propositions which are characterised by the fact that something is affirmed of an idea which is not *contained in* a given complex idea, but is rather a *necessary consequence* of it.[13] Locke's example is: the external angle of a triangle is bigger than either of the opposite internal angles. The relation of the outward angle to either of the internal opposite angles is no part of the idea signified by the name 'triangle', so 'this is a real Truth, and conveys with it instructive *real Knowledge*'.[14]

Unfortunately, Locke did not apply his trichotomy in his efforts to produce a coherent account of the status of propositions expressing causal relations. His reflections on cause and effect, and on what he calls 'powers', do not add up to a consistent theory. Causal relations are held to involve both an a priori element, residing in the notion of efficaciousness, and a contingent element, where Locke runs together the idea of efficacious cause with the notion of regular sequence.[15]

It was Hume who first convincingly broke the spell of the idea that an adequate account of causality can be built up only on the basis of the assumption that causal relations exhibit features of evident necessity.

The compulsion we feel in passing from the idea of a given cause to that of a given effect could be explained, Hume argued, by appealing to the notion of mental habits acquired through repetition. He was thereby able to eliminate the a priori element from a large segment of our knowledge of material reality. Nowhere, however, does Hume suggest that similar considerations can be brought forward in every sphere of material knowledge in such a way that it would be possible to eliminate entirely the a priori element from our knowledge of reality. He did, certainly, embrace a dichotomy between what he called *relations of ideas* and *matters of fact.* Knowledge of the former he conceived to be necessary, knowledge of the latter to be contingent. It is therefore tempting to read back into his writings a more modern view, according to which relations of ideas would be identified as mere connections among meanings or concepts, reflecting no corresponding connections between entities in the world.

Such an interpretation would however conflict with the details of Hume's doctrine of ideas. Consider, for example, his account of the interrelations among our ideas of colour:

It is evident, that even different simple ideas may have similarity or resemblance to each other; nor is it necessary that the point or circumstance of resemblance should be distinct or separable from that in which they differ. *Blue* and *green* are different simple ideas, but are more resembling than *blue* and *scarlet;* though their perfect simplicity excludes all possibility of separation or distinction.[16]

It is, in other words, impossible to establish the truth of propositions expressing relations of this kind by any *analysis* of the constituent ideas, since the latter are absolutely simple: 'No point of view is conceivable from which one could say that two colours and their dissimilarity contradict each other in the logical sense.'[17] And nor, either, is there any suggestion that our acceptance of the evident truth of colour propositions is merely a matter of acquired habits of thinking. Rather, such propositions are seen by Hume as reflecting objectively existing interrelations among the phenomena themselves; they are true, in his words, from the 'very nature' of the ideas in question. Similar interrelations are recognised by Hume also in other spheres: sounds, tastes and smells, like colours, 'admit of infinite resemblances upon the general appearance and comparison, without having any circumstance the same'.[18] He also applies the same account to the propositions of mathematics.

Hume's category of non-analytic propositions expressing necessary relations of ideas has, however, as a result of the influence of Kant's erroneous estimation of the significance of Hume's work, been almost completely ignored by successive generations of commentators, who have identified Hume's *ideas* with the quite different category of the Kantian *concept*. What is characteristic of the latter is that it is purely epistemological: it belongs to a sphere which is, in the framework of Kant's dualist metaphysic, entirely separated from the ontological sphere of the so-called things in themselves. Within his dualist framework Kant was able to develop a conception of all relations amongst concepts as falling into two exhaustive classes: either they are merely analytic, or — if synthetic — they are a matter of epistemological structure imposed upon the world of experience by the operations of the mind. From this it follows that we can know a priori only what is analytic or what we ourselves read into our knowledge.

Hume's philosophy does not, however, embrace a dualistic metaphysic of this kind. His non-analytic propositions rather straddle the boundary between the two spheres of what would normally be called the epistemological and the ontological. And neither sphere can meaningfully be held to have priority over the other. The proponents of positivist doctrines may therefore rightfully adopt Hume as an ancestor only by imposing upon his philosophy an alien metaphysic. Freed from its ballast of Kantianism, Hume's doctrine of ideas offers a much more sympathetic prospect for those who would take seriously the idea of an a priori component in our knowledge of reality.

4. Foundations of Austrian Apriorism

It is interesting to note that this non-Kantian interpretation of Hume's doctrine of ideas was first coherently expounded within the Austrian tradition of philosophy.[20] Not, however, by the logical positivists of the Vienna Circle who, along with Mises, fell under the sway of the Kantian conception of a priori knowledge, but by members of an earlier generation of philosophers influenced by Brentano.[21] The affinities between Menger's economic and Brentanian philosophies of value have been discussed in detail by Fabian and Simons and by Grassl in their papers in this volume. Here I wish to show that the theory of the a priori developed by Brentano and his successors (above all by the early phenomenologists) throws significant light upon the significance and practicability of Menger's general methodology.

We have already pointed out the Aristotelian flavour of some of Menger's writings. This Aristotelianism was not an isolated phenomenon in Austria in the second half of the nineteenth century. The Austrian school and university system had succeeded in keeping alive a general spirit of Aristotelian realism during the period in which intellectuals in Germany had fallen under the influence of the idealism, historicism and methodological collectivism that had followed in the wake of Kant and Hegel. This isolation of Austria from German philosophical currents was part of a deliberate policy pursued by the Imperial authorities, a policy designed to seal off the Empire from what were conceived as pernicious liberal and cosmopolitan influences from the outside world.[22] In philosophy, in particular, the institutes of learning in the Empire had imposed upon them a rigid and uniform syllabus, constructed around watered-down versions of the Aristotelian and scholastic philosophies, with the result that creative innovation was almost stifled.[23] With the rise of liberalism in Austria in the nineteenth century, intellectuals were gradually encouraged to experiment with new ideas; but these experiments inevitably took place against a philosophical background alien to, and in part also critical of, the principal intellectual currents prevailing in Germany. Menger's *Grundsätze der Volkswirtschaftslehre* was among the first of such experiments, and the aprioristic, anti-historicist, individualistic methodology which it expounds would at that time have been possible only in Austria.[24] I shall seek to show that it forms the counterpart, in the social sciences, of the aprioristic methodology inspired by Brentano and his followers in the field of psychology.

Brentano himself grew up in (Catholic) southern Germany where, as a young priest, he studied theology and philosophy in the scholastic tradition. When he came to Vienna in 1874 he had already published a dissertation on the ontology of Aristotle,[25] a book on Aristotle's psychology,[26] and a long essay on Aristotelian epistemology.[27] Brentano continued to be affected by Aristotle's thought throughout his life, and it is significant that he found in Austria a receptive audience for the philosophical doctrines which he had begun to develop against this background.[28]

Central to these doctrines is the notion of an a priori discipline of what Brentano called descriptive psychology.[29] The first task of descriptive psychology is to establish the characteristics of and the principal subdivisions among mental phenomena (to isolate, in the mental sphere, what we called natural kinds or species). It might be thought that we could attain to this knowledge by experimental methods. But experimental observation and measurement, if they are to be scientifically valuable at all, can properly begin only when it has been established what precisely the experimenter is seeking to observe and measure. Brentano therefore argued that experiment must be preceded by a prior determination of the fundamental kinds of mental phenomena on the basis of what he calls their 'natural affinities'.[30]

Mental phenomena may be relatively elementary or relatively complex. The second task of descriptive psychology is to determine the laws governing the interconnections of phenomena, and specifically governing the ways in which complex phenomena may be built up out of or on the basis of more simple phenomena.[31] Brentano shows, for example, that it is impossible that phenomena of preference (love, hate, desire, aversion, and so on) be built up directly on the basis of immediate sensory impressions. Such phenomena can arise only where sensory impressions are accompanied by phenomena of judgement.

Such laws have their origins in psychology, but they are not without more general significance. The laws governing the sphere of phenomena of preference, for example, are seen by Brentano as providing objective principles for the science of ethics.[32] The laws governing the sphere of phenomena of judgement (laws relating specifically to the opposition between correct and incorrect judgement) are similarly held to provide objective principles for the science of logic.[33]

Now Brentano's descriptive psychological laws, like the propositions expressing necessary relations of ideas in Hume's philosophy, do not express purely epistemological interconnections amongst concepts. Rather, they capture structural interconnections amongst the objectively existing elements and complexes of the psychological sphere itself, interconnections which are reflected in our knowledge of the natural affinities obtaining in this sphere. They are not imposed upon the phenomena in any Kantian sense. And the given laws are synthetic, not analytic. It does not follow axiomatically from our *concepts* of love, hate, feeling, desire, and so on, that these phenomena cannot arise directly on the basis of sensory presentations. Yet this structural property of the phenomena of preference is nevertheless capable of being evidently grasped by anyone who is familiar with experiences of the kinds in question.

The parallels with Menger, in the above, will by now be obvious. In a famous passage from the *Untersuchungen über die Methode der Sozialwissenschaften* Menger wrote:

Theoretical economics has the task of investigating the *general nature* and the *general connection* of economic phenomena, not of analysing economic *concepts* and of drawing the logical consequences resulting from this analysis. The phenomena, or certain aspects of them, and not concepts, their linguistic image, are the object of theoretical research in the field of economy. The analysis of the concepts may in an individual case have a certain significance for the *presentation* of theoretical knowledge of economy, but the goal of research in the field of theoretical economics can only be the determination of the general nature and the general connection of economic *phenomena.* It is a sign of the slight understanding which individual representatives of the historical school have for the aims of theoretical research, when they see only *analyses of concepts* in investigations into the *nature* of commodity, into the *nature* of economy, the *nature* of value, price and similar things, and when they see 'the setting up of a system of concepts and judgements' in the striving after an exact theory of economic phenomena.[34]

5. Husserl's Theory of the A Priori

It is not enough, however, to show that Brentano and Menger share a common methodology or that their methodologies share a number of crucial common traits. It is necessary to determine the precise nature of this methodology and to provide a coherent account of the theory of essences and kinds on which it rests. Only then will we be in a position to counter the positivist's arguments against the possibility of a non-tautologous a priori.

Such an account of essences or kinds and of the a priori interconnections between them is not provided by Brentano, whose methodological writings, like those of Menger, are concerned with the applications of the doctrine of a priori kinds in a specific field. And it is not provided either, in a form which would meet contemporary standards of philosophical rigour, in the writings of Aristotle and the scholastics. The outlines of a suitable account are, however, to be found in the early, pre-phenomenological works of Brentano's most important student, Edmund Husserl. Husserl began his intellectual career as a mathematician but became increasingly interested in philosophical issues relating to the foundations of logic and mathematics. His decision to become a philosopher was primarily influenced by Brentano, whose lectures he attended in Vienna in 1884–6. From 1887 to 1901 Husserl was *Privatdozent* in Halle. In 1891 he published a book entitled *The Philosophy of Arithmetic. Psychological and*

Logical Studies,[35] a work which still falls within the scope of Brentano's project of an a priori discipline of descriptive psychology. In the years which followed he published a series of articles on the foundations of psychology and on the philosophy of logic and mathematics in which he began to work out the principles of the more general theory of the a priori which the Brentanian enterprise, or any similar enterprise, would presuppose.[36] He sought especially to take account of an extension of Brentano's ideas which had been worked out by his colleague in Halle, Carl Stumpf, also a fellow student of Brentano. This general theory was presented, alongside contributions to philosophical psychology, to logical theory and to the philosophy of language, in the two volumes of his *Logical Investigations,* published in 1900–1.[37] The theory is, as we shall see, consistent in many respects with the theory underlying Brentanian descriptive psychology, but Husserl goes far beyond Brentano in the generality of his method.

It is the third Logical Investigation, 'On the Theory of Wholes and Parts', a work which bears further traces of the Aristotelianism characteristic of nineteenth century Austrian philosophy, which is most important for us here. Brentano, as we have seen, conceived the theory of descriptive psychology in terms of laws specifying the various possible interconnections and combinations of mental phenomena into complexes of various kinds. Menger, too, employed such a 'compositive' method. The objects of the social sciences he conceived as wholes or complexes

> which are structurally connected, which we learn to single out from the totality of observed phenomena only as a result of our systematic fitting together of the elements with familiar properties, and which we build up or reconstruct from the known properties of the elements.[38]

For Menger, as for Brentano, these 'elements' can hardly be conceived by analogy with absolutely simple atoms. 'Composition' is not aggregation of disconnected and mutually independent atoms into heaps. The complexes which we learn to recognise are, rather, structured or integrated wholes of interdependent elements which themselves exhibit various structural properties and relations and are capable of being grouped, like the wholes they constitute, into types or species.

These structural interconnections are intrinsically intelligible: they are capable of being grasped as evident by anyone who has familiarity with the domain in question — at least to the extent that what Menger calls exact knowledge, in psychology or in the social sciences, is possible at all.[39] They are, that is to say, a priori connections. It was the contribution of Husserl in the *Logical Investigations* to have stated precisely the nature of these a priori connections in a way which enables us to determine the detailed formal geography of the synthetic a priori domain. Where his aprioristic predecessors had offered little more than lists of examples of purported synthetic a priori propositions, Husserl offers a non-trivial explication of what it is for a proposition to *be* synthetic and a priori, in terms of a general theory of a priori or intelligible connections between objects *in the world*.

His ideas grew out of a distinction introduced by Stumpf between dependent and independent contents of mental experience.[40] An independent content is any part or element of a complex experience which can be thought or imagined as existing in separation from the remaining elements of the given complex. A dependent content is any part or element which cannot be thought or imagined in isolation from its surrounding complex. That part of a mental image of a horse which is an image of the head of the horse is, in Stumpf's terms, independent. An image of the shape or colour of the horse is, in contrast, dependent: it is impossible to imagine the specific colour-array of this specific individual horse except as the colour-array *of* the horse: *this* colour-array cannot be presented in separation (though of course a qualitatively exactly similar array may be capable of being so presented).

Husserl pointed out, first of all, that Stumpf's distinction can be recognised not merely in the sphere of mental contents but also in other dimensions of reality.[41] He then saw that it was possible to eliminate from Stumpf's definitions the reference to contingently existing capacities for thinking and imagining in such a way as to produce an objective, ontological distinction between two kinds of part or element, which he called, respectively, *pieces* and *moments*.[42] A piece is simply any element of a whole which, of its nature, can be removed or isolated from its surrounding whole and still continue to exist. A moment is any element which, of its nature, cannot exist except in the context of its surrounding whole.

The words 'can' and 'cannot', in the above, carry the force of modal possibility and necessity: it is in principle possible of any arbitrarily demarcated slice-shaped segment of an apple that it be extracted from, and that it should continue to exist independently of, the remaining segments. It is however impossible of the specific individual *shape* of the apple that it should similarly exist independently of the apple as a whole.

The qualifier 'of its nature' signifies that we are dealing here with *de re* possibility and necessity, with possibility and necessity which is intrinsic to, or rooted in, the kinds or natures of the objects and object-parts in question.[43] Relations between objects and their pieces and moments of the types here considered are therefore intelligible only to the extent that there are natural divisions between kinds of objects and object-parts. Thus there is a natural division between the promise and social acts of other kinds. And it is in principle impossible that an utterance of the form 'I promise to do such-and-such', *of its nature as a promise,* should exist except as part of a larger whole which includes also an appropriate intention (a psychological moment of the promiser), and an appropriate tendency to realise the given content. (It is, conversely, equally impossible that this specific intention should exist except as bound up with an utterance of the given form.)[44]

Husserl now advances a further generalisation of Stumpf's initial theory of dependent contents. He points out that relations of necessary dependence of the types distinguished by Stumpf obtain not only between the parts of a single whole, but also between objects not comprehended within any independently recognisable surrounding complex object.[45] A husband, for example, by his nature as a husband, cannot exist without a wife. This wider sense of moment or 'dependent object' may be defined — without any reference to the relations of part and whole — as follows: *a* is a moment of *b* if and only if *a* is necessarily such that, by its nature, it cannot exist unless *b* also exists.

A commodity or economic good is a dependent object in this generalised sense. A commodity cannot, of necessity, exist, unless there exist also appropriately directed valuing acts which depend in their turn upon specific subjective beliefs and intentions of individual subjects. A medium of exchange cannot, by its nature, exist, unless there exist also economic value, economic transactions, and a generally dispersed readiness to accept.

Dependence relations between moments in this generalised sense, or between moments and independent objects, may be *one-sided* (where *a* cannot exist unless *b* also exists, but not conversely). But they may also be reciprocal (two- or *n*-sided, for any $n > 1$). Husband and wife are in this sense two-sidedly dependent on each other.[46]

Moments may, by their nature, depend either upon one single independent object, or they may depend upon a manifold of dependent and/or independent objects of a more or less precisely determinate structure. A *debt*, for example, is a moment of a two-object manifold made up of debtor or creditor. A debt, by its nature, cannot exist unless debtor and creditor also exist.

Moments may be *mediate* or *immediate:* *a* is an immediate moment of *b* if and only if *a* is a moment of *b* and there is no *c* such that *a* is a moment of *c* and *c* a moment of *a*. Otherwise *a* is a mediate moment.[47]

Moments may be *extended*, for example in space and/or time. But they may also be non-extended. A debt, for example, endures through some time interval, however short; payment of a debt may, in contrast, be of instantaneous duration. Extensive moments may, like individual material objects, be *pieced*, either actually or in thought; a claim, for example, may be subdivided into constituent claims; a productive process may be subdivided into constituent operations, and so on.

The distinctions between one-sided and reciprocal moments, between moments dependent on a single object and (relational) moments dependent on an object-manifold, between mediate and immediate moments, and between extensive and non-extensive moments, distinctions capable of being recognised in every sphere of reality, were first rigorously isolated by Husserl in his third Logical Investigation. They enable us to construct a highly elaborate taxonomical theory of the different possible forms of objects and dependence relations existing in the world, a theory which turns out to have a mathematical elegance and precision of its own.[48]

Husserl now advances a twofold claim to the effect that: firstly, all synthetic a priori connections (all intelligible connections between objects in the world) are mediate or immediate relations of necessary dependence between dependent and independent objects;[49] and secondly, all synthetic a priori propositions, in whatever sphere, are capable of being derived from propositions expressing such dependence relations.[50]

6. Against Positivism

This account of the a priori connections existing in reality can be used to elucidate, in a simple and immediate manner, the nature of aprioristic claims such as those made by Brentano and Menger on behalf of their respective disciplines.[51] But its principal importance from our present point of view is that it provides not, as in earlier discussions, a mere list of examples of purported synthetic a priori truths, but a stable and coherent demarcation of the entire realm of the synthetic a priori which can be exploited to meet the various arguments put forward by positivist and analytic philosophers against the very idea of an intelligible structure of reality.

The most powerful of these arguments originated in work in the philosophy of mathematics around the turn of the century, and specifically in the so-called logicist programme.[52] The logicists were able to demonstrate that certain classes of purportedly synthetic propositions of mathematics were in fact capable of being established as theorems of formal logic. This they achieved effectively by eliminating each defined term (substituting *definiens* for *definiendum*) from the given propositions, and exhibiting the resultants as logical tautologies. The success of this method for certain restricted classes of a priori propositions led certain philosophers — particularly philosophers influenced by Wittgenstein's *Tractatus Logico-Philosophicus* — to advance the working hypothesis that all candidate synthetic a priori propositions could similarly be exhibited as logical tautologies.[53] This working hypothesis became entrenched as a philosophical dogma, first of all because it eliminated in one stroke so many niggling mysteries surrounding the old-fashioned view of the a priori, and secondly because, where its advocates were confronted only with lists of disconnected examples of purported synthetic a priori truths, even isolated cases of successful application of the method could sustain the belief that it could, in principle, be made to work in the general case. Propositions which proved recalcitrant to the method could either be dismissed as meaningless, or reassigned to the category of a posteriori truths.[54] It was therefore possible to ignore or camouflage the fact that those philosophers who persisted in their efforts to apply the method to new classes of propositions lying outside the mathematical sphere had consistently failed to produce detailed resolutions of the appropriate kind, even for the simplest examples of purported synthetic a priori propositions. No resolutions enjoying general acceptance amongst philosophers have been forthcoming even for propositions expressing simple colour relations. Yet these propositions are neither meaningless, nor — by the arguments in sections 2 and 3 above — are they a posteriori.

Wittgenstein himself began slowly to recognise the inadequacy of the original hypothesis, and in his later writings he moved away from the idea that those truths hitherto commonly accepted as synthetic and a priori — whether in the psychological sphere or in the spheres of language and other social phenomena — can be exhibited as logical tautologies. He developed instead a conception of the given truths as 'truths of grammar', and whilst the immediate connotations of this talk of grammar may sustain the assumption that we are still dealing with propositions true purely by virtue of the ways we talk and think, the details of Wittgenstein's exposition sometimes carry the implication that the given propositions are made true also, or in part, by objectively existing determinations of reality.[55]

The positivist-analytic programme for the elimination of the synthetic a priori can by now, in fact, be said to have failed. Only the memory of its initial successes, and the convenience of the idea that it has succeeded, sustain it as a (never too closely examined) presupposition of the older generation of analytic philosophers and of those writers on scientific methodology who have fallen under their influence.[56] Already in 1910–11, however, Husserl had provided the means for the construction of an argument why the programme must necessarily fail. This is provided in an unjustly neglected essay, first published as an appendix to his *Formal and Transcendental Logic* of 1929, entitled 'Syntactical Forms and Syntactical Matters: Core Forms and Core Matters'. Let us assume that we have in fact satisfactorily eliminated all the defined (logically complex) terms from the a priori propositions of some given theory — for example, from the theory of economics. The resultant propositions will consist entirely of what Husserl calls 'core terms', some of which will be formal ('object', 'property', 'and', 'not', and so on), some of which will be material ('subject', 'action', 'end', 'exchange', 'desire', or still more primitive terms relating to the ultimate subject-matter of economics). In some cases the resultant proposition will be analytic: a desire to exchange is, analytically, a desire; an action of a subject is, analytically, an action.[57] But some, at least, of the resultant propositions must, if the initial theory is to be coherent at all, express non-trivial relations holding between core matters (for example that an exchange is an exchange between subjects; that an exchange is an action performed by subjects; that an exchange is necessarily compatible with a desire to exchange on the part of the exchanging subjects, and so on). Now these latter propositions, or propositions like them but containing still more primitive economic terms, because they contain no trivially eliminable core matters, can be exhibited as analytic only if some at least of their constituent material expressions can be defined, logically, in terms of others. But this is to contradict the hypothesis that, on the level of core forms and matters, *all* defined terms have been eliminated.

This is to present only the skeleton of Husserl's theory of syntactic forms and matters. The theory itself implies also a detailed account of the nature of the relations between formal and material terms on the one hand, and the corresponding formal and material moments of objects existing in the world on the other. Even in this condensed version, however, the argument has important lessons for our understanding of the ways in which an aprioristic methodology may be applied in the construction of scientific theories. It tells us, most importantly, that an a priori scientific theory can be coherently constructed out of propositions which are uniformly analytic only if the theory is committed to at most *one* core matter: propositions expressing non-trivial interrelations between several core matters are, by definition, synthetic. It is the recognition of this fact which lies at the bottom of efforts in the foundations of mathematics to establish that all mathematical propositions can be expressed without remainder in terms of the single not purely logical notion of *set*. And it underlies also von Mises's insistence, against the background of his view that all a priori propositions of economics are analytic 'laws of thought', that the a priori element in economic theory can be constructed entirely in terms of the single material notion of *action*. The Misesian vision of economics as an edifice generated entirely by conceptual (logical) analysis of this single notion, with its apparent implication that the resultant theory must either be trivial (able to tell us nothing about reality), or magical (consisting of truths spun out of nowhere), has done much to inhibit the acceptance of the more general aprioristic claims made on behalf of Austrian economics. The suspicion has remained — in spite of von Mises's own claims for his method — that other core notions, in addition to the concept of action, have been smuggled into his theory on the way, and that the theory is therefore not purely analytic. It is the most important lesson of Husserl's work that Austrian economists, armed with the conception of synthetic a priori (intelligible) connections between parts and moments in the world, can properly abandon the official Misesian conception of their discipline as a part of the analytic theory of human action and conceive it instead precisely in Menger's terms: as a synthetic a priori theory of the whole family of kinds and connections manifested in the phenomena of economic life.

7. Perception Knowledge and Entrepreneurship

We shall conclude this essay with an application of the Husserlian method to one problem fundamental to contemporary research in Austrian economics, the problem of entrepreneurship. We shall consider, in particular, the theory of the entrepreneurial role recently advanced by Israel Kirzner on the basis of the work of Mises and Hayek.[58] Kirzner conceives the role of the entrepreneur as residing essentially in his ability to *see* economic opportunities which have for one reason or another been overlooked by other economic agents. One consequence of this conception is that there is an important sense in which the entrepreneur, unlike other participants in the economy, *does no work*. For the opportunities which he sees — the economic ends and the means for realising these ends — are already there, on the face of economic reality, even though no other economic agent has as yet perceived them. The role of the entrepreneur is thus sharply to be distinguished from, for example, that of the manager, whose function consists in the material organisation of the factors of production for an already predetermined end.[59] It is of course clear that both roles, perhaps along with others, may be invested in a single person. And it is also clear that, because the entrepreneurial function may be exercised in such a way that it is dispersed amongst slices of managerial activity, it may not always be possible to distinguish in practice where entrepreneurship ends and organisation begins. But it seems nevertheless true that managerial activity presupposes entrepreneurial activity; economic organisation directed towards some end cannot exist unless this end has been determined.

It is one principal virtue of Kirzner's analysis that it enables us to see the precise sense in which entrepreneurship, unlike managerial activity, is not a *factor* (input) of production, but rather a *presupposition* of production. The entrepreneur does not *do* anything, and therefore — in contrast to the manager — he can receive no wage.[60] He receives, rather, the residue, not calculable in advance, of the process of production which he sets in train, and it is the possibility of this pure or entrepreneural profit which sustains the entrepreneur in his state of alertness.

But what, now, is the status of these propositions concerning the nature of the entrepreneurial role? Are the differences between entrepreneurial, managerial, and other kinds of economically relevant activity analytic differences only; are they imposed upon the underlying phenomena as part of the conceptual framework of economic theory? Or are they differences of *kind*, discovered in the world? Kirzner himself seems to adopt the former view. He sees his theory as having the capacity to provide non-trivial knowledge of economic phenomena as a result of the fact that it contains an empirical element: the extent to which the purely conceptual propositions of the theory correspond to reality Kirzner, like Hayek, sees as a matter of empirical inquiry.[61] The substance of his account is however by no means alien to the original Mengerian conception of economics as an a priori theory of kinds and connections in the world. We can indeed translate the purportedly analytic propositions of his theory into the Aristotelian–Husserlian vocabulary in a way in which will make manifest the sense in which these propositions may properly be said to relate not to the relations between our concepts, but to connections between specific kinds of dependent and independent objects *in the world*.

Instances of entrepreneurial activity constitute, from the Husserlian perspective, a species or natural kind (and this is true even if, in particular cases, the entrepreneurial nature of an action is unclear or unrecognised).[62] The dependence-structure of this kind may be described as follows. Entrepreneurial activity is dependent, first of all, on the perception of a certain kind of structural moment of material reality as this is, at some given time, articulated by the existing economic relations. It is dependent further on the knowledge or belief engendered by the given perception that this structural moment *is* an economic opportunity (will generate a stream of profits). And it is dependent also, like the given moments of perception and knowledge, upon a specific individual — the entrepreneur — who is endowed with an appropriate background knowledge of the economic articulation of the relevant area of material reality. (It is essential to entrepreneurial activity that the associated perception and knowledge should be invested in a single subject.) Now perception and knowledge of an economic opportunity can be said to serve as the basis for properly entrepreneurial activity only if they give rise, in subsequent actions of economic subjects, to a tendency to realise the given opportunity: the activities of an individual who constantly perceives opportunities overlooked by other economic agents are entrepreneurial only to the extent that they are dedicated, in a substantive manner, to the exploitation of these opportunities. Entrepreneurial activity is therefore dependent also upon a tendency to realise appropriate changes in the economic articulation of that segment of reality towards which entrepreneurial perception and knowledge are directed.[63]

These relations are represented in Figure 1.1.[64]

Each frame designates a particular moment or independent object bound, mediately or immediately, into a single complex structure by relations of dependence. Links connecting broken to solid walls of the constituent frames signify that the object pictured by the broken frame is one-sidedly dependent upon the object pictured by the associated frame.[65] Propositions expressing these relations, or propositions logically derivable from these, are synthetic (they picture objectively existing determinations of reality) and a priori (their truth is evident to anyone who is familiar with the domain in question). It is a synthetic a

Figure 1.1: The Dependence Structure of Entrepreneurship

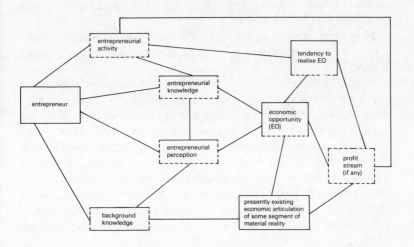

priori truth, for example, that a stream of pure entrepreneurial profits can by its nature exist, only if there exist also both entrepreneurial activity and a tendency to realise some associated economic opportunity. (There are, of course, no dependence relations in the opposite direction: entrepreneurial activity need not in every case generate profits.) This and other a priori truths may be read off immediately from the diagram. The absence of mediate or immediate dependence relations between certain elements in the diagram signifies that, as a matter of a priori necessity, the existence of the given elements is *compatible* with the non-existence of the remainder.[66]

One important difficulty confronting Kirzner's theory relates to the specification of the precise nature of the two moments of background knowledge and entrepreneurial perception. Entrepreneurial perception amounts, we will remember, to seeing *what is already there*. The entrepreneur does not create new objects or relations, but merely recognises what has been overlooked. But how can this notion serve as the basis of an adequate account of entrepreneurial activity, when processes of production are necessarily directed towards the future (the more ramified the productive network which is set in train, the further forward in the future will be the appearance of the ultimate end-product)? It is surely clear that the entrepreneur, in determining what are the worthy (profit-worthy) ends of economic activity, must of necessity anticipate the *future* needs of ultimate consumers; but future needs or desires are precisely not 'already there' in the sense which would seem to be required by Kirzner's theory.

How, then, are we to make sense of Kirzner's account of knowledge and perception in such a way as to preserve the insights of his theory?

It must be stressed, first of all, that the background knowledge which is principally relevant in the economic sphere is not what philosophers have called propositional or discursive knowledge.[67] Relevant background knowledge may be gleaned, certainly, from the reading of, say, stock-market reports, technical specifications, catalogues, market surveys, and so on. But then, in so far as the knowledge which is thereby acquired might serve as the seed-bed for entrepreneurial activity it is not knowledge in the form of propositions (knowledge which might serve as the basis for *calculation* in the Robbinsian sense[68]) which is acquired. It is, rather, a specific kind of *practical* knowledge which forms the background of entrepreneurial activity.

Practical knowledge has been brought to the attention of philosophers in recent times, on the one hand by Ryle, with his distinction between *knowing how* and *knowing that;*[69] and on the other hand by Heidegger, whose philosophy rests centrally on a view of the structure of our ordinary experience as determined primarily by the hierarchies of interdependent *objects for use* (tools, equipment) with which we are continually bound up in our everyday activities.[70] Propositional knowledge is simply that part of our knowledge which we are capable, at any given stage, of articulating into sentences. Practical knowledge is knowledge of how to *do* certain things, knowledge of a kind normally acquired by training and by experience (for example the knowledge of how to sit at table, of how to speak one's native language, how to use a pair of scissors, drive a car, or read a stock-market report). A given body of practical knowledge may or may not be capable of being converted into propositional knowledge, and it seems clear that individuals differ in their capacity to effect this kind of conversion (in either direction). People differ, for example, in their capacities to acquire practical knowledge through instruction (through the medium of sentences) rather than through example.

The practical knowledge which is the presupposition of entrepreneurial activity is of two kinds. On the one hand it is general knowledge of the various ways in which, in a given social and institutional environment, an economic opportunity may be brought to realisation. On the other hand it is specific *area* knowledge of a given segment of reality. Our use of the geographical term 'area' here is not entirely metaphorical.[71] An individual (again to differing degrees) is familiarly said to know his way around the area in which he lives. This knowledge is capable of being converted, in part, into propositions — for example, where we are called upon to direct a stranger on his way. But it is primarily practical: knowing one's way about signifies knowing *how* to get where one wants to be, knowing *how* to satisfy one's everyday needs; and this knowledge is normally not propositionally mediated. We do not need to think out our route to the bathroom, or to the railway station, each morning, any more than a skilled carpenter needs to think out the everyday operations which he performs with a chisel.

The practical knowledge which we have of our immediate neigh-bourhood consists, then, not merely of geographical knowledge (knowledge of the ground-plan of the streets and buildings). It consists also of a knowledge of the mesh of interrelations between these streets and buildings and the array of activities which take place in and around them. But now this kind of non-propositionally articulated area knowledge may clearly apply also to areas or segments of reality not purely geographical. Any individual who has *worked himself into* a given field, or discipline, or into a culture or language, has thereby acquired a corresponding area knowledge, has acquired what might be called a cultural physiology,[72] which forms the cognitive background of his thoughts and actions. A horticulturalist, for example, may be said to know his onions: he has acquired a body of area knowledge relating to onions and to the cultivation of onions, which enables him to classify onions of different strains on the basis of physiognomical properties which he may never find it possible to put into words. A poet may, on the basis of his area knowledge of poetic devices and intentions and of the structure of the language in which he writes, find himself deleting a line or a whole poem simply because it strikes him as being, in a not further specifiable way, somehow wrong.

But now certain kinds of practical area knowledge of presently existing reality are, unlike the knowledge of the horticulturalist and the poet, in a certain sense future-directed. A doctor, for example, will sense the future course of a disease as an integral part of his coming to understand its presently existing symptoms. And it will now be clear how, on this basis, we can make a sense of the Kirznerian account of entrepreneurial activity: the cognitive background of entrepreneurial perception is precisely one species of such future-directed area knowledge. It relates not merely to the presently existing state of things, but also to those possible future states of reality which are signalled, more or less inchoately, in the present.

The implications of these reflections on Kirzner's theory are not entirely trivial. They help us to explain, for example, how it is that economic agents may differ so radically in their entrepreneurial success. An individual may of course stumble by accident on a profit opportunity, that is, upon a mismatch between what the resource market has to offer and what consumers will prove to be prepared to pay: profit opportunities are, after all, on Kirzner's account, already in full view to anyone who cares, or is able, to cast his gaze in the appropriate direction. The opportunity has only once to be revealed in order for it to be manifest to other economic agents, who are then able to recognise that it had been there all along. But it would be impossible, by appeal solely to this notion of accidental recognition, to explain how it is that certain individuals seem to be in a position to score *repeated* successes in their entrepreneurial activities. Such individuals, it may now be asserted, are individuals who exhibit a peculiarly strong capacity for the acquisition of future-directed area knowledge of the appropriate kind.[73]

This account suggests also one possible explanation of the fact that certain kinds of immigrants seem to exhibit a disproportionately high degree of entrepreneurial success. The immigrant, in working himself into the culture and environment which is to be his new home, will bring with him assumptions and capacities, capacities for *seeing*, will bring an alien cultural physiology, derived from his native background. This will imply, in suitably propitious circumstances, that the new area knowledge which he acquires on the basis of the old will be free of certain habitual blind spots which have characterised the perceptions of members of the already entrenched society.[74]

These are, however, little more than loose remarks. A complete a priori theory of entrepreneurship would have to take account of the essential differences between entrepreneurial activity itself, which depends necessarily upon a future-directed area knowledge of an appropriate kind, and those forms of quasi-entrepreneurial activity which, because they rest on accident or error, exist independently of such knowledge.[75] It would have to take account of the differences between entrepreneurial perception which issues forth in appropriately directed economic activity, and quasi-entrepreneurial perception which stops short at the point where the knowledge gained might be put into practice.[76] It would have to be supplemented by a priori theories of non-entrepreneurial economic activity and of the types of non-future-directed knowledge on which it rests.[77] And these, in turn, would require as their basis a general a priori theory of action and of the consciousness of time, some elements of which, at least, are to be found in the writings in which Husserl applied his own a priori methodology to problems in psychology and in the philosophy of action.[78]

Notes

1. I should like to thank Israel Kirzner, Jeremy Shearmur, Peter Simons, and other participants in the Liberty Fund Seminar on Austrian Economics and its Philosophical and Historical Background held in Graz on 27–31 July 1980, for their assistance in the working out of the ideas put forward in this paper.
2. See Friedman (1953) for the definitive statement of this position.
3. In this respect the social sciences may resemble cosmology, or meteorology: see Hayek (1964).
4. See the methodological writings of Ludwig von Mises (especially Mises 1962 and the early chapters of Mises 1949). Rothbard (1979) is a survey of the Austrian criticisms of methodological positivism. See also Shand (1984, Chapters 1 and 2).
5. It may initially appear that there is some confusion involved in the idea that one and the same proposition can be established both empirically and by a priori means. A moment's reflection reveals, however, that this must be the case for every a priori truth. The proposition $2 + 2 = 4$, for example, can be recognised as true, a priori, by anyone who is familiar with the objects (2, 4, addition, equality) in question. But it can also be empirically established, e.g. by a mechanical process of counting out coins (though then of course other, more deep-seated a priori truths will serve as presuppositions).
6. It is Ludwig Lachmann who has most relentlessly criticised the predictive claims customarily made on behalf of economic theory — see especially Lachmann (1977, part 2). Compare also Shackle (1972).
7. Only comparatively recently has the nature of the *Methodenstreit* between Menger and the German historical school of economics come to be understood as a philosophical dispute between Aristotelianism on the one hand, and the crude empiricism/inductivism of Schmoller on the other. See Kauder (1965); Hansen (1968); Hutchison (1973); Bostaph (1978).
8. Walras (1965, p. 3).
9. The expresson 'natural kind' has recently established itself as a technical term of analytic philosophy where it connotes, for example, biological species (horse, cyprus tree, orange, caddis-fly, and so on: see for example, Wiggins (1980, Chapter 3). Natural kinds in the analytic-philosophical literature are, however, normally treated as one or other variety of logical fiction. Here we shall adopt a realist perspective, that is to say we shall take the view that an adequate description of any segment of material reality must involve reference not only to the individual objects to be found within it but also to the kinds which these objects exemplify. It is a distinguishing mark of natural kinds that they exhibit both *norm instances* and various — more or less natural — deviant instances. On norm kinds see Wolterstorff (1980) and the remarks in Smith (1986). On kinds in general, especially in relation to Aristotelian metaphysics, see Loux (1976).
10. The idea that propositions of the given kind are laws of thought has grown up as a result of the fact that the familiarity we have of the basic kinds is so basic to our thinking about the associated phenomena that we cannot *think round them*.
11. To be more precise, Mises (1949, Chapters 1, 2, 7, *passim*) holds economics to be

founded on one single a priori axiom, the so-called 'fundamental axiom of action', together with a small number of additional empirical postulates such as: leisure is a consumer good.

12. J. Locke, *Essay Concerning Human Understanding,* Book IV, Ch. VIII.

13. Ibid., §8.

14. Ibid.

15. Ibid., Book II, Ch.XXI.

16. D. Hume, *A Treatise of Human Nature,* Book I, Part I, section 7, footnote.

17. Reinach (1911, p. 176) (cited according to the English translation).

18. D. Hume, *Treatise,* Book I, Part I, section 7, footnote. Simple ideas in general, Hume goes on, resemble each other in their simplicity: 'And of this we may be certain, even from the very abstract terms *simple idea.* They comprehend all simple ideas under them. . . . And yet from their very nature, which excludes all composition, this circumstance in which they resemble, is not distinguishable or separable from the rest. It is the same case with all the degrees in any quality. They are all resembling, and yet the quality, in any individual, is not distinct from the degree.'

19. See A. Reinach (1911, p. 169) and the arguments there given.

20. On Austrian philosophy, see Haller (1979; 1981); Nyiri (1981); Smith (1978 1981).

21. Most important for us here is the 1911 paper by one of Husserl's most important students, Adolf Reinach. But see also Meinong (1882); Linke (1901); Salmon (1929); Davie (1977); Murphy (1980); and Willard (1984). That Hayek, too, fell under the sway of Kantian influences has been forcefully argued by John Gray (1984).

22. See Mises (1969). Only one philosophical or scientific work of importance was produced within the Empire in the first half of the nineteenth century. This was the *Wissenschaftslehre (Theory of Science),* of Bernard Bolzano.

23. Of the principal German philosophers only Leibniz and Herbart, both of whom exhibit realist, syncretist elements in their philosophies, were officially recognised in Austria.

24. See Mises (1969); Smith (1981); and the extremely useful piece by Rothbard (1975) on the scholastic background to Austrian economics.

25. Brentano (1862).

26. Brentano (1867).

27. Brentano (1872).

28. Brentano's influence after his move to Austria was no longer confined to a narrow circle of priests and theologians. Among those who attended his lectures in Vienna were, besides Husserl, also Meinong, Ehrenfels, Masaryk, Twardowski and Freud; see Haller (1981).

29. See Brentano (1924). Brentano characterised his methodology as empirical, but by this he meant simply that 'experience alone is my teacher' (Foreword); and he held the empirical method to be entirely compatible with a certain ideal or aprioristic point of view. 'Empirical', for Brentano, connotes something different from 'experimental'.

30. Brentano (1924, p. 63 (Eng. trans. p. 44)).

31. Ibid., p. 64 ff. (Eng. trans. p. 45ff).

32. See Brentano (1889).

33. Brentano was not, in this, guilty of psychologism, the view that logic is a branch of empirical psychology as normally conceived (see the 'Prolegomena' to Husserl's *Logical Investigations),* since the laws of (descriptive) psychology are, for Brentano, necessary, evident laws. See Mulligan and Smith (1985).

34. Menger (1883, p. 6n. (Eng. trans. p. 37n.)).

35. Husserl (1891).

36. These essays have been reprinted in Husserl (1979). See especially Husserl (1894).

37. The second edition of the work, published in 1913-22, contains revisions

introduced by Husserl to bring the work into closer conformity with his later, properly phenomenological philosophy. Nowhere in his later writings, however, does Husserl abandon the logical and methodological standpoint set forth in this work. See Smith and Mulligan (1982).

38. Hayek (1952, p. 67) and Hayek (1943). See also Lachmann (1969, pp. 152ff).

39. See Menger (1883); Hutchison (1973); Bostaph, (1978); Back (1929) offers a detailed statement of Menger's methodology in the *Untersuchungen* which makes clear the similarities to Husserl's methodology of synthetic a priori laws.

40. See Stumpf (1873), especially section 5, 'The Theory of Psychological Parts' and section 6, 'On the Nature of Psychological Parts'. Stumpf's work is a critique of psychological atomism and specifically of atomistic theories of spatial perception. It is discussed in more detail in Smith and Mulligan (1982, section 2).

41. Husserl (1900–1, Investigation 3, section 5).

42. Ibid., sections 1ff. See also Smith and Mulligan (1982); Smith (1981b); Sokolowski (1967—8; 1971; 1974); Simons (1982); and Mulligan, Simons and Smith (1984).

43. See Husserl (1900–1, section 14). *De re* necessity and possibility is contrasted with *de dicto* necessity and possibility. A proposition is *de re* necessary if and only if it is necessary in virtue of the essences or natures of the object(s) in question; a proposition is *de dicto* necessary if and only if it is necessary by virtue of the meanings of the terms which it contains.

44. On the a priori laws relating to the natural kind *promise* (and to other, related social act-kinds) see Reinach (1913), where Reinach also sketches a theory of what we have called 'a priori tendencies'. Karl Duncker (1941, section 13) has pointed out that such a tendency is a necessary accompaniment also of states of desire. On Reinach's work in general see Smith (1982a) and also the papers collected in Mulligan (1986).

45. Husserl (1900–1, sections 14ff).

46. Ibid., section 16.

47. More precisely: a is a mediate moment of b if and only if a is a moment of b and there is some c such that a is a moment of c and c a moment of b (see ibid., sections 14 and 16). A mediate moment a of an object b may also be immediately dependent on b, where there are two or more systems of dependence relations between a and b.

48. See the recent work by Kit Fine (1985) on dependence and the theory of closure algebras.

49. Husserl did not advance the converse thesis, that all dependence relations between moments are synthetic. Some, he held, were analytic, for example, the relation between a husband and a wife, between a master and his servant, or between a king and his subjects (ibid., section 11f.). It would however take us too far afield to discuss here the demarcation criterion between analytic and synthetic dependence relations advanced by Husserl.

50. The class of synthetic a priori propositions thus includes all those propositions logically entailed by propositions expressing dependence relations. But it includes also propositions expressing the *compatibility relations* obtaining between objects of different kinds in virtue of the fact that they may, as a matter of a priori necessity, enter into dependence relations with each other. A speck in the visual field need not be red, but it must have some colour, selected from the continuum of different kinds of moment which are intrinsically compatible with the moment *visual speck* and interchangeable with the moment *red*. Qualitative continua of this kind can be recognised in every sphere of sensory perception. Compatibility relations generate also, however, moment continua articulated not qualitatively, but quantitatively: by the relations of more or less (more intense than, more probable than, more imminent than, more guilty than, more valuable than, and so on). The synthetic a priori laws governing continua of this latter variety are familiar to Austrian economists in, for example, the theory of time preference (see Mises

(1949), Chapter 18) and compare Smith (1981b, section 3).

51. On the role of the theory of parts and wholes in Brentano's philosophy see Chisholm (1978); Smith and Mulligan (1982; 1985) and Brentano (1933 and 1982). The affinities between Husserl's theory and the work of Menger are evident on almost every page of Menger's methodological writings. Consider, for example, Appendix VII of the *Untersuchungen*, in which Menger discusses Aristotle's view that the individual 'of his nature as a *civilised* man' is dependent upon the existence of the state; or those passages in the letter to Walras of 1884 in which Menger characterises his own 'exact' method as 'analytic-compositive' (as involving not only the analysis of complexes into their constituent elements but also — precisely as in Husserl's theory — the consideration of how elements may become connected into more complex wholes) (Walras (1965, p. 5)). These affinities between Husserl and Menger were evident already to Hayek's contemporaries, Schütz and Kaufmann, in pre-war Vienna, and Hayek writes that he was often blamed by Schütz 'for the blind spot which prevented me from seeing how much help I could derive from Husserl for my work' (personal communication of Prof. von Hayek). Kaufmann was, like Schütz, a former disciple of Husserl, but became increasingly associated with the Vienna Circle; and his earlier, sympathetic treatment of Husserl's theory of dependence relations in the field of general methodology (Kaufmann 1930, Chapter 1) gave way to a more critical appraisal when he came to consider the possible applications of the theory to the social sciences (1934). In his paper on the synthetic a priori in economics (1937) he defends a more or less orthodox logical positivist position. The dissertation of Otaka (1932), written under Husserl, contains a detailed survey of holistic methodologies in the social sciences. It may be supplemented by the writings on part–whole relations listed in Smith (1982b).

52. This programme was initiated by Frege and Russell, and its most definitive statement is the 3-volume *Principia Mathematica* by Whitehead and Russell (1910–13). The aim of logicism was to establish, in a formally rigorous way, that mathematics is derivable from logic, an aim which was strictly realised only for certain restricted classes of mathematical propositions. Subsequent investigations in the foundations of mathematics have, however, been crucially marked by the logicist thesis and many of its most important results arise precisely from the question why logicism must fail.

53. Thus at *Tractatus* 6.3751, for example, Wittgenstein asserts that 'the simultaneous presence of two colours in the visual field is impossible, in fact logically impossible, since it is ruled out by the logical structure of colour', a thesis which was upheld by the members of the Vienna Circle (see, for example, Schlick (1930–1)), and by analytic philosophers of the post-war generation. (Delius (1963) is the most valuable survey of the relevant literature and includes a sympathetic discussion of Husserl's treatment of the synthetic a priori.)

54. This strategy proved successful only because, given the predominance of the positivistic tendency amongst philosophers in England and America, and the virtually complete annihilation of rigorous philosophy in the German-speaking world, no group or school was in a position to present a coherent case in favour of the synthetic a priori. A climate was created within which it was considered respectable only to produce ever narrower delineations of the class of purported synthetic a priori truths. The peculiarity of Husserl's position is that he defended a view of the synthetic a priori as comprehending more, far more, than even Kant had believed.

55. Thus Wittgenstein writes: 'Essence (*das Wesen*) is expressed by grammar' (1953, p. 371). Later he says: 'It is grammar which says what kind of object anything is' (1953, p. 373). Grammar expresses not empirical properties of objects (feelings, beliefs, images, thoughts, and so on) but essential properties: 'Could someone have a feeling of ardent love or hope for the space of one second — *no matter what* preceded or followed this second? — What is happening now has significance — in these surroundings. The surroundings lend it its significance. And the word 'hope' refers to a phenomenon of human life. (A smiling mouth *smiles* only in a human face.)' (1953, p. 583). 'Could one

teach a dog to simulate pain? Perhaps it is possible to teach him to howl on particular occasions as if he were in pain, even when he is not. But for this to be proper simulation there would still be missing the proper surroundings' (1953, p. 250). The simulation of pain, as a certain specific *kind* of phenomenon, can, of necessity, exist, only against a specific *kind* of background. Necessary relations of this kind are also called by Wittgenstein 'internal relations' (see Gier (1981, pp. 83ff.)), as opposed to, for example, causal relations, which Wittgenstein (1975, p. 63f) characterises as 'external'. Wittgenstein's grammar may be described as a theory of the internal relations between language, on the one hand, and action (and all the other phenomena of human life) on the other. It is interesting that Wittgenstein also uses the word 'phenomenology' to describe this kind of investigation, an investigation which is 'midway between science and logic' (1977, p. 15); see also Spiegelberg (1968); Gier (1981, Chapter 5); Smith and Mulligan (1982, section 4).

56. Especially since the publication of Kripke (1972), analytic philosophers have become increasingly more sympathetic to the idea of a synthetic a priori element in scientific theory (or, correlatively, to the idea of material necessity in the world). See for example, Wiggins (1980); Brody (1980); Chisholm (1976); and, from a different perspective, Harré and Madden (1975). Some of the relations between contemporary essentialism and Husserl's theory of part and whole are discussed in Simons (1982).

57. These propositions are analytic because the modifiers 'to exchange' and 'of a subject' occur only trivially, that is, they can be replaced, in such a way that the truth of the original is preserved by *any* grammatically similar modifier. (See Husserl, 1900–1, third Logical Investigation, sections 11–12) and Smith and Mulligan (1982, n. 77, part 3).)

58. See especially the papers collected in Kirzner (1979, part 3) and also Kirzner (1973; 1985).

59. Decision-making, in the framework of Austrian economics, therefore comprehends two distinct processes. On the one hand it is a matter of 'mechanical computation of the solution to the maximization problem implicit in the configuration of . . . given ends and means', and on the other hand is '*the very perception of the ends-means framework* within which allocation and economizing is to take place'. (Kirzner, 1973, p. 33.)

60. The knowledge which is acquired by the entrepreneur in his perception of an economic opportunity is thus radically distinct from those types of knowledge which we may choose to acquire (as a result of a previous entrepreneurial decision), knowledge which may properly be treated as something like an input or a tool. Ignorance is therefore correspondingly ambiguous: it may mean lack of command over a needed tool, or 'the sheer failure to utilize a resource available and ready to hand' which has simply not been noticed (see Kirzner, 1978, p. 130).

61. See Kirzner (1979b).

62. We must stress, once again, that the idea of a natural kind brings with it the possibility of deviant instances (see n. 9 above). It might be thought that this admission robs the theory of its significance: *P* is, as a matter of necessity, true of all instances of kind *K* unless (because the instances in question are deviant instances) it is not. However the ways in which an instance may deviate from the norm are themselves subject to a priori laws. And it is at the point where reflection on the kinds of possible deviations begins (reflection which yields a priori propositions of a higher order of complexity than the relatively simple propositions of the general theory), that the Husserlian methodology reveals its most powerful cutting edge (see n. 64 and n. 75 below).

63. See n. 44 above. A priori tendencies make themselves felt also in economic laws which assert, for example, that there is a tendency for any given good to acquire a single price throughout a given market.

64. Figure 1.1 pictures the ways in which the constituent parts and moments of what might be called *successful* economic activity are (in Wittgenstein's terms) 'internally

related' to each other. Entrepreneurial activity may, as a matter of necessity, be unsuccessful (may fail to generate a stream of pure entrepreneurial profits). It would be a simple matter to construct a picture of the more general case, incorporating both successful and unsuccessful entrepreneurship. Even this diagram would however necessarily involve, as a constituent moment of the moment of entrepreneurial knowledge, a *belief* that (with a greater or lesser probability) a profit stream will be generated.

65. Smith (1981) and Smith and Mulligan (1982; 1983) contain a preliminary statement of the formation rules for dependence-diagrams of this kind, together with a discussion of the range of possible applications of the directly depicting language which the diagrams constitute.

66. See n. 50 above.

67. It will already be clear (from, for example, n. 64 above), that 'knowledge' in the present context is to be understood in a sense loose enough to comprehend also beliefs, including false beliefs.

68. See Kirzner (1979), e.g. Chapters 1, 2 and 10.

69. Ryle (1949), Chapter 2.

70. Heidegger (1962). Husserl's work, too, especially in the later period, is consistent with a view of knowledge as centred primarily on action or practice, and not on any storehouse of propositions 'in the mind' (see Føllesdal (1979)).

71. It corresponds to one technical use of the term 'area' in contemporary linguistics, for example by Radden (1978).

72. Our use of the term 'cultural physiology' is designed to draw attention to the fact that area knowledge is not principally a matter of the conscious following of rules, but rather of the complex web of skills, habits, and reflexes which, through drilling and practice, becomes part of our make-up as human beings. Both von Hayek and Wittgenstein have exploited the notion of cultural physiology in their writings, but von Hayek unfortunately to some extent confused subliminal regularities with conscious rule-following (see, for example, Hayek (1963) and the criticism in Steele (1981); on Wittgenstein and cultural physiology see Nyíri (1977; 1979; 1982), see also Polanyi (1958); Oakeshott (1962); and the final section of Smith (1985)).

73. Kirzner himself has recognised at least part of what is involved here: '. . . the ability to learn without deliberate search is a gift individuals enjoy in quite different degrees'. See also Mises (1949), p. 325: 'Economists must never disregard in their reasoning the fact that the innate and acquired inequality of men differentiates their adjustment to the conditions of their environment.'

74. This proposition will apply particularly to those immigrants whose prior cultural background is stable and well-established. It is erroneous to suppose that entrepreneurial ability, like creative abilities of other kinds, is associated with instability or deviance. Such abilities are rather, to an even greater extent than ordinary human skills and practices, dependent upon the acceptance of established systems of conformity. See Nyíri (1977; 1979). There are, of course, other factors tending to encourage entrepreneurial activity on the part of (certain kinds of) immigrants: immigrants tend, for example, to be closed off from salaried employment to a greater extent than the members of the native community.

75. Such forms of quasi-entrepreneurial activity are examples of essentially possible deviations from the natural kind of entrepreneurship proper, discussed in n. 62 above.

76. The foreclosure of economic activity may be encouraged by certain kinds of institutional practices (of the type which may occur, for example, in the controlled economies of Eastern Europe). But the ways in which institutional measures may generate deviant forms of entrepreneurial activity are themselves governed by a priori laws: sée Reinach (1913, Chapter 3), in which Reinach discusses the relation between his a priori laws relating to the various *natural* kinds of legal phenomena and the treatment of such phenomena in actually existing systems of positive law. 'That a claim expires

through being fulfilled is', Reinach argues, 'just as self-evident a truth as any logical or mathematical axiom. But if it should prove expedient, why should not a system of positive law introduce a restriction according to which certain claims expire only when their having been fulfilled has been reported at the nearest office of the county court?' (Reinach, 1913, p. 802). The possibility of a restriction of this kind is, Reinach claims, intrinsic to the structure of a claim, where restrictions such as 'A claim expires only when the claimant has shot his next of kin' are incompatible with this structure.

77. See the illuminating discussions of the structure of human work in Rossi-Landi (1975), Chapter 2, section 2.3.2.

78. See Føllesdal (1979); Smith and Mulligan (1982); Hoche (1973).

Bibliography

Armstrong, D.M. (1978). *Universals and Scientific Realism*, 2 vols, Cambridge: Cambridge University Press.

Back, J. (1929). *Die Entwicklung der reinen Ökonomie zur nationalökonomischen Wesenswissenschaft*, Jena: Fischer 1929.

Bostaph, S. (1978). 'The Methodological Debate Between Carl Menger and the German Historicists', *Atlantic Economic Journal, 6,* 3-16.

Brentano, F. (1862). *Von der mannigfachen Bedeutung des Seienden nach Aristoteles*, Freiburg: Herder, English translation, *On the Several Senses of Being in Aristotle*, by R. George, Berkeley: University of California Press, 1975.

Brentano, F. (1867). *Die Psychologie des Aristoteles, insbesondere seine Lehre vom Nous Poietikos*, Mainz: Kirchheim; English translation, *The Psychology of Aristotle; in particular his doctrine of the active intellect*, by R. George, Berkeley: University of California Press, 1977.

Brentano, F. (1872–3). Review of Friedrich Kampe, *Die Erkenntnistheorie des Aristoteles*, in *Zeitschrift für Philosophie und philosophische Kritik, 59* (1872), 219–38; *60* (1873), 81–127.

Brentano, F. (1889). *Vom Ursprung sittlicher Erkenntnis*, Leipzig: Duncker and Humblot; English translation, *The Origin of Our Knowledge of Right and Wrong*, by R.M. Chisholm, London: Routledge, 1969.

Brentano, F. (1924). *Psychologie vom empirischen Standpunkt*, 2nd edn, 2 vols, ed. O. Kraus, Leipzig: Meiner; English translation, *Psychology from an Empirical Standpoint*, ed. L.L. McAlister, London: Routledge, 1973.

Brentano, F. (1933). *Kategorienlehre*, ed. A. Kastil, Leipzig: Meiner; English translation, *The Theory of Categories*, by R.M. Chisholm and N. Guterman, The Hague: Nijhoff, 1981.

Brentano, F. (1982). *Deskriptive Psychologie*, ed. R.M. Chisholm and W. Baumgartner, Hamburg: Meiner.

Brody, B.A. (1980). *Identity and Essence*, Princeton: Princeton University Press.

Chisholm, R.M. (1976). *Person and Object. A Metaphysical Study*, London: Allen and Unwin.

Chisholm, R.M. (1978). 'Brentano's Conception of Substance and Accident' in R.M. Chisholm and R. Haller (eds), *Die Philosophie Franz Brentanos*, Amsterdam: Rodopi, 197–210.

Davie, G. (1977). 'Edmund Husserl and "the as yet, in its most important respect, unrecognised greatness of Hume" ' in G. Morice *et al.* (eds), *David Hume*. Bicentenary Papers, Edinburgh: Edinburgh University Press, 69–76.

Delius, H. (1963). *Untersuchungen zur Problematik der sogenannten synthetischen Sätze apriori*, Göttingen: Vandenhoeck and Ruprecht.

Duncker, K. (1941). 'Pleasure, Emotion and Striving', *Philosophy and Phenomenological Research,* 1, 391-430.

Fabian, R. (ed.) (1985). *Christian von Ehrenfels: Leben und Werk,* Amsterdam: Rodopi.

Fabian, R. and Simons, P.M. (1986). 'The Second Austrian School of Value Theory' in this volume.

Fine, K. (1985). 'Husserl's Theory of Dependence', unpublished MS.

Føllesdal, D. (1979). 'Husserl and Heidegger on the Role of Actions in the Constitution of the World' in E. Saarinen *et al.* (eds), *Essays in Honour of Jaakko Hintikka,* Dordrecht: Reidel, 365–78.

Friedman, M. (1953). 'The Methodology of Positive Economics' in M. Friedman, *Essays in Positive Economics,* Chicago: Chicago University Press.

Gier, N.F. (1981). *Wittgenstein and Phenomenology,* Albany: State University of New York Press.

Gray, J. (1984). *Hayek on Liberty,* Oxford: Blackwell.

Haller, R. (1979). *Studien zur österreichischen Philosophie,* Amsterdam: Rodopi.

Haller, R. (1981). 'Wittgenstein and Austrian Philosophy', English translation of Chapter XII of Haller (1979), in Nyíri (1981, 91–112).

Hansen, R. (1968). 'Der Methodenstreit in den Sozialwissenschaften zwischen Gustav Schmoller und Karl Menger: seine wissenschaftshistorische und wissenschaftstheoretische Bedeutung' in A. Diemer (ed.), *Beiträge zur Ent-wicklung der Wissenschaftstheorie in 19. Jahrhundert,* Meisenheim am Glan: Anton Hain.

Harré, R. and Madden, E.H. (1975). *Causal Powers. A Theory of Natural Necessity,* Oxford: Blackwell.

Hayek, F.A. von (1937). 'Economics and Knowledge', *Economica, 4,* 33-54; repr. in Hayek (1949, 33–56).

Hayek, F.A. von (1943). 'The Facts of the Social Sciences', *Ethics, 54,* 1–13; repr. Hayek (1949, 57–76).

Hayek, F.A. von (1949). *Individualism and Economic Order,* London: Routledge.

Hayek, F.A. von (1952). *The Counter-Revolution of Science. Studies in the Abuse of Reason,* Glencoe, Ill.: Free Press; repr. by Liberty Press, Indianapolis, 1979.

Hayek, F.A. von (1962). 'Rules, Perception and Intelligibility', *Proceedings of the British Academy, 48;* repr. in Hayek (1967, 43– 65).

Hayek, F.A. von (1964). 'The Theory of Complex Phenomena' in M. Bunge (ed.), *The Critical Approach to Science and Philosophy,* New York: Free Press; repr. in Hayek (1967, 22–42).

Hayek, F.A. von (1967). *Studies in Philosophy, Politics and Economics,* London: Routledge.

Heidegger, M. (1962). *Being and Time,* Oxford: Blackwell, English translation of 7th German edn by J. Macquarrie and E. Robinson.

Hoche, H.–U. (1973). *Handlung, Bewusstsein und Leib. Vorstudien zu einer rein noematischen Phänomenologie,* Freiburg: Alber.

Husserl, E. (1891). *Philosophie der Arithmetik. Psychologische und logische Studien,* vol. I (only volume published), Halle: Pfeffer.

Husserl, E. (1894). 'Psychologische Studien zur elementaren Logik', *Philosophische Monatshefte, 30,* 159–91; repr. in Husserl (1979, 92–113); English translation by D. Willard, *The Personalist, 58* (1977), 295–320.

Husserl, E. (1900–1). *Logische Untersuchungen,* 1st edn, 2 vols, Halle: Niemeyer.

Husserl, E. (1913–22). *Logische Untersuchungen,* 2nd edn, 2 vols, Halle: Niemeyer; English translation, *Logical Investigations,* by J.N. Findlay, London: Routledge, 1970.

Husserl, E. (1928). 'Vorlesungen zur Phänomenologie des inneren Zeitbewusstseins', ed. M. Heidegger, in *Jahrbuch für Philosophie und phänomenologische Forschung, 9,* 367-498; English translation, *The Phenomenology of Internal Time-Consciousness,* by J.S. Churchill, The Hague: Nijhoff, 1964.

Husserl, E. (1929). 'Syntaktische Formen und syntaktische Stoffe, Kernformen und Kernstoffe', Appendix to 'Formale und transcendentale Logik', *Jahrbuch für Philosophie und phänomenologische Forschung, 10,* 269–74; English translation in, *Formal and Transcendental Logic,* The Hague: Nijhoff, 1969, 294–311.

Husserl, E. (1979). *Aufsätze und Rezensionen (1890–1910),* ed. B. Rang, The Hague: Nijhoff.

Hutchison, T.W. (1973). 'Some Themes from *Investigations into Method'* in J.R. Hicks and W. Weber (eds), *Carl Menger and the Austrian School of Economics,* Oxford: Clarendon, 15–37.

Kauder, E. (1965). *A History of Marginal Utility Theory,* Princeton: Princeton University Press.

Kaufmann, F. (1930). *Das Unendliche in der Mathematik und seine Ausschaltung. Eine Untersuchung über die Grundlagen der Mathematik,* Leipzig and Vienna: Deuticke; English translation, *The Infinite in Mathematics,* ed. by B.F. McGuiness, Dordrecht: Reidel, 1978.

Kaufmann, F. (1934). 'Soziale Kollektive', *Zeitschrift für Nationalökonomie, 1,* 294–308.

Kaufmann, F. (1937). 'Do Synthetic Propositions *a Priori* Exist in Economics?', *Economica, 4,* 337–42.

Kirzner, I. (1973). *Competition and Entrepreneurship,* Chicago: University of Chicago Press.

Kirzner, I. (1978). 'Economics and Error' in L. Spadaro (ed.), *New Directions in Austrian Economics,* Kansas City: Sheed Andrews and McMeel, 57–76, as repr. in Kirzner (1979a, 120–36).

Kirzner, I. (1979a). *Perception, Opportunity and Profit. Studies in the Theory of Entrepreneurship,* Chicago: University of Chicago Press.

Kirzner, I. (1979b). 'Hayek, Knowledge and Market Processes' in Kirzner (1979a, 13–33).

Kirzner, I. (1985). 'Prices, the Communication of Knowledge, and the Discovery Process', in K.R. Leube and R. Zlabinger, *The Political Economy of Freedom. Essays in Honor of F.A. Hayek,* Munich: Philosophia, 193–206.

Kripke, S. (1972). 'Naming and Necessity' in D. Davidson and G. Harman (eds), *Semantics of Natural Language,* Dordrecht: Reidel, 253–355 and 763–69; 2nd revised edn, *Naming and Necessity,* Oxford: Blackwell, 1980.

Lachmann, L.M. (1969). 'Methodological Individualism and the Market Economy' in E. Streissler *et al.* (eds), *Roads to Freedom. Essays in Honour of Friedrich A. von Hayek,* London: Routledge, 89–104; as repr. in Lachmann (1977, 149–65).

Lachmann, L.M. (1977). *Capital, Expectations and the Market Process. Essays on the Theory of the Market Economy,* ed. W.E. Grinder, Kansas City: Sheed Andrews and McMeel.

Linke, P.F. (1901). *D. Humes Lehre vom Wissen. Ein Beitrag zur Relationstheorie im Anschluss an Locke und Hume,* Leipzig: Engelmann.

Loux, M.J. (1976). 'The Concept of a Kind', *Philosophical Studies, 29,* 53–61.

Meinong, A. von (1882). *Hume-Studien II. Zur Relationstheorie,* Vienna: Braumüller, repr. in Meinong's *Gesamtausgabe,* vol. II, Graz: Akademische Druck- und Verlagsanstalt, 1971, 1-172.

Menger, C, (1871) *Grundsätze der Volkswirtschaftslehre,* Vienna: Braumülter, repr. as vol. I of Menger, *Gesammelte Werke,* ed. F.A. von Hayek, Tübingen: Mohr, 1968; English translation, *Principles of Economics,* by J. Dingwall and B.F. Hoselitz, Glencoe, Ill.: Free Press, 1950.

Menger, C. (1883). *Untersuchungen über die Methode der Socialwissenschaften und der politischen Okonomie insbesondere*, Leipzig: Duncker and Humblot; repr. in Menger, *Gesammelte Werke*, vol. II (1969); English translation, *Problems of Economics and Sociology*, by F.J. Nock, Urbana: University of Illinois Press, 1963.

Mises, L. von (1949). *Human Action. A Treatise on Economics*, New Haven: Yale University Press (based on Mises, *Nationalökonomie. Theorie des Handelns und Wirtschaftens*, Geneva: Editions Union, 1940; repr. Munich: Philosophia Verlag, 1980).

Mises, L. von (1962). *The Ultimate Foundations of Economic Science. An Essay on Method*, Princeton: Van Nostrand.

Mises, L. von (1969). *The Historical Setting of the Austrian School of Economics*, New Rochelle: Arlington House.

Mulligan, K. (ed.) (1986). *Speech Act and Sachverhalt: Reinach and the Foundations of Realist Phenomenology*, Dordrecht/Boston/Lancaster: Nijhoff.

Mulligan, K. and Smith B. (1985). 'Franz Brentano and the Ontology of Mind', *Philosophy and Phenomenological Research, 45*, 629-44.

Mulligan, K., Simons, P.M. and Smith, B. (1984). 'Truth-Makers', *Philosophy and Phenomenological Research, 44*, 287–321.

Murphy, R.T. (1980). *Hume and Husserl. Towards Radical Subjectivism*, The Hague: Nijhoff.

Nyíri, J.C. (1977). 'Wittgenstein's New Traditionalism', in *Essays on Wittgenstein in Honour of G.H. von Wright (Acta Philosophia Fennica, 28)*, Amsterdam: North-Holland, 503–12.

Nyíri, J.C. (1979). 'Wittgenstein's Spätwerk im Kontext des Konservatismus', in H.J. Heringer and M. Nedo (eds), *Wittgensteins geistige Erscheinung (Ludwig Wittgenstein Schriften*, Beiheft 3), Frankfurt: Suhrkamp, 83–101; English translation, 'Wittgenstein's Later Work in Relation to Conservatism', in Brian McGuinness (ed.), *Wittgenstein and his Times*, Oxford: Blackwell, 1982, 44–68.

Nyíri, J.C. (1982). 'Wittgenstein 1929–1931: Die Rückkehr', *Kodikas, 4–5*, 115-36. Partial English translation as 'Wittgenstein as a Conservative Philosopher', *Continuity, 8*, 1–23.

Nyíri, J.C. (ed.) (1981). *Austrian Philosophy: Studies and Texts*, Munich: Philosophia.

Oakeshott, M. (1962). *Rationalism in Politics and Other Essays*, London: Methuen.

Otaka, T. (1932). *Grundlagen zur Lehre vom sozialen Verband*, Vienna: Springer.

Polanyi, M. (1958). *Personal Knowledge. Towards a Post-Critical Philosophy*, London: Routledge.

Radden, G. (1978). 'Can "Area" be taken out of the Waste-Basket?' in W. Abraham (ed.), *Valence, Semantic Case and Grammatical Relations*, Amsterdam: Benjamins, 327–37.

Reinach, A. (1911). 'Kants Auffassung des Humeschen Problems'. *Zeitschrift für Philosophie und philosophische Kritik, 141*, 176–209; repr. in Reinach (1921, 1–35). English translation by J.N. Mohanty in *Southwestern Journal of Philosophy, 7* (1976), 161–88.

Reinach, A. (1913). 'Die apriorischen Grundlagen des bürgerlichen Rechts', *Jahrbuch für Philosophie und phänomenologische Forschung, 1*, 685–847; repr. in Reinach (1921, 166–350).

Reinach, A. (1921). *Gesammelte Schriften*, Halle: Niemeyer; new edition forthcoming, Munich: Philosophia Verlag.

Rossi-Landi, F. (1975). *Linguistics and Economics*, Paris and The Hague: Mouton.

Rothbard, M.N. (1957). 'In Defense of "Extreme Apriorism" ', *Southern Economic*

Journal, 23, 315–20.
Rothbard, M.N. (1975). 'New Light on the Prehistory of the Austrian School' in E.G. Dolan (ed.), *The Foundations of Modern Austrian Economics*, Kansas City: Sheed and Ward, 52–74.
Rothbard, M.N. (1979). *Individualism and the Philosophy of the Social Sciences*, San Francisco: Cato Institute.
Rug, R. and Mulligan, K. (1985).'Theorie und Trieb. Bemerkungen zu Ehrenfels' in Fabian (1985), 214–46.
Ryle, G. (1949). *The Concept of Mind*, London: Hutchinson.
Salmon, C.V. (1929). 'Central Problems of David Hume's Philosophy', *Jahrbuch für Philosophie und phänomenologische Forschung, 10*, 1929, 299–449.
Schlick, M. (1930–1). 'Gibt es ein materiales Apriori?' in *Wissenschaftlicher Jahresbericht der philosophischen Gesellschaft an der Universität zu Wien für das Vereinsjahr 1930/31*; repr. in *Gesammelte Aufsätze 1925–36*, Vienna: Gerold, 1938 (repr. Hildesheim: Olms, 1969), 20–30; English translation in *Philosophical Papers*, vol. II, Dordrecht: Reidel, 1979, 161–70.
Shackle, G.L.S. (1972). *Epistemics and Economics*, Cambridge: Cambridge University Press.
Simons, P.M. (1982). 'The Formalisation of Husserl's Theory of Wholes and Parts' in B. Smith (1982, 113–59). Vienna: Holder-Pichler-Tempsky.
Smith, B. (1978). 'Wittgenstein and the Background of Austrian Philosophy' in *Wittgenstein and his Impact on Contemporary Thought*, Dordrecht: Reidel, 31–35.
Smith, B. (1981a). 'The Production of Ideas: Notes on Austrian Intellectual History' in B. Smith (ed.), *Structure and Gestalt. Philosophy and Literature in Austria-Hungary*, Amsterdam: Benjamins, 211–34.
Smith, B. (1981b). 'Logic, Form and Matter', *Proceedings of the Aristotelian Society*, Supplementary Volume 55, 47–63.
Smith, B. (ed.) (1982). *Parts and Moments. Studies in Logic and Formal Ontology*, Munich: Philosophia.
Smith, B. (1982a). 'Introduction to Adolf Reinach, On the Theory of the Negative Judgment' in B. Smith (1982, 289–314).
Smith, B. (1982b) 'Annotated Bibliography of Writings on Part-Whole Relations since Brentano' in B. Smith (1982, 481–552).
Smith, B. (1984). 'Acta cum fundamentis in re', *Dialectica, 38*, 157–78.
Smith, B. (1985). 'The Theory of Value of Christian von Ehrenfels' in Fabian (1985, 150–71).
Smith, B. (1986). 'On the Cognition of States of Affairs' in Mulligan (1986).
Smith, B. and Mulligan K. (1982). 'Pieces of a Theory' in Smith (1982, 15–110).
Smith, B. and Mulligan, K. (1983). 'Framework for Formal Ontology', *Topoi, 3*, 73–85.
Sokolowski, R. (1967–8). 'The Logic of Parts and Wholes in Husserl's *Investigations*', *Philosophy and Phenomenological Research, 28*, 537-53; repr. in J.N. Mohanty (ed.), *Readings on Husserl's Logical Investigations*, The Hague, Nijhoff, 1977, 94–111.
Sokolowski, R. (1971). 'The Structure and Content of Husserl's *Logical Investigations*', *Inquiry, 14*, 318–47.
Sokolowski, R. (1974). 'Parts and Wholes' in R. Sokolowski, *Husserlian Meditations*, Evanston: Northwestern University Press, 9–17.
Spiegelberg, H. (1968). 'The Puzzle of Wittgenstein's *Phänomenologie* (1929–?)', *American Philosophical Quarterly, 5*, 244–56.
Steele, D.R. (1981). 'Spontaneous Order and Traditionalism in Hayek', unpublished MS.
Stumpf, C. (1873). *Über den psychologischen Ursprung der Raumvorstellung*,

Leipzig: Hirzel.

Walras, L. (1965).   *Correspondence of Léon Walras and Related Papers*, ed. W. Jaffé, vol. II, Amsterdam: North-Holland.

Whitehead, A.N. and Russell, B.A.W. (1910–13).   *Principia Mathematica*, Cambridge: Cambridge University Press.

Wiggins, D. (1980).   *Sameness and Substance*, Oxford: Blackwell.

Willard, D. (1984).   *Logic and the Objectivity of Knowledge*, Athens, Ohio: Ohio University Press.

Wittgenstein, L. (1953).   *Philosophical Investigations*, Oxford: Blackwell.

Wittgenstein, L. (1961).   *Tractatus Logico-Philosophicus*, with translation by D.F. Pears and B.F. McGuinness, London: Routledge, 1961 (1st German edn, 1921).

Wittgenstein, L. (1975).   *Philosophical Remarks*, English translation by R. Hargreaves and R. White, Oxford: Blackwell.

Wittgenstein, L. (1977).   *Remarks on Colour*, translated by L.L. McAlister and M. Schättle, Oxford: Blackwell, 1977.

Wolterstorff, N. (1980).   *Works and Worlds of Art*, Oxford: Clarendon.

2 THE SECOND AUSTRIAN SCHOOL OF VALUE THEORY

Reinhard Fabian and Peter M. Simons

1. Introduction: General Questions

The *first* Austrian school of value theory, starting out from Carl Menger (also Friedrich von Wieser, Eugen von Böhm-Bawerk), is well known and well documented, and we shall not discuss it in detail in this paper. Also well known and researched are the marginal utility theories put forward simultaneously with the appearance of Menger's *Grundsätze der Volkswirtschaftslehre* in England by W. Stanley Jevons, and in Switzerland by Léon Walras, as are the subsequent developments in economics in Austria (Schumpeter, Mises, Hayek), England and America (Marshall, Edgeworth, Clark) and Switzerland (Pareto). The immediate pre-history of Menger's theory is also well known, especially its relation to Gossen and Daniel Bernoulli. The parallels to be found in Bentham were first documented in 1901 by Oskar Kraus, and later histories of value theory by Rudolf Kaulla (1906), his teacher Lujo Brentano (1908), the elder brother, incidentally, of one of our chief protagonists, and again Kraus (1937) have traced in detail the rise of the theory of marginal utility (see also Kauder, 1965).

Far less well-documented is a remarkable parallel blossoming of value theory in Austrian *philosophy*, most of it concentrated into a mere 25 years around the turn of this century. In depth and breadth this development outstrips both the other near-contemporary movements in philosophical value theory in Europe: the Baden or South-West German school of neo-Kantians (Windelband, Rickert, Bauch and others) and the slightly later developments in the phenomenological movement (especially Scheler and N. Hartmann). The fountain-head of this other Austrian school of value theory was the philosopher Franz Brentano (1838–1917), who taught at the University of Vienna from 1874 to 1895. Brentano, his pupils and grandpupils together contributed immeasurably to the philosophy and psychology of modern times. Some of Brentano's students (e.g., Carl Stumpf, Edmund Husserl) made their careers and reputations in Germany, but those who will concern us here, the value theorists, remained within the borders of the

Danube monarchy. Following Eaton (1930, p. 16) and Rescher (1969, p. 50) we shall call them collectively the *second* Austrian school of value theory. The suggestion of a parallel to the Menger school is intentional, for not only have we here two flourishing schools of value theory in Austria; there are doctrinal parallels and scientific and personal interactions between the two schools. The basic ideas of the principal members of the second school, their development and their interaction with those of the first, are the main topics of our essay. Despite its philosophical importance, the value theory of the phenomenological school will not be dealt with here, firstly because this development took place outside Austria, but more crucially because, being somewhat later, it both presupposed the work of the second Austrian school, and did not enjoy the mutual interaction with economics which so uniquely characterises the latter. The person linking the two schools, Edmund Husserl, was less interested in value theory for its own sake, and published no major work in the area, although he canvassed in outline the idea of a formal axiomatics of value to parallel that of logic. It is mainly the application of Husserl's phenomenological method by others to the area of value which is known, and which has been influential.

To describe the philosophical value theorists stemming from Brentano as a 'school' is somewhat misleading, for they were at variance on many points of doctrine, including such basic questions as whether there are absolute values. Furthermore the scientific and personal relations between various individuals and groups within the Brentano school were, as we shall see, often less than totally cordial and co-operative. However, insofar as they can all trace their philosophical ancestry clearly back to Brentano and they are all agreed on the vital importance of a general, all-embracing philosophical theory of value, to include as special cases economic, ethical, aesthetic and other values, there are crucial ties binding them together. We shall therefore continue to refer to them as a school; the internal divisions and differences will be dealt with further below.

At the outset of this investigation, two general questions occurred to us concerning this movement, to which we have sought the answers. Firstly, why did there develop at this time in Austria a strong philosophical discipline dealing with value *in general*? Secondly, why was there then so much fruitful cross-fertilisation between different disciplines, in particular between philosophy, psychology, economics and jurisprudence? The answers which can be given to these questions are corroborated in detail in the body of the essay, but to give an overall view of our findings, we shall set out here a brief summary.

In answer to our first question, the emergence of the general theory of value can be attributed in two respects to Franz Brentano: to his theories and to his influence as a teacher. The then orthodox classification of mental phenomena into thinking, feeling and willing was derived from Kant. Brentano by contrast revived and strengthened the classification, going back through Descartes and Augustine to Aristotle, into ideas (presentations, *Vorstellungen*), judgements, and a third large class, often given the ungainly title 'phenomena of love and hate' but which it is easier to call, following a suggestion of Anton Marty, '*interests*'. Interests may be positive (liking, loving, desiring) or negative (disliking, hating, shunning) in the same way that judgements can be classified into positive (affirming) and negative (denying), a parallel exploited to the full by Brentano. More crucially, from our point of view, 'interests' subsumes the phenomena of feeling and willing into one class. This then opens the way for a general division between *cognitive* philosophy, relating to judgements, and a general philosophy of *value*, sometimes called 'axiology', to include the study of all feelings, esteemings, action, emotions, and the objects of such acts. With this the study of all acts of *valuing*, both positive and negative, is brought together, and along with this study goes naturally the investigation of values themselves.

Certainly not all of Brentano's students followed him in this: in particular Christian von Ehrenfels repartitioned interests into two basic classes of feeling and willing. Nevertheless he, like the others, continued to study values in general: once inaugurated, the new general discipline of value theory was able to continue under its own momentum. The idea of a general value theory in fact pre-dates Brentano's work. It can be found already in the writings of Hermann Lotze, a thinker whom Brentano knew and respected. The germ of such a theory is even present in Bentham. But it is Brentano who is usually — and rightly — credited with being the first to develop such a theory in detail.

The fact that, wherever Brentano students studied value theory, they studied it in its generality, can best be attributed to the force of Brentano's example as a teacher and person. His lectures on practical philosophy in the University of Vienna were massively popular, and were regularly attended by students from faculties outside philosophy. The clarity and naturalness of the idea of a general study of value kept its hold on his students even after they had diverged from their teacher over other matters.

Turning to our second question, there is no single reason for the cross-fertilisation between disciplines, rather a number of interrelated factors. Firstly, there was the growing confidence of the fledgling science of psychology in Europe in the second half of the nineteenth century, with Brentano himself not least among the pathfinders. Psychology was at that time only beginning to develop to the position where it could hive itself off from philosophy as an independent discipline. Thus it was natural for students of Brentano, the author of the famous *Psychology from an Empirical Standpoint* (1874), to take an interest in, and indeed contribute to, empirical psychology. We can here mention merely such facts as that the person considered to be the father of Gestalt psychology is Brentano's student Ehrenfels; that another Brentano student, Alexius Meinong, founded, in Graz in 1894, the first laboratory for the experimental study of psychology in the Habsburg Empire, an honour which, had circumstances been more favourable, would certainly have gone to Brentano himself; and that the philosopher Carl Stumpf is best known as the author of a massive two-volume treatise, *Tonpsychologie*, on the psychology of music. Nor was psychology then, as it is now, a curricular subject taught apart from philosophy. That there was a close relationship between philosophy and psychology then seemed perfectly natural. Indeed, psychology was itself in the ascendent within philosophy: it was often canvassed as the fundamental philosophical discipline, competent to assess the credentials of other branches of philosophy, an idea characteristic of the British empiricists Locke, Hume and Mill, and transmitted with emphasis by Brentano. Furthermore Brentano's division of psychology into a ratiocinative, a priori, descriptive part, and an experimental, a posteriori, genetic part, with the former being the more fundamental of the two, meant that the groundwork of psychology was the task of philosophers, as had been the case in Aristotle's *De Anima* and in the studies of 'human nature' made by the British empiricists.

Secondly, the institutional structure of Austrian universities meant that students were as a matter of course exposed to lectures by leading figures in areas outside their main field of study. Austrian universities normally consisted of four faculties: philosophy, theology, medicine and law. In the philosophy faculty were taught not only philosophy, but also mathematics and the natural sciences, and history. Economics was taught in the Law Faculty. By requirement of the *Studienordnung* then in force, law students had also to attend lectures in philosophy, some basic elements of which they would be expected already to have mastered before entering university, since one of the subjects studied in the *Gymnasium* was entitled 'philosophical propaedeutics'. Thus a powerful teacher like Brentano could be expected to capture good students for philosophy from other subject areas, as, for example, he did in the case of Husserl, whose doctorate was in mathematics, and Meinong, whose doctorate was in history. Students who attended Brentano's lectures would very often have also attended those of Menger in the Law Faculty.

We must also remember that the academic world of the later nineteenth century was much smaller than it is today. Further, whereas the German Empire had inherited from its smaller predecessor states a multitude of small universities, there were far fewer in Austria: these were mainly in the three capitals, Vienna, Prague and Budapest, with old German-speaking universities in Graz and Innsbruck, as well as the long-established Jagiellonian University in Kraków. Only towards the end of the century did the number begin to grow appreciably, with universities in the Slav areas such as Lemberg (Lwów), Agram (Zagreb), and Czernowitz being founded in 1875. So there were relatively fewer professorial chairs, and the main protagonists of our essay could be expected to know of, and often indeed know, each other well. In addition to the normal professional connections and personal friendships of the academic world, there are in our case also historical accidents linking the two schools, especially through Böhm-Bawerk, who was not only Friedrich von Wieser's brother-in-law, but also related by marriage to Meinong; moreover, for many years von Wieser was the next-door neighbour of his fellow Professor von Ehrenfels in Prague.

It is very easy to discern the influence of the economists on the philosophers, since they cite, and even start out from the works of the former. Influences in the other direction are harder to detect, but they do exist, as we shall see below. First of all, however, we shall examine in greater detail the main figures of the second Austrian school, in particular Brentano, Meinong, Ehrenfels and Kraus. Because of the importance of the personal and cultural ties in the second Austrian school, we shall include not only brief accounts of the relevant works of the main protagonists but also short biographical sketches.

2. Franz Brentano

Biography

The life of Brentano was more than usually eventful and controversial for that of an academic. The details have been recounted before by his students, in particular detail by Oskar Kraus and Carl Stumpf, so we shall give a rather brief outline here.

Franz Clemens Honoratus Hermann Brentano (b.1838, Marienberg, d.1917, Zurich) was the second son of a Catholic writer, Christian Brentano, who, significantly in view of the religious controversy to surround Brentano through his middle and later life, was expelled in the same year from Prussia for supporting the Bishop of Cologne in a conflict with the Prussian government. He was a nephew of the Romantic poet Clemens Brentano and the authoress Bettina von Arnim, whose husband Achim was Clemens Brentano's *Wunderhorn* collaborator. Brentano was raised at a fine house in Aschaffenburg, and was schooled in Catholicism by his deeply religious mother. His elder brother, the distinguished economist Lujo, spent much less time under this influence and developed quite different interests and attitudes. Brentano studied in Munich, Würzburg and, between 1858 and 1859, worked intensively in Berlin under the Aristotle scholar and logician Adolf Trendelenburg. It was to Trendelenburg that he dedicated his first book, *Von der mannigfachen Bedeutung des Seienden nach Aristoteles*, which appeared in 1862.

He then studied theology in Munich and Würzburg, where he was ordained in 1864, and he habilitated in Würzburg as *Privatdozent* in 1866, holding a now famous disputation in the *Aula* in which he defended 25 Latin theses, by various accounts getting much the better hand against his interlocutors, and deciding one of his audience, a young law student called Carl Stumpf, to study philosophy with him. Stumpf remained one of his closest friends, although they saw much less of each other in later life, and was the first of his enviable series of famous students. Stumpf's 'Reminiscences of Brentano' provide a graphic account of Brentano's time at Würzburg. The date of Brentano's disputation coincided unhappily with the Prussian attack on Aschaffenburg, and Würzburg itself was attacked only two weeks later. Throughout his life Brentano cherished the idea of a Greater Germany in the old South German sense, and he was bitter in his criticism of the new Prussian-led *Reich*, which he was convinced was destroying what was best in German life and would lead to catastrophic consequences.

In 1870 Brentano experienced a religious crisis of conviction, which also coincided with the eventually successful attempt to declare the dogma of papal infallibility. Bishop Ketteler of Mainz, one of the opponents of the proposed dogma, got Brentano to write an influential paper against it. At the same time Brentano was having doubts about other points of dogma, in particular the Trinity, which he came to believe was contradictory. It was characteristic of Brentano that internal, intellectual arguments carried more weight with him than external events, even where the latter turned out the way he did not want. Characteristically also, he was not content either with such half-way houses as old Catholicism or Protestantism, but broke with Christianity altogether, although he postponed leaving the priesthood, which entailed also leaving the Church, until early 1873, mainly out of consideration for his mother. His doubts were conveyed to Stumpf, who had entered a seminary, under Brentano's influence, with the idea of taking up the cloth, and again under Brentano's influence left the seminary and gave up the idea of becoming a priest. For some reason Brentano did not exercise a similar influence upon another student, the Swiss-born Anton Marty, but Marty later heard of Brentano's change and himself gave up the faith: such was the way that Brentano's presence could act at a distance. Brentano was held up in Würzburg as a champion of the Church's cause, which made his position there increasingly untenable, especially as it began to leak out that he had had a change of heart. In 1872 Brentano travelled to London, where he met Herbert Spencer. He also corresponded with Mill, whose works he greatly admired. While he was away he was made *Extraordinarius* at Würzburg. At this time he and Stumpf were deep in work on matters psychological: their ideas were often worked out in tandem, and Stumpf's 1873 book on the psychology of spatial perception was both influenced by and influenced Brentano's own interest in psychology.

By leaving the church, Brentano succeeded in sowing mistrust among clerics, but without managing to free himself from the mistrust of anti-clerics. He looked around for a chair, rejecting the idea of Leipzig because the library had no modern literature, and in 1874, after representations by his older friend and colleague Hermann Lotze, he was appointed *Ordinarius* in philosophy in Vienna. In the same year there appeared his most famous and influential work, *Psychology from an Empirical Standpoint*, which made his academic reputation. It was, according to Stumpf, only after he went to Vienna that Brentano began to occupy himself in earnest with ethical and value-theoretical matters. He remained Professor for only six years. He decided to marry in 1880, and it was pointed out to him that certain High Court decisions implied that marriage of ex-clergy was not allowed. The case was not however clear, and the liberal view was that the High Court interpretation was a bad one; but to be safe Brentano acquired Saxon citizenship and married in Leipzig. Because of this he had previously to resign his Professorship, and he returned as a *Privatdozent*, although everyone expected that he would soon be reappointed as professor. However, despite repeated representations, this never happened. The case became a *cause célèbre*, and Brentano a nationally-known figure as a result. He was undoubtedly handled very shoddily by the authorities. He remained in Vienna for a further fourteen years, but eventually, sadly, left, to take up residence in Italy, after the death of his first wife Ida in 1893. He remarried in 1897. Deprived of the chance of teaching, he lived mainly in Florence, summering at a house he owned at Schönbühel in der Wachau on the Danube, a house which stood over that river very much as his childhood home had stood over the Main. From 1903 an unsuccessful cataract operation left him partially sighted, and in his later years he became totally blind. His ideas were still developing however, and he developed a new metaphysical position, sometimes called 'reism', according to which the only category of existent is that of Thing *(res)*, understood as including both spatial things and also non-spatial, immaterial souls. In doing this he was led into opposition to those of his students who, starting out from his earlier teachings, acknowledged other categories, in particular the category of 'state of affairs', and also those of his students such as Husserl who had developed ontologies partially platonistic in character. Brentano's later philosophy, though that of an ageing man, yet reveals an agile and innovative mind. In its concern with ontological parsimony, coupled with a *Sprachkritik* whereby expressions appearing to designate entities other than things are treated as misleading, and paraphrased away, it foreshadows later developments in analytical philosophy, and in particular the ideas of the Polish reist Tadeusz Kotarbiński, who went further than Brentano, for example in denying the existence of immaterial things. The later Brentanian philosophy is ontologically at the opposite extreme from that of Meinong. Its ontological parsimony captured the unswerving, often evangelical adherence of the second generation of his students and followers. It should be pointed out, however, that Brentano's new views on language and ontology made relatively little difference to his established position on ethics. Brentano's consolations in his last years were his unswerving faith and trust in God, and also contacts with his younger followers, particularly Oskar Kraus and Alfred Kastil, who were to edit his *Nachlass*. Although they were actually pupils of Marty, and never heard Brentano lecture, they followed his new teachings to the extent of disagreeing with their former teacher. Brentano was forced to leave Italy because of war propaganda, and he died in Zurich in 1917.

Brentano's life as a teacher will be investigated below, but first we shall present his major principles in value theory.

Brentano's Work on Value

Little of Brentano's work on ethics and value theory was published in his lifetime. The most important of the works which did appear is the short book *Vom Ursprung sittlicher Erkenntnis*, published in 1889. This contains the text and notes to a famous lecture delivered to the Vienna Law Society in that year. The lecture was originally entitled 'Von der natürlichen Sanktion für recht und sittlich'. The book was translated into English in 1902, as *The Origin of the Knowledge of Right and Wrong*, and it deeply impressed G.E. Moore, who wrote an enthusiastic review (1903b). The lecture contains in miniature the ideas which Brentano had long been expounding at greater length in his Vienna University lectures on practical philosophy. It is through these lectures, published posthumously in 1952 as *Grundlegung und Aufbau der Ethik*, that Brentano's ideas took hold on his students. The lectures, in the form presented in this book, were given every Winter semester between 1876 and 1894 except when Brentano had leave of absence. Kraus suggests that even if only the Law Society lecture had survived, it alone would have assured Brentano a place among the great philosophers, and that it represented the most significant forward step in ethics since antiquity. Even the somewhat less partisan Moore remarked: 'In almost all points in which he differs from any of the great historical systems, he is in the right... It would be difficult to exaggerate the importance of this work.' (McAlister 1976, p. 177.)

We summarise here briefly Brentano's basic principles (for further details, see Chapter 5). Since, as Brentano argues, '[t]o understand the true source of our ethical knowledge, we must consider the results of recent investigations in the area of descriptive psychology' (1889, p. 11), we start with his psychology. Although Brentano described his approach as empirical, this does not here mean experimental, but rather anti-speculative. Brentano described himself as belonging to the 'empirical school', and he was certainly an empiricist in the sense that he believed that all concepts have their origin in intuitive presentations (1889, section 18). He valued highly the results of the British empiricists, especially Mill, as against the works of the German idealists, which he regarded as representing the most degenerate phase of the cycle of birth, development, stagnation and deterioration which he believed to repeat itself through the history of philosophy. But he was also very willing to listen to and learn from such rationalist philosophers as Descartes and Leibniz. Furthermore his descriptive psychology is a priori, and is the direct forerunner of Husserl's more elaborate phenomenology. *Psychology from an Empirical Standpoint* appears today as a purely conceptual and descriptive investigation, belonging to what might be called philosophical psychology or philosophy of mind.

Brentano's basic principle is classificatory: all mental phenomena divide into three fundamental classes. He gives credit for the rediscovery of this Aristotelian division to Descartes. The classes are: ideas *(ideae, Vorstellungen)*; judgements *(judicia, Urteile)* and interests, or love and hate *(horexis, voluntates sive affectus, Gemütstätigkeiten, Lieben und Hassen)*. Bretano denies that judgements and ideas form a single class, as associationists thought. The mere combination or association of ideas does not involve a position-taking, an affirmation or denial, a type of binary opposition which is characteristic of judgement. Nor can he agree with Kant that presentations or ideas require cognitive thought. The mere passive living-through of an idea is for Brentano not something intellectual, nor does it presuppose intellectual position-taking. However judgements without the ideas which form their matter are not possible for Brentano. Similarly interests presuppose judgements, and so also ideas. Interests comprise a wide range of phenomena including hope, fear, regret, desire, wish, resolve, will, action, satisfaction, dissatisfaction, pleasure, pain, and so on. Brentano denies the then current division of this class into willing and desiring. He does not deny that these are different, but argues that there is here a continuous spectrum of phenomena which shade smoothly into one another, in which there are no sharp demarcation lines, let alone divisions of principle.

Brentano's second point is to stress the analogies between judgement and interest. On these analogies he places much weight. Just as it is self-contradictory simultaneously to affirm and deny the same thing, so it is self-contradictory in the sphere of interests simultaneously both to love and to hate the same thing (in the same respect). The laws governing the emotional sphere Brentano likens to logic, an idea later to be developed by others. He uses the word *'richtig'* (correct) to cover both spheres, and argues that we can experience in ourselves such correctness.

Just as there are some things which we can be certain are true, because they are transparently *evident* to us — we can have no doubt concerning the correctness of their affirmation — so there are some things which we can be certain are good, it being similarly a matter of transparent evidence in the emotional sphere, and we can have no doubt that it is correct to love them. Brentano's theory of the self-illuminating nature of evidence is clearly inspired by Descartes. It is in virtue of such evidence that the foundations of ethics are a priori, notwithstanding the fact that the concepts concerned are derived from experience. Brentano carefully distinguishes evidence from instinct and habit in both spheres. On the basis of evidence Brentano believes he can establish certain absolute values. As examples he gives knowledge, joy (other than *Schadenfreude*, joy at the suffering of others), pleasure, the love of the good. Their polar opposites are of course evidently bad. He does not deny that it is possible to find people who love the bad and hate the good: it is all too easy to discover cruelty, brutality, malice, and so on. But he regards such attitudes as basically perverse. Brentano recognises that his short list is not particularly illuminating or practically helpful, but remarks that obviousness is by no means the same as triviality. When dealing, as here, with the foundations of a subject, such obviousness is a desideratum, as it is in logic. We see here the beginnings of the idea of a formal codification or axiomatisation of these basic principles, the possibility of which was first clearly apprehended by Brentano's students Meinong and Husserl. Meinong's own first faltering steps along this path led, through the ground-breaking work of his student and successor, Ernst Mally, to the development of what we now call deontic logic *(Sollenlogik)*.

Brentano distinguishes between those things which it is correct to love for their own sake, that is, which are good in themselves, as ends, and those which are good solely as means to the attainment of such ends. This distinction between primary (intrinsic) and secondary (extrinsic) goods is important in two respects. Firstly, it means that economic goods are always secondary, so the investigation of economic goods and of economic value presupposes, as its a priori foundation, the descriptive psychology setting out the principles for primary goods. Secondly, the distinction is Brentano's main bulwark against ethical and value-relativism: it allows him to acknowledge the existence of relativity, namely in the sphere of secondary goods, which vary according to time, place and circumstance, while denying that the primary goods are also relative. Primary goods are all psychic in nature, whereas secondary goods need not be. The latter are what he calls practical or useful goods. He is also thereby able to distinguish that which is best in itself from that which is the best we can attain. By virtue of our limitations we usually remain ignorant of what is best in itself, and may indeed make mistakes, in a sense analogous to that of factual mistakes of judgement, about what is good. The highest maxim of practical philosophy is to choose the best we can attain and strive for its attainment. Brentano recognises that this too is not particularly informative, but it rules out some philosophies, such as that of Kant, from being adequate foundations for ethics. He recognises also the familiar objection that we cannot know for sure what is the best we can attain because of ignorance and uncertainty about the future, but is not deceived into thinking it an important objection, because it holds for all practical philosophies alike, except such degenerate ones as regard it of no intrinsic importance *what* we strive for, merely *that* we strive for something. It requires no great effort of imagination to see what Brentano's reaction to Heidegger and existentialism would have been. In this connection he acknowledges the part that estimation of probabilities has to play in practical philosophy. But he is resolutely against a form of intellectualism, of a sort developed later by Meinong, which would conceive value-mistakes as mistakes of judgement.

Brentano is also anti-hedonist. He acknowledges the value of the work of certain modern hedonists such as Bentham in some respects, but, as a good Aristotelian, he could hardly be expected to espouse hedonism. There are qualitatively different kinds of value and disvalue, which are not arithmetically comparable. He is nicely ironical about the possibility of exact measurement:

> Consider how ridiculous it would be if someone said that the amount of pleasure he has in smoking a good cigar is such that, if it were multiplied by 127, or say by 1077, it would be precisely equal to the amount of pleasure he has in listening to a symphony of Beethoven or in viewing one of Raphael's madonnas! (1889, section 33.)

In this respect he is dubious of the correctness of Fechner's psychophysical law in general, and certainly denies that it could ever be used in the measurement of emotions. Any quasi-behaviouristic attempt to measure degree of feeling by measuring involuntary movements 'is like trying to establish the exact day of the month by studying the weather' (1889, n. 41). This point is interesting in that there seem to be certain historical connections between Fechner's work and that of the marginal-utility theorists. Brentano must consistently also deny that the value of primary goods falls as these accumulate, whatever may be the case for secondary goods. Brentano is willing to acknowledge that the incomparability of different kinds of value poses a practical problem in making decisions: he does not wish to hide this. Nor, wisely, is he willing to offer any detailed guidance on such choices. The matter is too complicated to belong to the foundations of ethics.

The most important disanalogy between judging and interest consists in the fact that interests, unlike judgements, admit of comparisons of degree. Whereas one thing cannot be more true than another, one thing can certainly be more good, that is better, than another, and *mutatis mutandis* for 'false' and 'bad'. Whereas an action could be neither good nor bad, but merely indifferent, Brentano does not recognise any possible alternative status for judgements outside truth and falsity (a disanalogy which Brentano came to see only *after* the appearance of the *Ursprung*). Brentano's account of 'better' is perfect both in its simplicity and in its coherence with his other principles. It invokes the concept of *preference*, with which we are all evidently acquainted. A thing *A* is better than a thing *B* (*B* is worse than *A*) just when it is correct to prefer *A* to *B*, and incorrect to prefer *B* to *A*. This simplicity should not disguise the profundity of Brentano's principle. We need only compare it with the other initially plausible idea that something is better which is worthy of *greater* love for its own sake, which Brentano, with good reason, rejects. He also offers several valid principles of preference, insight into which is derived from acts of preferring which are experienced as being correct. They include (i) preference of something good to something bad; (ii) the very Leibnizian idea of preference of the existence of something good to its non-existence; (iii) preference of the non-existence of something bad to its existence; (iv) preference of more intense pleasure to less intense pleasure; (v) preference of less intense pain to more intense pain; (vi) preference of longer-lasting to shorter-lasting joy or pleasure; (vii) preference of shorter-lasting to longer-lasting pain. Again, Brentano makes no apology for the transparent obviousness of these principles.

For the highest practical good, that is, good concerning what we can attain, Brentano follows a broadly utilitarian line, in that he holds that secondary goods are summable, and that the greatest overall sum is to be sought.

> To further the good throughout this great whole so far as possible — this is clearly the correct end in life, and all our actions should be centred around it. It is the one supreme imperative upon which all the others depend. It is thus a duty to give of oneself and even on occasion to sacrifice oneself. Any given good, whether in ourselves or in others, is to be loved in proportion to its value and is to be loved

equally wherever it may be found. Envy, jealousy and malice are ruled out. (1887, section 35.)

In a footnote, Brentano later qualifies this apparently uncompromising altruism by making the familiar claim that normally the most effective way to further the overall good is by caring first for oneself and, in concentric circles, one's own family, city and country. But it must be noted that Brentano's readiness to accept utilitarian ideas regarding subordinate rules, that is, in the sphere of the practically attainable, and his similar readiness to accept their relativity, far from making him a relativist, rest on and presuppose the absolute primary goods. This conviction of the absoluteness of primary values is supported by Brentano's theism, and here again his views on the relationship between God, the absolutely and perfectly good in Himself, and the world, are reminiscent of Leibniz: God, not the world, is the correct object of our supreme love. Thus in the injunction to love God above all and the recognition that all goods, whether our own or our neighbour's, are to be loved proportionately only to their value, he finds rational justification for the first two commandments.

Brentano as Teacher, the Two Generations, and Anton Marty

Brentano was a great teacher: there can be no doubt of that. All of his students who have written about him describe the tremendous impact his teaching had on them. He was of striking appearance: tall, thin, with a strong but ascetic face and an impressive mane of hair and penetrating eyes. Even after giving up the cloth he wore simple, dark clothes, and was said to have retained throughout his life a faintly priestly air. His personal grace and charm made him a sought-after guest in Viennese society. Again and again, his students describe his effect on them as that of a metamorphosis. He was never worsted in verbal combat, being a master of dialectic. Yet with his students he was not cruelly dismissive or contemptuous, provided they were seriously looking for the truth and not merely babbling. He could draw profound insights out of a student's fumbling attempts, and so instil confidence. He could never have enough time for his students: he would invite them out for walks with him, when only philosophy would be discussed, and he would then be oblivious of his surroundings. He would even continue discussing points at dinner when notable guests arrived unexpectedly. Husserl describes eloquently Brentano's inner certainty that he had a mission to fulfil, to found and to propagate a truly scientific philosophy.

His lectures were hugely successful, attracting literally hundreds of students from all faculties, and not just those who had to attend. They were nevertheless demanding, and the fainter-hearted would drop out. In terms of the number and quality of his successful students, he has no peer in modern times: one must look back to antiquity for comparisons. His lecturing style was regarded by those who heard him as a model of perfection: clear, incise, serious throughout. He would examine positions from both sides, giving pros and cons, before making the solution known, always with reasons, very much in the style of Aquinas's *Summa*. He would always induce his students to trade vague metaphors for crystal literalness. His preoccupation with clarity and detail at the expense of system-building in the grand German manner likens him in some respects to modern analytic thinkers, and indeed, in his later years his metaphysical reism was underpinned by a *Sprachkritik* which is wholly twentieth-century in spirit.

His concern for the intellectual and spiritual welfare of his students extended even to the details of their personal lives, and he would counsel them minutely on the best course of action they should take. Even when students were not in his presence, his influence was felt to be working on them and guiding them. It was thus more than usually tragic, firstly that he should have to give up supervising doctoral dissertations and habilitations on losing his chair, then later that he should have to give up teaching altogether.

He was rather slow to publish his findings, preferring to work his ideas out and discuss them rather than rush into print. This had, as Stumpf notes in his reminiscences, a somewhat detrimental side-effect. His students were forced either to quote from unpublished works or to paraphrase them, with the attendant risk of misinterpretation. Since Brentano was rather touchy about misrepresentation and what he considered ill-informed attacks on his work, his relationships with some of the older students, who went their own way and later disagreed with him, were occasionally clouded. He was also somewhat credulous, and accepted unfavourable reports readily, only for these to evaporate as soon as he had a reunion with the figure concerned. These problems have a later parallel in Wittgenstein, who was similarly both unready to publish yet sensitive to misinterpretation.

The power of his personality and his crushing dialectic drove some of the more independently-minded of his students into silence in his presence. They were, as Husserl relates, unwilling to air cherished but inchoate ideas only to have them swiftly dispatched by Brentano. So several of his older students developed a cautious reserve, for which they all expressed regret later in life, for they found that on reunion with

Brentano, they could always recapture a warm personal friendship, even if they could not secure his agreement, or even understanding, of their own ideas. Brentano often did not read the works of his students, but relied on verbal reports, which were necessarily somewhat distorted. Husserl recounts how, after dedicating to Brentano his first book, *Philosophie der Arithmetik*, in 1891, he had to wait until 1905 for a letter of thanks: Brentano had either not looked at the book or had merely glanced through it, and had forgotten to thank Husserl for the dedication until coming back to the book again much later.

It is perhaps significant that those of his pupils with whom he was on the best terms were those who chose an area of work somewhat aside from Brentano's cherished domains of metaphysics, psychology and ethics. Stumpf declares that one of his motives for choosing the psychology of sound as an area of investigation was that it was one in which he could work without fear of crossing Brentano's unpublished writings, and he notes that it was the same with Marty in the philosophy of language and Kraus in the philosophy of law. By contrast, those philosophers such as Husserl, Meinong and Höfler who remained more or less within Brentano's main concerns, were far more distanced personally and professionally from their teacher. Brentano took disagreements somewhat hard, and could be unfair to those who disagreed with him. This was the converse of his concern for his student's intellectual welfare and his keen desire for truth.

The problem of personal and professional distance was considerably exacerbated by the development, after Brentano had given up teaching, of a 'second generation' school of younger philosophers, who followed with avidity the later Brentanian turn to reism and *Sprachkritik*. The link between the first, direct generation of students whom Brentano had taught in Würzburg and later Vienna, and the later group, was the Swiss philosopher Anton Marty (1847—1914). Marty came of a notable family of clerics in Schwyz and he became a student of Brentano in Würzburg in 1867, the oldest of Brentano's major pupils after Stumpf. Marty became Professor at the new university in Czernowitz; in 1880 there followed a call to Prague, where Marty began to specialise in the philosophy of language, becoming in a sense Brentano's ambassador to that territory. His theory of autosemantic and synsemantic expressions, of which there are parallels in Husserl, was a chief tool of Brentano's later *Sprachkritik*.

Marty himself made no original contributions to value theory, his main published work being the *Untersuchungen zur Grundlegung der allgemeinen Grammatik und Sprachphilosophie* of 1908, in which, like Husserl, he advocated a rational grammar and semiotics somewhat in the tradition of the school of Port-Royal. Here he does indeed treat of expressions connected with interests (which usage he advocated), such as commands, expressed wishes, questions, requests, and other such speech acts. The whole class he calls 'emotive' or interest-demanding expressions. Apart from this, Marty merely expounds and defends Brentano's triple classification of mental phenomena and presses its parallels with a classification of linguistic expressions. Further, there is no evidence from Marty's *Nachlass* that he was at any time preoccupied with or even particularly interested in ethics or value theory for their own sakes. The chief interest for us here is his role in transmitting in a pure and unexpurgated form Brentano's principal ideas to his own students. He would refer them on from himself to Brentano as authority. He was effectively a clearing-house for Brentano's ideas in Prague, a role which he continued to play after Brentano himself had given up teaching. His most notable students were Oskar Kraus (of whom more below), Alfred Kastil, Emil Arleth and also, for a brief period, Franz Kafka (cf. B. Smith (1981)). Kraus and Kastil were the most fervent of the followers of Brentano in this second generation, and ended up as his posthumous editors, a task whose magnitude and importance should not be underestimated. Arleth is less well known, because he died relatively young in 1909 at the age of 53, as Professor of Philosophy in Innsbruck, to which he had been called in 1906. His main work, *Die metaphysischen Grundlagen der aristotelischen Ethik* of 1903, was instrumental in bringing to the attention of the Prague Brentanians the extent to which Brentano's ideas resembled those of Aristotle. He was succeeded at Innsbruck by Kastil, who had himself also written a shorter work on knowledge of the good in Aristotle and Aquinas in 1900. Kastil wrote what is still the best book on Brentano's philosophy (1951). Kraus also, though originally from a juristic background, having studied and received his doctorate under Wieser, was to stress the similarities between Aristotle and the later theories of Brentano and the economists of the marginal-utility school.

Through continual close contact with Marty, and frequent visits to Brentano in Florence and Schönbühel, the younger students kept abreast of Brentano's later developments, and like his older students were completely captivated by him, though they did not attain anything like the same independence of thought. Indeed, they were instrumental in sharpening the divide between Brentano and his older students by their fervour. The division cut especially deep between the Prague

Brentanians and the Graz school of Meinong, and to a slightly lesser extent, the phenomenological school of Husserl. Acrimonious exchanges in print can be seen on both sides. The second generation's tone was not infrequently evangelical: others were accused of having fallen *(abgefallen)* from the true way of Brentano's thought. The divide extended even to matters of taste. Brentano, whose ideal in music was Gregorian chant, and who detested Wagner and all that he stood for, had it pointed out to him that Höfler and Ehrenfels were both convinced Wagnerians. Ehrenfels, the former student of Bruckner, wrote mediocre Wagnerian heroic dramas, yet in fact Ehrenfels himself occupied, as in various things, an intermediate position. For many years a colleague of Marty in Prague, he retained the friendship of his former teacher Brentano, yet was also on good terms with Höfler and Meinong.

Of those who continued the tradition of value theory into a third generation, we may mention Kraus's student Georg Katkov, whose *Untersuchungen zur Werttheorie und Theodizee* of 1937 appeared in the series published by the Brentano Society.

Excursus: Aristotle's Value Theory

We have mentioned in various places the extent to which Brentano's true guide and teacher was Aristotle. Since Aristotle was part of the Austrian intellectual background in the nineteenth century, both through the classes in philosophical propædeutics which were an important part of the grammar-school curriculum and also via the less direct influence of the church, it is interesting to note that, as Emil Kauder ('Genesis of the Marginal Utility Theory: From Aristotle to the End of the Eighteenth Century', *Economic Journal, 63* (1953), 638—50, reprinted in Kauder, *A History of Marginal Utility Theory*, Princeton: Princeton University Press, 1965, 3—29) has pointed out, Menger, too, and later Austrian economists such as Böhm-Bawerk and Mises, were decidedly Aristotelian in their tenets, in contrast to Jevons and Walras outside Austria. The parallels between Menger and Brentano in terms of their common relation to Aristotle are something which we have not gone into in detail, but they would provide a fruitful ground for historical enquiry. However, to facilitate comparison, it is worth seeing Aristotle's basic principles set out clearly on their own. For the outline of the following exposition we are indebted chiefly to Kraus (1937).

1.   The word 'good' and its cognates are ambiguous. There is that

which is valuable in itself, and that which is willed for the sake of something else.

2. That which is willed for the sake of something else is the *useful* and must be distinguished from the good in itself.

3. The opposition between affirming and denying in judgement corresponds to that of loving and hating in the realm of emotions (*horexis*). As there is correct or incorrect judging, so there is correct or incorrect loving and hating.

4. We must distinguish the good in the sense of that which is truly good, valuable, worthy of love, from that which is merely likeable, desirable, liked or desired. Aristotle sometimes, but not consistently makes a threefold distinction, between the truly good (*kalon, agathon*), the useful, and the pleasant. The latter distinction was very influential in separating practical from aesthetic values in later philosophy.

5. Among goods, we must distinguish the attainable from the unattainable.

6. Primary goods or values, those worthy of love in their own right, are all psychical in nature and are directly knowable. As examples Aristotle gives pleasure of the senses, 'noble' enjoyments, knowledge, and virtuous occupation. He quotes with approval a saying of Eudoxus, that pleasure is much to be wished, because no one asks what it is good for.

7. Secondary goods or values comprise bodily goods, such as health and strength, and 'external' goods, such as honour, the possession of friends, and last, and least, wealth.

8. The highest good is *eudaimonia* (*Glückseligkeit*: the English word 'happiness' is an unsatisfactory translation, but there is no better).

9. Some advantages accrue through the accumulation or summing of goods. Aristotle cites a number of principles of preference, codified by Arleth, which are exactly those we gave above in expounding Brentano. But there are also goods, including *eudaimonia*, which cannot be secured by accumulation of other goods.

10. Aristotle distinguishes the good in abstraction from questions of attainability (*agathon*) and likewise the better in abstraction from attainability (*beltion*), from the practically good (*prakton agathon*) and practically better (*hairetouteron*). The practically good or better depend on circumstance, so are relative and impermanent.

11. A physical possession is a tool (*organon*) for the attainment of good or prevention of evil. All physical possessions are secondary goods. They possess two kinds of value: use value and exchange value. Their value is relative. It is only in respect of such goods that we can describe a person as fortunate or unfortunate in his circumstances.

12. So the value of generosity is proportionate not to the amount given but rather the proportion of the gift to the possessions of the giver.

13. External goods are not in all circumstances and for everyone equally, or even positively, valuable. One and the same object or collection of objects may represent different values to different people.

14. External goods, like all tools, have their limitations. Objects useful in isolation or small quantities may be useless or even detrimental to their possessor if in over-plentiful supply (such is the case when we speak of an excess or surfeit). The value of such a good is relative to circumstances, and these circumstances include the state of supply of other goods of like sort.

15. Primary or mental goods, on the other hand, can never be in over-plentiful supply. One cannot have an excess or surfeit of knowledge, joy, pleasure or virtue.

16. A good A is more valuable than a good B when A makes a more valuable compound when added to something else than B does, and leaves a less valuable residue when subtracted from a compound than B does. (The anticipation of Menger is here uncanny.)

17. Goods with greater adaptability are, other things equal, better than less adaptable goods.

18. Rare goods are more valuable than common ones, without regard to questions of utility. So gold is more valuable than iron despite the greater utility of iron. Kraus recalls Adam Smith's remark that nothing is more useful than water, but it has practically no monetary value. (It is well observed that Smith lived in Britain rather than the Kalahari!)

From these remarks the similarities to Brentano will be obvious. Kraus has certainly brought out the likenesses and left the differences unstressed, but that was the intention. There is, for example, nothing in Aristotle corresponding to Brentano's marked emphasis on evidence

(Evidenz), nor is the analogy between logic and the rules governing admissible valuations developed by Aristotle. But to an extent to which Brentano was perhaps not even fully conscious, his basic tenets are to be found already two thousand and more years before him in his one true master Aristotle.

It is hoped that these parallels will facilitate the drawing of similar comparisons between Aristotle and the Austrian economists.

3. Alexius Meinong

Biography

There is very much less to report of Meinong's life than of Brentano's. Most of it was spent quietly and diligently in study and teaching, mostly at the University of Graz. Meinong travelled very little, almost invariably submitting papers to congresses, when asked, *in absentia*. He was in no way a controversial or even publicly notable figure, and his energies were concentrated exclusively into his work.

Alexius Meinong, Ritter von Handschuhsheim (b.1853, Lemberg Lwów, d.1920, Graz) was born of a noble family of public servants. His grandfather emigrated from Germany to Austria, and Alexius was born in Galicia solely because his father's work had taken him there. He was educated in Vienna, where he entered the University in 1870. He entered the Law Faculty, but eventually wrote his doctoral dissertation in history, on one Arnold of Brescia, in 1874. Philosophy was, however, his second subject, and he attended Brentano's lectures. As he recalls in his *Selbstdarstellung*, 'Earlier, I had attended there, for two semesters, lectures on economics by Carl Menger, perhaps his first, and this, no doubt, must have been of help to my later work on the theory of value.' (*Gesamtausgabe* VII, p. 5.) Meinong's surmise that these were Menger's first lectures is correct. His *Meldungsbuch*, showing the courses he attended, reveals that he took courses given by Menger in the winter semester of 1872—3 and the summer semester of 1873, and a comparison with the *Vorlesungsverzeichnis* of Vienna University shows that the first lectures by Dr Carl Menger were in the winter semester of 1872–3, on *'Bank- und Kreditwesen'*, and the summer semester of 1873, on *'National-Ökonomie'*. Meinong later attended Brentano's lectures on *'Alte und neue Logik'* in the summer semester of 1875, but he tells us that his decision to specialise in philosophy was made independently of any influence of Brentano. Indeed, this independence from his teacher was an abiding feature of

Meinong's development. While praising the way in which Brentano 'gave lavishly from his riches, as an example, as a conscientious teacher and kind adviser' (ibid.), Meinong noted, like others, that because of Brentano's forceful personality, the fledgling independence his students might acquire was wont to be jealously guarded. Meinong was, even at a very early stage in his career, perhaps the most independent of Brentano's major students. This led to coolness and misunderstandings 'whose consequences have been with me deep into my later work' (ibid., p. 6). In his short autobiography, written three years after the death of Brentano and shortly before his own, Meinong acknowledges his own fault in this and expresses deep regret that he was never so close to Brentano as were others. That this was written after Brentano's death was often pointedly mentioned by the second generation. Meinong's closest associations however were with his pupils, especially Alois Höfler and later Stephan Witasek.

His independence shows itself already in his *Habilitationsschrift, Hume-Studien I*, done under Brentano's supervision in 1877. Neither in this, nor in the second Hume-study, which appeared in 1882, is there any explicit reference to Brentano, though Meinong's investigations of Hume's nominalism and theory of relations were undertaken at Brentano's suggestion. Meinong taught at Vienna as *Privatdozent* from 1878 until 1882, acquiring on the way two students from the wider Brentano circle who were later to follow him to Graz, Höfler and Ehrenfels. His appointment as *Extraordinarius* in Graz in 1882 came to him, as he says, 'completely unexpectedly'. He had already given some rudimentary demonstrations in psychology in Vienna, and in 1886–7 started the first course in experimental psychology in Austria. In 1889 he was appointed *Ordinarius*, and married in the same year. His lectures on value theory and ethics of 1884–5 were, significantly, attended by Ehrenfels. In 1894 the lectures on psychology, which had been interrupted in 1889 because of poor accommodation and equipment, began again in a new laboratory, the first of its kind in Austria, of which Meinong was Director. In 1894 his compendious *Psychologisch-ethische Untersuchungen zur Werttheorie* appeared. Although written from what he later acknowledged was a psychologistic position, this was perhaps his most influential work on value theory in his lifetime. He sent a copy to Husserl, who had not the time to read it straight away, but in a letter to Meinong of 5 April 1902, Husserl writes, 'The Easter vacation I have been working on a completely new version of my ethics lectures, and have studied with *great use* your Psych.-eth. Unters. z. Werttheorie' (Meinong;

Philosophenbriefe, p. 107). Schuhmann's *Husserl-Chronik* shows that a rash of manuscripts on value theory do indeed date from this time.

Meinong spent much of his energy on questions of empirical psychology in the 1890s, and only slowly did he begin to realise that his more ontological and phenomenological investigations were crystallising into a new subject, which he came to call *Gegenstandstheorie* (theory of objects), rather than ontology or metaphysics, terms which were considered taboo by many philosophers at the time. It is perhaps ironical that the work by which Meinong is best known in the Anglo-Saxon philosophical sphere, *Über Annahmen* (1902), is primarily a work of philosophical psychology. Its chief aim is to establish the existence of a hitherto unidentified kind of mental act, the assumption, which lies between presentations (ideas) and judgements. Assumptions are like judgements in having presentations as their basis, and in exhibiting positive or negative polarity. Unlike judgements and like presentations, they do not contain a moment of conviction or assertion. The same idea can be found in the more austere setting of Frege's *Begriffsschrift*. The objects of assumptions, as of judgements, are what Meinong calls 'objectives', and *Über Annahmen* owes its fame primarily to its investigation of objectives, the distinctions between being and so-being, existence and subsistence, the doctrine of the *Aussersein* of the pure object, and Meinong's account of the meaning of sentences. Many of these ideas found sympathetic readers in England and America: one such reader, and the most influential, was Bertrand Russell, whose influence turned the tide against the positive reception of Meinong's work when he began to disagree with Meinong's views. Only slowly is Meinong's reputation as a great philosopher emerging from the twilight into which it was cast by Russell, and his works beginning to find champions and sympathetic interpreters to assist the admirable efforts of J.N. Findlay. Even so, the emphasis remains heavily on object theory: the rich analyses in psychology, epistemology and value theory still tend to be overlooked. (The collection *Essays on Meinong*, edited by Simons, is an attempt to rectify this imbalance.)

In 1904, to mark the tenth anniversary of the psychology laboratory, Meinong and his students published a famous collective volume, *Untersuchungen zur Gegenstandstheorie und Psychologie*, to which he contributed a programmatic essay, 'Über Gegenstandstheorie'. In 1913 and 1914 his students, under the direction of Höfler, edited two volumes of *Gesammelte Abhandlungen* to mark his sixtieth birthday, bringing together his earlier writings on psychology and object theory.

In 1914 he handed over the direction of the psychology laboratory to Stephan Witasek, whose early death only six months later he describes as the greatest blow of his personal and professional life: he had intended Witasek to be his literary executor. A third collective volume on value theory was never published because of the war. In 1914 Meinong received a call to Vienna, but, realising that he had not many years to live, he preferred to continue his fruitful and accustomed course in Graz. He was also that year elected to the Vienna Academy of Sciences as a Fellow. When he died he was working on a revision of his early book on value theory, purging it of its psychologism and bringing it up to date with his later discoveries. The work was almost ready for the press, and was edited by his successor at Graz, Ernst Mally, in 1923 as *Zur Grundlegung der allgemeinen Werttheorie.*

Like his own teacher Brentano, Meinong was an attentive and successful teacher, taking great pains to foster within the circle of his students a spirit of co-operation in their scientific endeavour. He was very ready to learn from his students, co-operating with Höfler in the writing of the latter's *Logik*, and incorporating suggestions and improvements made by Mally into his object theory. His relations with all of them were warm, and his autobiography shows a touching pride and affection for the members of his school. Although he and Husserl held many parallel views, they were not in close contact, and it was a source of regret to Meinong that such parallels could not be developed in greater co-operation. His notes on Husserl's *Ideen* of 1913 (in R. Fabian and R. Haller (eds), *Kolleghefte und Fragmente*, 1978, p. 287–324; English translation in M.-L. Schubert Kalsi, *Alexius Meinong on Objects of Higher Order and Husserl's Phenomenology*, The Hague: Nijhoff, 1978, p. 209–47) show that he found Husserl's later idealistic turn both alien and unnecessary, and yet perceived close parallels with his own writings, which were nevertheless somewhat obscured by the tendency of both writers to develop their own distinctive terminologies. He remained however on cordial terms with Husserl. Only with Brentano and the second generation did his relations become soured.

Meinong's Works on Value

Apart from the works already mentioned, Meinong published a number of other important works in value theory: an 1895 paper 'Über Werthaltung und Wert'; the short but programmatically important 'Für die Psychologie und gegen den Psychologismus in der allgemeinen Werttheorie', sent by Meinong to the 1911 Bologna International

Philosophers' Congress and appearing in *Logos* in 1912; the treatise 'Über emotionale Präsentation', which appeared in 1917 under the auspices of the Vienna Academy of Sciences, and carried the new direction forward; and the posthumous 'Ethische Bausteine', which first appeared in 1968 in the new *Gesamtausgabe*. The third volume of this, *Abhandlungen zur Werttheorie*, realised at last the project of Meinong's students which the war had prevented, and totals over 700 pages on value theory. This should give the lie to the one-sided reception Meinong has had, especially in the Anglo-Saxon world, where from Russell onwards only his object-theory — and this under a relatively narrow interpretation — has received attention. But his other concerns, especially theoretical psychology, epistemology and value theory, together amount to much more than his work on object theory, however much this formed, in his mature publications, the central part of his philosophy. It is significant that both his first and his last major treatise were on value theory, to which he felt able to return after the intensive first decade of the century spent developing the theory of objects. Furthermore, a cursory glance at the frequency of Meinong's *Schlagwörter* shows that *'Wert'* and its cognates is almost twice as common as *'Gegenstand'* and its cognates. It is impossible, in this short space, to do justice to the subtlety and complexity of Meinong's value theory. He can truly be said to have built the first considerable edifice on the foundations laid by Brentano. Nor can we do more than point out the way in which he developed his views from the psychologically oriented to the more objective and crystalline world of 'non-personal' (Meinong's way of avoiding the term 'absolute') values, developed in his last years. For the following exposition we have drawn on Wolf (1972).

Meinong's first sentence in value-theory goes 'For as long as there has been research into political economy, value has constituted one of its most eminent subjects.' His first footnote cites Menger's *Grundsätze der Volkswirtschaftslehre*. But thereafter he strikes out on his own, section 2 being entitled 'Extra-Economic Value'. He claims that the right to investigate the foundations of value theory, as even economists will admit, belongs not to economics itself but to psychology. Furthermore, value is a basic concept, not to be explained through concepts such as utility, biological need, cost, or work, all of which, according to Meinong, already presuppose value. Value is not self-sufficient, but is constituted through subjective value-experiences. This subjective basis was later loosened by Meinong after he had self-consciously rejected what he was later happy to call his early 'psychologism', but while Meinong's objectivism or ontological realism in the realm of object theory is renowned, even notorious, he did not follow this path to the same degree in value theory. While he was indeed ready in his later life to accept non-personal values, he was also concerned to keep a place for the personal and relative values with which he had started out. Even in the early writings Meinong makes a distinction between those values which can be said to endure in the valued object, and those which fluctuate according to the state of the person valuing, which difference he calls that between objective and subjective value.

The basic value-experiences, in Meinong's eyes, are *feelings*. Desires he sees as being too specific, since they relate only to the future. In a controversy with Ehrenfels which lasted for several years in the 1890s, and which is a model of fruitful, friendly disagreement, Meinong was forced to modify his position and accept desires as an 'incidental' value experience. Ehrenfels pointed out that if an object is valued for the feelings it can arouse in us, then Meinong cannot explain how we value things which do not exist, such as perfect justice. Meinong responded by allowing that we value things which we desire, but this is to be explained counter-factually by saying that we *would* have the appropriate feelings if the object *were* to exist. So Meinong retains feelings as the primary value experiences. However, not all feelings are for Meinong *value*-feelings: this holds only for those which, in a sense explained by Meinong, have judgements as their presuppositions. But there are indeed values corresponding to feelings without presupposed judgements, so we must distinguish between value-feelings which do and those which do not presuppose judgements: value-feelings in the wider sense include aesthetic feelings, pleasure feelings, and what Meinong calls knowledge feelings and logical feelings. Emotional value-experiences always have *some* presupposition, but this does not have to be a judgement: it could also, as in the case of pleasure, be an idea (*Vorstellung*). Meinong does not, however, abide strictly by Brentano's classification of mental phenomena, since, as we saw above, he holds that there is another basic kind of mental phenomenon besides ideas, judgements and interests, namely assumptions.

Value experiences present (*präsentieren*) something more than that which can be grasped intellectually, through judgements and assumptions, that is precisely a moment of value. The object which *bears* this moment must, however, according to Meinong, be grasped intellectually. Since pure understanding must remain blind to value, the objects of judgements and assumptions, Meinong's 'objectives', cannot be the same as the objects of valuing experiences: such objects Meinong calls 'dignitatives' in the case of feelings and 'desideratives' in the case of desires. But a proper valuing experience not only has an intellectual presupposition, it only comes to expression through an intellectual act of predication, while yet retaining its emotional core. The value is fully grasped only in a *value-judgement*, which term Meinong, unlike Brentano, takes at its face value. In this, value is like perception, which again, for Meinong, is only completed in an appropriate perceptual judgement. Dignitatives and desideratives therefore present themselves to the intellect, though they are the *objects* of emotive acts, and yet must be further distinguished from the *bearer* of the value, which is an objective. Whereas the later phenomenologists say that values are *grasped* through feelings, for Meinong they are only presented through feelings, which here exercise a 'quasi-intellectual' function. Thus Meinong, in contrast to the simplicity of Brentano, develops a theory which is labyrinthine in its complexity, weaving intellectual and non-intellectual acts inextricably together.

Meinong, from 1894 onwards, held to a general position in the philosophy of mind, according to which anything which is present to mind, any object of consciousness, is present for us solely in virtue of the existence within our experience itself of a side of our mental life which serves precisely to direct us to the object; this may be called the 'content' of the act. The distinction between content and object was first made by Brentano's Polish student Kasimir Twardowski (see his influential *Zur Lehre vom Inhalt und Gegenstand der Vorstellungen* of 1894), and was taken up by Husserl as well as Meinong. The distinction is already present in Höfler's *Logik* of 1890, in which Meinong assisted, where it is treated as an ambiguity in the term 'object'. No content is ever identical with its object, and objects may be non-mental and exist independently of the thinking subject, whereas contents may not. With the establishment of this distinction the possibility of a fully-developed theory of mind-independent objects first opened up for Meinong. The content is, speaking loosely, the representative (*Vertreter*) of its object. But the legitimacy of the representation function is guaranteed not by similarity, as Locke had thought, or any unexplained *adequatio intellectus et rei*, but by what Meinong describes as a parity in the possibilities of their variation: to different kinds of content belong different kinds of object and vice versa (rather, to use Wolf's metaphor, as different kinds of uniforms of soldiers correspond to the different countries they fight for). The *guarantee* that there is something actually out there corresponding to the relevant content is something which Meinong does not feel he needs to pronounce on, it being sufficient to note for descriptive purposes the natural confidence and trust we have in general in the legitimacy of presentation, for example in the perceptual sphere. This side-stepping of epistemological scepticism is reminiscent of Husserl's more ponderous and self-conscious procedures in phenomenology.

So whereas ideas present simple objects, and judgements and assumptions present objectives, and in each case the objects (using the word to cover generally both simple objects and objectives) are not a part of the act in question but have an existence beyond it, so too the objects of value-experiences have an existence beyond the acts of feeling and desiring which intend them. Meinong believes that there are nuances of feeling and desire which are analogous to the variations in a perceived object. So like Brentano before him, but in a very much more involved way, he exploits the analogies between valuing and other experiences. But his chief argument is the sheer similarity of factual and evaluative predications:

> I say of the sky at one time that it is blue, and at another that it is beautiful, and the sky appears to be no less ascribed a property in the latter case than the former, the one property being just as well conveyed by a feeling as the other by an idea, so we could not do better than ascribe the function of presentation, which everyone ascribes to ideas, to feelings. (Meinong 1917, p. 33.)

In this way Meinong, while being an epistemological realist with respect to values, is nevertheless an indirect realist, by contrast with the later direct value-realism of his student Mally, who insisted that we are directly acquainted with values, without the intercession of representative entities. But Meinong is, all the same, a realist; he refuses to countenance any reduction of 'X is beautiful' to 'I like X'.

In turning against psychologism in his later work on value theory Meinong came to regard it as a form of psychologism to insist on the subjectivity and relativity of all values: 'the value of an object consists in the fact that a subject takes, could take, or reasonably should take, an interest in the object' (Meinong 1912, p. 9; *Gesamtausgabe* III, p. 277). Meinong's arguments against psychologism and for non-personal, non-relative values, are as follows:

1.   There are clear cases, according to him, where we grasp values which are perfectly clearly not subject-dependent, as in the case

of certain ethical values.

2. What is valuable need not be experienced as such: for example, children very often simply are unaware of what is best for them.
3. The fact that we make value-*mistakes*, that is, errors of value-judgement, is only comprehensible if we accept that there are non-personal values: for example, a talisman with supposed magic powers may be ascribed a false subjective value.
4. The necessity to 'potentialise' the value concept, so that something is valuable not only if it *is*, but also if it *could* or (more problematically) *should*, be valued. Here Meinong the realist draws precisely the opposite conclusion to that of the dispositional phenomenalist who would claim that the possibility of a dispositional account makes realism dispensable.

There is unfortunately no space for us to go into any greater detail or examine the legitimacy of Meinong's obviously important but nevertheless often questionable conclusions. We do best to take leave of him with the following declaration of his belief in absolute values: 'once one has completely accepted emotional presentation, then non-personal values can be as sure as the visible, tangible external world'. (Meinong 1923, p. 154; *Gesamtausgabe* III, p. 634.)

The Meinong School

When Meinong was called to Graz in the Autumn of 1882, as a result of his four years of activity as *Privatdozent* at the University of Vienna, he was able to bring with him two students — Alois Höfler and Christian von Ehrenfels — who had also originally belonged to the larger circle of Brentano students and had completed their philosophical studies under Meinong. Even though Ehrenfels in his later philosophical development followed quite distinctive paths and goals (see below) and only Höfler committed himself directly to the direction of research defended by his teacher, still the two of them were bound up in a lifelong personal friendship with Meinong and can thereby be considered as the oldest and closest members of the Meinong school, also called the Graz school. Höfler's main philosophical interests lay in the field of logic, psychology (especially the psychology of education) and the philosophy of science. He also adopted the main tenets of Meinong's position in value theory, but himself wrote almost nothing of substance in this field. His principal aim, as he himself wrote in his autobiography

Die Philosophie des Alois Höfler (1921, p. 136n.), was to make more generally available the most original parts of Meinong's works.

The proper establishment and growth of the Meinong school did not however take place until Meinong had begun his long period of teaching and research activity in Graz. Among the many students whom Meinong collected around him (see Meinong 1921, pp. 99, 141–4), we must mention here above all those who have contributed important works in the fields of ethics and value theory. To these belong first of all Ernst Mally (1879–1944), who not only studied (to his Habilitation) under Meinong in Graz, but also served from 1925 to 1942 as Meinong's successor in the chair of philosophy. Whilst Mally was, in the beginning, very intensively involved in the working out of the Meinongian theory of objects and was at the time one of the first to take notice of the new developments in modern logic (Russell and Whitehead), he later distanced himself increasingly from Meinong's philosophy and set out in a new dynamic-holistic direction of his own. His most notable writings are the *Grundgesezte des Sollens* (1926), a pioneering work outlining principles of what later came to be called deontic logic, and a late work, *Erlebnis und Wirklichkeit* (1935). The *Grosses Logikfragment* was edited in 1971 from Mally's *Nachlass*, in which are also to be found the as yet unpublished lecture-notes on value theory. Mally's value-theoretical position is characterised by the priority of the emotional over the intellectual and by its concentration on the concept of objective value. Among the later students of Meinong is Franz Weber (1890–1975), much encouraged by Meinong in view of his considerable philosophical promise. Weber acquired his doctorate in Graz in 1917 and in 1920 he was called to Ljubljana to be the first philosophy professor in the newly-established Slovenian University. His main writings (*System der Philosophie* (1921); *Ethik* (1923), *Ästhetik* (1925)) were all published in the Slovenian language under the transliterated name France Veber. It is only in Terstenjak (1972) that we find for the first time large works in the German language. The basic tenets of Weber's value theory closely approximate those of his teacher Meinong. Weber however conceives the relation between feeling and value as being essentially more differentiated, in that he sees the bases for evaluation as lying in the various kinds of feelings; there is then built up on the second level a realm of value-feelings proper, in the form of 'reactive' value-positions (happiness, sadness) and 'judicative' value-positions (pleasure, displeasure). For Weber, as for Meinong, value is in the end an absolute property of the valued object, independent of the valuing subject, a view which he also shares with

Brentano, with whom he also agrees that the necessary differentiation of correct and incorrect values is given on the basis of the judicative feelings. Finally we mention in this context two further philosophers who, though not themselves active in Graz, nevertheless stand close to the value-theoretic tradition founded by Meinong. The first of these is Ernst Schwarz, in whose treatise *Über den Wert, das Soll und das richtige Werthalten* (1934) particular weight is laid on the objectivity of value and the strict separation of value from feeling. The second is Josef Klemens Kreibig (1863–1917), *Privatdozent* in Vienna from 1898 who, originating also in Brentano's circle, shows in his work *Psychologische Grundlegung eines Systems der Werttheorie* (1902) strong influences not only of Meinong but also of Ehrenfels, who was also a personal friend. It is instructive to see the range of influences beyond the confines of these, his closest associates, by quoting the acknowledgments from the foreword of Kreibig's book, which illustrates our point that it was typical of works of its time to draw on more than one discipline for their material:

> The author has to thank a number of workers for important stimulation, above all v. Meinong and v. Ehrenfels, whose works masterfully inaugurated the psychological investigation of value. In the effort to bring to account the developmental side of this phenomenon, Friedrich Jodl's psychology, as well as the writings of Spencer's rich developments, proffered themselves. Also turned to good account were Fechner's aesthetics, Paulsen's ethics, individual works by Lehmann, Döring, Jonas Cohn, Wundt, and the works in political economy by the Menger school.

4. Christian von Ehrenfels

Biography

As the eldest of five children, Christian Freiherr von Ehrenfels (b. 1859, Rodaun near Vienna, d.1932, Lichtenau) was destined to take over the country estates which stretched in a wide circle around the Ehrenfels family seat in the Lower Austrian Waldviertel, north of the Danube. After a happy childhood spent at his father's castle Brunn am Wald, Ehrenfels began studies at the Hochschule für Bodenkultur in Vienna, but soon moved to the University, where from 1879 he registered with the Faculty of Law. For three years he attended not only the lectures of Franz Brentano, but also regularly heard the young *Privatdozent* Alexius Meinong, whose pupil and follower he soon became, and with whom he was to remain in close life-long friendship. Although Ehrenfels registered in the Faculty of Law, there is no indication that he heard Carl Menger lecture while he was in Vienna. The doctrines of the Austrian economists, which played so considerable a part in his scientific development, probably first became known to him through the Graz lectures of Meinong, who, as mentioned earlier, had himself got to know Menger in Vienna. In the summer of 1882 Ehrenfels interrupted his studies in Vienna in order to complete his military service in the 4th (Count Sternberg) Dragoon Regiment. He completed his philosophical education in 1885 under Meinong in Graz, with the dissertation *Über Grössenrelationen und Zahlen.*

In the meantime he had made a decision which was to have important consequences for his future life. In a memorable letter of 15 October 1882 Ehrenfels requested his father to be allowed to hand over his birthright to his younger brother, in order to be able to yield to an inner striving 'which is directed towards a thing to which I cannot give a name, as no one has yet invented one for it, but which is very close to religion' (F. Weinhandl 1960, p. 428). Throughout his life Ehrenfels was driven by this striving, and it manifested itself in the unique combination of three passionate interests which stamp his creative personality: philosophy, poetry and music. Above all the works of Richard Wagner wrought a powerful impression on the young Ehrenfels, who made the pilgrimage to Bayreuth on foot for the first performance of *Parsifal* in 1882, and remained all his life an ardent follower and promoter of Wagner's work. As early as 1885 he appeared in public for the first time with a work of drama; afterwards came a rapid succession of further theatrical works which appeared as a collection in 1895 under the title *Allegorische Dramen.* It always remained his most ardent wish to have these dramas set to music after the fashion of Wagner. To this end he took up private tuition in harmony and counterpoint with Anton Bruckner, but soon had to realise that his musical talents were not equal to the task. However, through the services of the composer Otto Taubmann at least one of his music dramas, *Sängerweihe*, did eventually receive musical performances (in Elberfeld in 1904 and in Dessau in 1909) and Ehrenfels retained from his lessons a theoretical grounding in music.

Ehrenfels' academic career began in 1888, when he habilitated in Vienna with the work 'Über Fühlen und Wollen'. Two years later appeared the essay 'Über "Gestaltqualitäten"' whose principal idea has shown itself to be so extraordinarily fruitful in psychology, giving rise to the twentieth-century movement of Gestalt psychology. This work is also expressly mentioned by Meinong (1921, p. 142) as being one of the most important works leading up to his own theory of objects: his article 'Zur Psychologie der Komplexionen und Relationen' (1891) is partly a commentary on Ehrenfels' article, partly a contribution of his own to the theme, and is just one illustration of the way in which the two philosophers stimulated and influenced one another. In the summer semester of 1891 Ehrenfels began lecturing at the University of Vienna, returning to the subject of his first course in a series of five articles under the title 'Werttheorie und Ethik' (1893–4); the subject was to stand in the centre of his scientific activity in the years following. The extensive two-volume *System der Werttheorie* (1897–8) represents the peak of his early creative period. During this time Ehrenfels, by now married, was called to the German University at Prague as the successor to Friedrich Jodl and in 1899 he was made *Professor Ordinarius* in Philosophy. His immediate philosophical colleagues in Prague at the time included Anton Marty, Emil Arleth and later Alfred Kastil, Oskar Kraus and Josef Eisenmeier. These together made up the core of the orthodox (mainly second generation) Brentano school, with whom Ehrenfels engaged in a series of controversies, exposing himself to sometimes bitter attacks. It is the more remarkable that Ehrenfels remained nevertheless on good personal terms with his former teacher Brentano throughout the feuds. Other men whose friendship he cultivated included Sigmund Freud, Friedrich von Wieser, Gerhard Hauptmann, Houston St Chamberlain and Thomas G. Masaryk, and his name is also to be found in the pages of Kafka's diaries.

Shortly after the turn of the century a wave of publications erupted from Ehrenfels' pen, in which he concerned himself with practical and social questions such as 'racial hygiene', sexual ethics and eugenics. In the conviction that Western civilisation was threatened with long-term biological decline unless drastic counter-measures were taken, Ehrenfels campaigned for the introduction of polygamy, in the belief that by this form of marriage the selection and propagation of the most virile would be possible, thereby facilitating the attainment of a more noble type of human being. Although his suggestions for reform met with no public sympathy, he continued to the end to hold on to certain basic tenets in his proposal for sexual reform, as emerges from his last work of this kind, 'Die Sexualmoral der Zukunft' (1930).

The outbreak of the First World War represented a decisive turning-point in Ehrenfels' life. Although he was able to bring out his metaphysical work *Kosmogonie* (1916), almost immediately thereafter he fell into a deep depression, which kept him from working for four years. The conquest of this illness was signalled by the appearance in 1922 of the work *Das Primzahlengesetz*. Here Ehrenfels undertook on the one hand to solve, with the help of the Gestalt concept, the problem of giving a law of the development of prime numbers, and on the other hand to supply a Gestalt-theoretical foundation for aesthetics. In 1925 he wrote a further, politically highly-coloured play, *Die Mutter des Legionärs*, which was performed in Prague. The play concerned reconciliation between the German and Czech peoples, and for that reason Ehrenfels dedicated it to his friend and fellow Brentano pupil, the Czech President Thomas G. Masaryk. In 1929, at the age of 70, Ehrenfels retired, and he died in 1932 at his home, a small castle in Lichtenau, Lower Austria.

The Philosophical Work

To do proper justice to the full extent of Eherenfels' literary output it would be necessary to present Ehrenfels not merely as a philosopher, but also as a dramatist and revolutionary social ethicist. In view of the limitations imposed by the present essay, we shall, however, confine ourselves to a brief statement of some of the most important philosophical ideas in Ehrenfels' writings.

Although the greater part of Ehrenfels' philosophical and literary achievements are today either little known, or more often simply forgotten, his name has in one respect found lasting fame in the history of ideas. Ehrenfels can incontestably be seen as the founder of Gestalt theory, a reputation founded on the publication in the year 1890 of the essay 'Über "Gestaltqualitäten" '. Under the stimulation of certain ideas which he had found in Mach's *Analysis of Sensations*, Ehrenfels undertook to make precise an idea — to which he gave the name *'Gestalt'* — within the framework of a scientific psychology. He develops his analysis on the basis of concrete examples: melodies and spatial figures, and shows with very clear arguments that such configurations cannot adequately be understood as the mere sum of their constitutent parts. The constituent elements, for example the individual tones of a melody, are indeed the indispensable foundation for the total phenomenon in question, but the tone-*Gestalt* built up on this basis represents a completely new category (namely that of a 'founded content', in the later terminology of Meinong), which can be explained neither solely in terms of the summation of the individual tones nor in terms of the relations holding between them. In answer to the question how the *Gestalt* arises out of its subordinate foundations, Ehrenfels inclines to the opinion of Mach, according to which the whole is itself given immediately, that is, simultaneously with the individual elements. A variant of this position was later taken over also by M. Wertheimer, W. Köhler and K. Koffka, but in opposition to this view stands the theory of Meinong and his school (V. Benussi, S. Witasek), according to which the *Gestalten* cannot be 'produced' without the help of characteristic mental activity. According to Ehrenfels the phenomena of our inner and outer mental world manifest an astounding variety of *Gestalt* qualities, which can firstly be classified into temporal (dances, melodies, salutes, spoken language) and non-temporal (shapes, table-settings, written language), and then lead further to *Gestalten* of higher order, complex structures whose fundamenta are not merely simple elements but are themselves complete *Gestalten*. Ehrenfels assumes that most mental processes, operating in accordance with associative laws, have to do with higher-order *Gestalten*, and that in particular human creative imagination reveals itself in the creation of such *Gestalten*. Finally, with the concept of '*Gestalt* height', introduced in his later writings, Ehrenfels sees the possibility 'of building the whole of aesthetics on the basis of *Gestalt* theory'. For 'what we call "beauty" is nothing other than "*Gestalt* height". The unbeautiful is that with a low level of structure (*das niedrig Gestaltete*). The ugly is that which is disharmonius, that is, that which includes *Gestalt* elements which contradict one another...' (Ehrenfels 1922, pp. 99–100). The problem of the nature of *Gestalten* was handled explicitly only in the early essay of 1890; Ehrenfels went on to give his theory a metaphysical-cosmological, and then also mathematical interpretation in *Kosmogonie* and in *Das Primzahlengesetz*. The properly psychological part of the theory, however, was not further advanced by Ehrenfels. This task fell to later specialist psychologists, and philosophically motivated psychological theorists, e.g. Karl Bühler and W. Metzger, up to recent times.

Ehrenfels and Value Theory

In a letter sent to Meinong in Summer 1891, Ehrenfels gives an indication of his philosophical intentions:

> What presents itself to me as my proper field of work, for a long time to come, is ethics, construed as a special branch of general value theory, along with, of course, the basic psychology of feeling and desire. I am planning for the coming years a fat work in three

volumes, which is also to set all the necessary learned apparatus in motion. The question of changes in valuation has apart from that brought me close to the problems of evolution; in short, it seems to me that I could keep going a very long way along this track. (A. Meinong, *Philosophenbriefe*, p. 77.)

Ehrenfels did indeed take energetic steps in carrying out this comprehensive programme. The psychological starting point for an ethical theory he had developed already in the *Habilitationsschrift* of 1887, 'Über Fühlen und Wollen'. Then in 1893–4 the provisional framework for a treatment of ethics inside general value theory was given in a series of five articles, after which, four years later, the two-volume *System der Werttheorie* brought Ehrenfels' systematic work in this area to a close for the time being (the original plan for a third volume — which was to have included further treatment of the problems of economic value theory — was not carried out). As far as his basic position on the problem of value is concerned, Ehrenfels was from the start a passionate advocate of the subjectivist point of view. The fact that value is so often treated as a property of objects can be traced back, he argues, to nothing more than misleading linguistic usage. According to Ehrenfels, value does not consist in an objective characteristic, which can truly be attributed to an object, but rather in a characteristic 'relation between an object and a subject, which consists in the fact that the subject either actually desires the object, or, if he is not convinced of its existence, would desire it'. (Ehrenfels 1897a, p. 65.) From this basic determination of the concept of value, according to which everything of value has subjective desirability as a defining characteristic, we can see not only the importance ascribed by Ehrenfels to the psychological theory of desire, but also an unavoidable opposition to Meinong's theory of value-feelings and similarly to Brentano's conception of the phenomena of 'correct love and hate'. Thus Ehrenfels takes special pains to show, as against the position found in Brentano's descriptive psychology, that feeling and desire do not fall into one and the same category of mental phenomena. His disagreement with Meinong which, as we mentioned above, caused Meinong to soften somewhat his position that value is based on feelings, had a similar, practically symmetrical effect on Ehrenfels. Ehrenfels compelled Meinong to analyse some value-statements counter-factually, and Meinong compelled Ehrenfels to do the same. Ehrenfels held originally that an object is valued in so far as it is desired, but Meinong pointed out that we value also objects which we already possess. So Ehrenfels was compelled to say that we do not *actually* desire these, but *would* do so if they did not exist, and this modified position is the one which appears in the *System*.

This opposition to his teachers, which was nevertheless confined to a scientific difference of opinion (it did not, as was otherwise usual amongst Meinong's and Brentano's pupils, affect personal relations), brought Ehrenfels to a position even more strikingly close than they to the standpoint of the Austrian economists. The concept of marginal utility developed by Menger and Wieser offered Ehrenfels an important starting-point for the concept of a *general* value theory, that is, one going beyond the specifically economic sphere. The concept of utility in general, understood as 'capacity for satisfying needs', pointed on the one hand to the aspect of desire, so decisive for Ehrenfels' treatment, and offered up at the same time a standard for the quantitative determination of value. In the analysis of the general concept of value Ehrenfels introduced the basic division between mediated and unmediated values, from which arises the most practically important distinction between intrinsic values (*Eigenwerte*) and extrinsic values (*Wirkungswerte*). Intrinsic value is possessed by those things which are desired solely for their own sake, whereas extrinsic value is possessed by things which are desired for the sake of their effect, that is, as means to certain ends. (The terminology of intrinsic and extrinsic value was incidentally later taken over by Meinong and also crops up in the work of Böhm-Bawerk.) Just as the value of a thing is constituted by its desirability, so also its worth corresponds directly to the strength or intensity of the desire. The determination of the strength of desire is derived by Ehrenfels from a special 'Law of Relative Advancement of Happiness', according to which the actual occurrence of striving or willing always increases the state of happiness in comparison with a state of not striving or willing; the strength of the striving results from the difference between the compared states of happiness. In this psychological theory it becomes most important to answer the question of the relation between feeling and desire. Ehrenfels holds, in total contrast to the Kantian conception, that it is not in reason but in feeling and feeling-disposition that we find the essentially influential element inducing desire and determining its intensity and direction. He defines feeling-dispositions as 'capacities for connecting determinate mental phenomena with determinate feelings of pleasure or displeasure' (Ehrenfels 1897a, p. 117). This point of view has very far-reaching consequences; it implies that all change in value leads back to change in feeling-dispositions, since all values have as their basis desires conditioned by feeling. Ehrenfels goes on to investigate in great detail the psychological causes and influences of the formation of values and movement in values, and finally draws on certain biological concepts ('development of valuations', 'struggle for survival among individual valuations') in order to further the explanation of these phenomena.

One of the most important branches of general value theory, and certainly the one most discussed in the philosophical tradition, is, of course, ethics. For Ehrenfels, ethics can only 'be conceived and carried on' as 'the psychology of ethical value-facts', so that the foremost task of a scientific ethics is the 'psychological investigation of matters of ethical fact'. (Ehrenfels 1898, p. 5.) The starting point for every such investigation consists in the phenomena, characteristic of ethics, of moral *approval* and *disapproval*. In each of these an ethical valuation is expressed, a valuation which is based, as already established for values in general, on particular desires. Since desire-dispositions are directly dependent on feeling-dispositions, an ethical valuation does no more than state the presence or lack of a desire- or feeling-disposition. From a consideration of the feeling- and desire-dispositions actually to be found in Western culture, Ehrenfels concludes that the dispositions positively valued are those whose 'increase above the actually occurring level would be necessary for the general good' (Ehrenfels 1889, p. 39). The striking circumstance that huge contrasts subsist between the ethical valuations of different cultures, and also between different epochs within one culture, is for Ehrenfels an obvious consequence of the psychologically regulated nature of value change. Ehrenfels then goes on to discuss thoroughly the tendencies affecting change in value formation and development within ethics, as he had already done for the general case. In the context of his theory of ethical value Ehrenfels occasionally uses the word '*Grenzfrommen*', meaning roughly 'marginal benefit' or 'marginal avail', which he understands as a wider form of marginal utility ('*Grenznutzen*'). Schumpeter (1954, p. 1058), wrongly translates this as 'marginal piety'; but '*Frommen*', (benefit, avail, profit) is simply an archaic near-synonym for '*Nutzen*', and not to be confused with piety (*Frömmigkeit*).

Ehrenfels' final large work after the writings on value theory was the *Kosmogonie*, published in 1916. After 14 years devoted almost exclusively to the discussion of social-ethical and eugenic questions, Ehrenfels returns in the *Kosmogonie* to problems of a theoretical nature, though still seeking consequences for the general concerns of humanity. The underlying idea of this work was precisely summarised by Felix Weltsch in his obituary of Ehrenfels (Weltsch 1932, p. 168):

The *Kosmogonie*, which Ehrenfels himself held to be his most important work (published in 1916), seeks nothing less than an explanation of the course of the universe. This is attempted on the basis of a dualistic hypothesis. The universe is a result of two opposed tendencies, that of a primeval formative urge (the unifying principle) and that of chaos, which stands opposed to the formative urge. The contributions of these two principles yields for Ehrenfels answers to a whole range of difficult metaphysical problems, such as causality, probability and time. According to Ehrenfels the unifying principle is quite without any consciousness of purpose: it is simply a striving to bring unity and order into the chaos, the order coming from the formation of new and ever higher structures [*Gestalten*]. This is the meaning of all that happens. Since this process is still far from ended, i.e., since the world is still in the process of creation, so that much is still dependent on chaos and can only be explained by the opposition of chaos, it is impossible rationally to fully comprehend the world. The world is combined out of order and chaos, fortune and misfortune, good and evil. This metaphysic has its predecessors in the struggle between Ormazd and Ahriman, in Manichaeism, in many gnostic views and in Jewish and Christian mysticism, and must clearly in every case issue in some kind of religious stance. The primeval formative principle is then called God, and God, who created and is still creating the world, came, so Ehrenfels considers in his final outlook, to consciousness in Man.

5. Oskar Kraus

Biography

The academic career of Oskar Kraus (b.1872, Prague, d.1942, Oxford) at the German University in Prague was hindered by his championing of Brentano's cause in the controversy over the latter's marriage. As a high-school student, Kraus believed in a utopian atheistic socialism. In 1890 he entered University; family circumstances compelled him to make his main subject law, rather than philosophy and natural science as he wished. He studied law under Jodl and philosophy under Marty. His first personal meeting with Marty took place in March 1891, when Marty recommended him to read

Brentano's *Ursprung* which had only recently appeared. Under Marty's influence, Kraus underwent what he described as 'a tremendous metamorphosis'. Among the members of the Prague Law Faculty the economist Friedrich von Wieser especially fascinated him. He read Wieser with zeal, and was converted from a Marxist to a psychologically based theory of value. His by then waning interest in socialism led him into minor trouble with the authorities at the University. He was compelled by Krasnopolski, Dean of the Faculty and Professor of Civil Law, to state in writing that he would not, while still a student, engage in any further political activities. Towards the end of 1894, Kraus led a protest meeting in the main hall before students and teachers, in which he championed Brantano's cause. Krasnopolski, who had already gone into print against Brentano, and whom Brentano later even had to sue for libel, was in the audience, and Kraus made of him a powerful enemy. In 1895 Kraus received his doctorate in law, and applied to habilitate under Wieser. His opponent Krasnopolski forced the faculty to choose between himself or Kraus's habilitation, and the case naturally went against the student. Kraus was forced to work instead at the office of the Procurator of Finance. The result was that he was encouraged by Marty to habilitate in philosophy instead, which he did in 1901 with a book on Bentham's value theory. As Kraus (1929, p. 9) put it: 'in the end the human *ressentiment* I had considered a heavy evil turned out to my good.' Shortly after this, he and Krasnopolski were reconciled, but Kraus had to continue his office work: 'For more than sixteen years I submerged every morning in the sea of files and dust at the Finance Procurator's so that I could breathe in the afternoons and evenings the purer air of philosophy' (ibid., p. 10).

He continued to have frequent discussions with Marty until the latter's death shortly after the outbreak of war in 1914, and he corresponded with Brentano, whom he met on several occasions from 1895 onwards. His devotion to his teachers shows in the fact that he took on the burden of editing the *Nachlass* of each, with Kastil's help. In 1909 he became an *Extraordinarius*, finally giving up his administrative work in 1911. In autumn 1916 he succeeded to Marty's chair in Prague, his appointment being one of the last governmental acts of the dying Emperor Franz Josef. After the war he remained in Prague.

The first President of the new Czech Republic, Thomas G. Masaryk, himself a former student of Brentano in Vienna, founded the Prague Brentano Society, with Kraus as president, and the Czech state financially supported the production of the Brentano *Gesamtausgabe*. The Society also produced a series of original monographs, the second of which was Kraus's largest work, *Die Werttheorien: Geschichte und Kritik*, which appeared in 1937. In 1938 the Brentano Society disbanded and Kraus fled from National Socialist central Europe to England, dying in Oxford in 1942. His fellow editor and fellow student under Marty, Alfred Kastil, described him as 'indisputably the finest and most fruitful mind of the second generation of [Brentano] students'.

Work and Signficance

As a philosopher, Kraus always remained within the orbit defined by Brentano's ideas and interests, and was until the end of his life a fervent and sometimes acrimonious defender of Brentano's later reistic philosophy, especially against members of the first generation and their followers. So his expositions of the ideas of Meinong and Ehrenfels are respectful but neither sympathetic nor exhaustive, and he even took Brentano's part against his former teacher Marty, especially over the theory of truth.

Because of his juristic background, together with his passion for Brentano's philosophy, Kraus was well positioned to appreciate both philosophical and economic theories of value, having been introduced to the latter by Wieser. His chief interests in philosophy were thus value theory, philosophy of law, and the history of philosophy. His principal importance for us here turns on his view of *preference* as the basic concept of value theory, and on his work on certain historical precedents for key doctrines of Austrian economics, most notably in Aristotle and Bentham. His writings influenced in some measure both Böhm-Bawerk and Engländer. The former probably knew of Kraus earlier, for he was Wieser's brother-in-law and also Finance Minister at the time of the affair over Kraus's habilitation.

The main foundations of Kraus's positive and historical views on value theory were laid by 1905, and he thereafter deviated only in details: thus his subsequent conversion by Brentano away from the correspondence theory of truth is of no relevance to us here. He was an able and clear summarist, though he is less reliable over those with whom he disagrees than those with whom he is in agreement, tending in the former cases to summarise just so much as is required to show where the authors in question have gone astray. We cannot do better in giving a broad perspective on his ideas than to quote at length from his 1929 *Selbstdarstellung:*

On the Philosophy of Value and Economics

My *Habilitationsschrift, Zur Theorie des Wertes*, a study of Bentham done in 1901, deals with the whole of philosophical and economic value theory. After setting out the several meanings of the term 'value' I give a critique of the doctrine of marginal utility, the chief merit of which was to try to get closer, in the only way possible, i.e. through psychological methods, to the problem of economic value, its greatest defects lying in the incompleteness of its psychology.

Nevertheless, every future advance will have to refer back to Menger, and certainly also to my analysis of economic value and its tracing back to the concept of preference (greater value). To account for what we think when we speak of economic value and the ascription of value it is not enough just to bring in the concepts 'utility' and 'scarcity', since we don't think of these when we speak of economic value; rather the concept always alludes to something involving the advantage or disadvantage of the hypothetical loss [*Verlust*], the reason for which may lie in scarcity or utility, but which is not conceptually identical with these. Also the concept of 'greater utility' is surely a preference concept. To ascribe economic value to a usable thing within my reach means: I judge it to be more or less precious, i.e. that I cannot without disadvantage forego it, be it irreplaceable, only partly replaceable, or replaceable only at some sacrifice (cost). I show further that the so-called valuation according to marginal utility signifies nothing other than valuation according to the principle of greatest advantage or least disadvantage. In particular I had to reject the theory of Wieser, who characterised the economic value of a supply of goods of the same sort as the product of marginal utility and number of units. Among those in the Austrian School it was Böhm-Bawerk (1909–14, vol. II, 2, p. 219) who agreed in this respect with my critique and protested his priority over other critics. Otherwise, among political economists Oskar Engländer has carried my criticism further — has taken up the idea of preference as the basic concept of the theory of economic value and built up the theory of costs and prices, and, following in particular Brentano and myself, set ethics in a closer connection with economic theory. In addition my book led to the demonstration that what marginal-utility theorists call 'Gossen's Law', according to which, with the increase in quantity of goods, each newly added atom must suffer a continual decrease in value, until this has sunk to nil, goes back to Bentham. Certainly Bentham made different applications of this proposition than Gossen and the marginal-utility theorists, in that he drew from it the conclusion that a more even distribution of a quantity of goods among many results in a far higher total value than the concentration of the same quantity of goods in the hands of one or just a few. F. Albert Lange accorded this law an enormous significance when he found it in an incomplete form in Bernoulli. Bentham on the other hand was derided by Marx as the 'genius of bourgeois stupidity'. How far this was unjustified can be gathered from the fact that the St Simonists and Thompson were influenced by Bentham's ideas. Finally I showed the connections between what are called Bernoulli's and Fechner's Laws, and the more careful and less flawed treatment of Bentham. The later histories of value by Kaulla and Lujo Brentano have considered these connections.

In a treatise, 'Die aristotelische Werttheorie', I gave a survey of the Aristotelian ethical and political-economic theories of value. By juxtaposing the theories of Böhm-Bawerk and Aristotle I showed that the latter in the *Ethics*, *Politics*, *Rhetoric* and especially in the *Topics*, anticipates the theories of the Menger school, and that he used the Mengerian method of differences, not the fictive algebraic method of value ascriptions. In the *Jahrbücher der Philosophie* (1914) there appeared a critical review of mine on 'Die Grundlagen der (gesamten) Werttheorie'. Unlike other attempted treatments, I distinguish strictly between emotional valuations and their supervenient intellectual value judgements and value knowledge; without preceding feelings no intellectual valuations (value judgements) are possible. At that time I already sought to distance myself from the fiction of a 'self-subsisting realm of values'. However I then still believed in the correspondence theory, which I today fiercely combat as a disastrous error. I had also not yet freed myself completely from the illusion of taking 'value and disvalue', if not actually as a property of a thing, still somehow as a 'hypothetical predicate'. It became clear to me only later that the 'universality', 'sempiternality', 'immutability', 'validity', 'absoluteness' and 'objectivity' of 'true values and preferences' is fully accounted for when it is realised that valuations of certain objects can be characterised as correct (justified), and that only valuations and preferences which agree with these, never any that are in conflict with them, can also be characterised as correct (justified). Things which are or can be objects of such justified feeling activities are called 'valuable', but without the value being added as a new property to its other qualities. A realm of ideal value-essences then shows itself to be a completely worthless hypostatisation. By contrast with attempts to set out novel types and species of intrinsic values (primary values), it must be said that there can only be 'immediate values' inside states of consciousness, that is only in our presentations, judgements and emotions (noetic and sensory). The 'ranking of values' is decided by our justified preferences. But whoever talks of an unalterable ranking of values, misunderstands Brentano's great discovery if he would interpret this as meaning that the most insignificant snippet of knowledge is preferable, on account of the 'majesty of truth', to the most considerable sum of sensory pleasures! It is merely true that given the choice of deciding which to renounce, the whole species 'sensory pleasure' or the class 'knowledge' — as Mill teaches — we would correctly decide to renounce the lower class of the merely sensory. In connection with justified preferences and the so-called axioms of value and preference, the principle of summation plays an important part. In this connection the mathematical concept of expected value has to be brought in for the appraisal of chances. It takes us, in the realm of practical reason, to the highest law that he who wishes to choose correctly must choose the best that is *attainable*. The ethics of value is 'material' in that it takes note of the objects of correct valuations; it is 'formal' in that it brings forward the moment of *correctness* (the right, enjoined or dutiful). Value theory devotes its attention to both *correlative* moments [of form and matter]; ethics looks after the material in the theory of the good, while the theory of duty puts the formal moment in the foreground. It concerns itself above all else with the correctness of emotional consciousness-object relations; the prime thing being the characteristic of correctness, justification. The theory of right also touches on this concept of correct, dutiful willing and choosing.

6. Mutual Influences between the two Austrian Value Schools

The decisive ideas for a new conception of economic value theory, developed first by Carl Menger, and further extended by Wieser and Böhm-Bawerk, introduced a new phase in the history of political economy. These three founders of the Austrian school not only renewed the discussion of fundamental problems in value theory in economics but also exercised a significant influence on the formation of the second school of value theory in Austria.

That the economists were able to exert such a fruitful influence on philosophical research may well have been due to a factor additional to those mentioned in our introductory section, which is above all of decisive import for the content of the theory. What clearly distinguishes Menger's *Grundsätze* as regards method, and likewise applies to the investigations of Wieser and Böhm-Bawerk, is the attempt to trace all economic phenomena back to their simple ultimate 'elements'. If true knowlege of the nature of the value of goods is to be attained, then it is the conviction of Menger and his school that this is only possible by going beyond the mere description of external facts to the roots of the phenomenon of value and uncovering 'the essence and final causes of value' (Menger, 1871, p. 87). It was Emil Kauder (1957, pp. 411-25) who made clear that this conception of essence *(Wesen)* makes conspicuous the striking influence that Aristotle's philosophy exercised on Menger's thought. In fact Aristotle is one of the few philosophical writers who is repeatedly cited in Menger's writings. Other direct parallels between Menger and Aristotle in economic value theory were first shown in detail by Oskar Kraus (see above).

When Friedrich von Wieser's first book *Über den Ursprung und Hauptgesetze des wirtschaftlichen Wertes* appeared in 1884, he indicated even in the book's title that he wished to develop a new theory of economic value very much along the lines prescribed by Menger's programme. Wieser emphasises, in conformity with Menger's intentions, that investigation of the value problem cannot confine itself to the mere external relations between goods but must above all penetrate to the deeper causes, i.e. to the 'essence of value' (Wieser, 1884, pp. 13, 37). In much greater detail even than Menger, Wieser treats the connections between the value of goods, subjective estimations of value, and the satisfaction of human needs. He arrives at the basic position that the value of a good is founded in subjective interest, that economic man turns to those objects which he takes to be useful and important for the satisfaction of his needs. It is therefore a requirement of an economic theory of value that it contain an explanation of *acts of human valuation*. From the recognition that the constitutive moment of every valuing — the essence of value — lies in a certain mental relation of the subject to economic goods, Wieser is led finally to the conclusion that 'the doctrine of value is, if we have correctly circumscribed its task, applied psychology' (Wieser, 1884, p. 39). This provocative statement naturally did not meet with general agreement but was rather the occasion for extended controversy (see on this subject the summary in Rosenstein-Rodan (1927, pp. 1207–

1212)). Not only the opponents of the Austrian school but also some later representatives of marginal-utility theory expressly denied such a close connection between psychology and economics. When Wieser attempted to counter the objections that had been raised, in particular by Schumpeter, he saw himself compelled to take up a position on several basic methodological questions. Wieser's arguments on the problem of method in the economic and social sciences are sufficiently well known and their range and significance has been discussed in detail (e.g. by Mises, Hayek, Lachmann), so it is not necessary to go into details here. We mention just one point in connection with the psychological foundations of economics. If Wieser holds investigations in psychology to be an ineliminable part of economic research, he nevertheless does not wish to assert by this that economic psychology is a necessary presupposition for economic theory. The knowledge that is furnished by subjective value theory is self-sufficient, and was attained quite independently of the results of particular psychological experiments. How then does the economist attain the psychological insights relevant for value theory? Wieser's answer is that human consciousness houses a

> treasury of experiences possessed by everyone who engages in practical economy, and which every theoretician therefore already finds within himself without having to summon them by any special scientific means. . . . How could economic theory neglect to draw from a source which is so easily accessible, so infinitely rich and of such reliable purity! (Wieser, 1914, p. 133).

This implied conviction of the reliability of 'inner experience', which was shared by many other scientists, not only in the Brentano, Meinong and Husserl schools, has of course since been questioned by philosophers and psychologists from a number of different points of view. While there are signs in sciences such as linguistics of a revival of a similar conviction, the appeal to that which may only be experienced introspectively, whether immediately through inner perception or less directly through memory, is still widely held not to satisfy the criteria of intersubjective testability and controllable observation which are required of a science that is to be counted as empirical. This circumstance certainly contributed to the fact that, for a long time after Wieser's work, the relations between economics and psychology were broken off. Only more recent investigations, such as that of G. Katona (*Psychological Analysis of Economic Behavior*, New York: McGraw-

Hill, 1951) have shown that the application of psychologically-based methods can help to attain a better understanding of many microeconomic processes.

When detailing points of content in the theories of Menger and Wieser it should above all be made clear that the classical works of these Austrian economists exhibit a notable openness towards philosophical and psychological questions. This is one of the chief reasons why they attracted philosophers such as Ehrenfels, Meinong and Kraus, and stimulated them to further research. Kraus has himself attested how full of 'philosophical spirit' were Wieser's lectures (Kraus,1901, p. v), and we can also read directly in Wieser (1889, p. x): 'What needs to be given is a philosophy of value which requires words, not numbers'. It is no accident that Wieser lays emphasis on words, and reveals explicitly for the first time his disinclination to accept the mathematical treatment of marginal utility, a tendency which can be found implicit already in his first work of 1884. There he indicated in the first few pages that it is necessary to clarify the meaning of the basic concepts which are employed in everyday language before the proper investigation of value phenomena can be begun. Wieser requires such preliminary linguistic work not only for value-theoretic investigation. He emphasises their importance also for all areas of social science: a notable standpoint, anticipating in certain respects the method of linguistic analysis in contemporary philosophy.

Having pointed out the various internal and external factors whereby Austrian economics had a sustained effect on philosophy we must now consider whether and to what extent the Austrian economists also exhibit reactions to the work of philosophers. In general it can be shown that such an influence from both philosophy and theoretical psychology did obtain, although exerting a weaker and more uneven impression. If we consider once more Menger's work from this perspective, then it is immediately clear that the alterations and additions which are made in the second edition of the *Grundsätze der Volkswirtschaftslehre* (Menger 1923) contain no reference to the publications of the Brentano or Meinong schools. It would however be premature to conclude from this fact alone that Menger took no notice of the simultaneous researches in the neighbouring disciplines. Basing his opinion on personal information from Karl Menger Jr., Emil Kauder indicates rather that Menger (Sr.) undertook after 1900 to try and provide a psychological foundation for his theory, and therefore studied in detail the works of W. Wundt, Brentano, Ehrenfels and Kraus (Kauder 1965, pp. 89, 121). This interest in Austrian philosophers is clearly confirmed in Menger's correspondence with Meinong, Ehrenfels and Höfler, which is preserved in their respective *Nachlässe* in the University of Graz. It can be seen then that from the very beginning reciprocal connections between the two schools were built up, although this circumstance left immediately visible traces only on one side, namely in the philosophical literature.

A somewhat different picture to that of Menger can be gathered from the writings of Wieser that appeared after the turn of the century. In these, particularly in his investigations on the 'Theorie der gesellschaftlichen Wirtschaft' (1914), we find the value-theoretic works of the Austrian philosophers expressly cited. Nevertheless Wieser avoids entering into the content of the arguments of these authors, which may indeed appear surprising, considering that Wieser enjoyed the friendship of Ehrenfels over many years and was also directly connected with Kraus (who had studied with him in Prague). The reason for this otherwise unusual attitude can however simply be found in the fact — mentioned above — that Wieser in particular laid emphasis on the point that the knowledge necessary for the psychological foundations of economic value theory can be obtained independently and without the help of scientific psychology. By sharply delimiting economics from psychology Wieser also wanted to counter the accusations held against him by critics, according to which the then new-born science of psychology was far from possessing secure and generally-accepted foundations. So we can characterise Wieser's relationship to the second value school as follows: he certainly knew the representatives of this school well, and was even personally very close to some, but did not allow himself to get involved in discussing their ideas in print.

The Austrian economist who, on his own account, sought positive interaction with the psychologists and was, by contrast with Menger and Wieser, also prepared to carry the exchange into the scientific arena, was Eugen von Böhm-Bawerk. Following the path struck out by Wieser, Böhm-Bawerk emphasised vigorously the conviction that economics cannot dispense with psychology in its explanation of the basic phenomena of economic value. The third edition of his major work *Kapital und Kapitalzins* (Böhm-Bawerk 1909–14, vol. II, book 3 and *Exkurse* X–XI) furnishes ample proof of Böhm-Bawerk's considerable interest in psychological questions, and also demonstrates the extent to which he is concerned to bring into the framework of his account writings on value theory such as those of Kraus, Ehrenfels and Meinong. (On the relationship to Kraus see also

Kraus (1937, pp. 357–83).) Nevertheless Böhm-Bawerk preserves the right to undertake his own investigations into problems on the borderline between economics and psychology without having to take account of particular results of the latter. He argues for such 'boundary-crossing' (Böhm-Bawerk 1909–14, vol. II, pp. 322–30) on the grounds that, firstly, scientific psychology has still dealt very little with certain special problems affecting economics, and secondly, that even in matters of primary importance, such as the theory of feelings, no unified position had emerged from psychology. (Böhm-Bawerk (1909–14, vol. II, pp. 326–8), cites copiously from Witasek (1908).) The problem which Böhm-Bawerk found especially important, and which he attempted to solve with the help principally of psychology, is that of the determination of the magnitude of value. The essence of value, according to Böhm-Bawerk's definition, lies in the significance of goods for the individual's 'welfare'. From the valuations actually carried out on the goods available, there emerges a mirror-image of our welfare interests inasmuch as the magnitude of a good's value depends on the magnitude of the marginal increase in welfare which can be achieved by means of the good. 'A good will have a high value if an important advance in our welfare depends on it, and a low value when it brings only an insignificant welfare profit.' (Böhm-Bawerk 1886, p. 19). Welfare profit comes about through the satisfaction of our needs, and this means precisely the increase of pleasure and decrease or avoidance of displeasure. Since, however, the available goods do not suffice for the satisfaction of all our needs, it is necessary for us as rational economists to undertake to rank our needs in order of importance. This ranking then forms the foundation for determining the magnitude of value assigned in each case to a good. Böhm-Bawerk expresses this in psychological terms as follows:

> the value of a good is to be measured according to the magnitude of the difference in welfare, the difference of pleasure and pain, which goes with the possession or non-possession of the good. So it is ultimately magnitudes of feeling and of sensation with which we calculate, according to our theory. (Böhm-Bawerk 1909–14, vol. II, p. 331.)

The problem of the measurability of magnitudes of value or utility which Böhm-Bawerk here raises was a much-disputed topic in marginal-utility theory. Even the Austrian economists came to very different conclusions regarding it. We do not here need to go more closely into details, as this chapter on the history of economic theory has been presented many times before (see, for example, Kauder (1965, pp. 191–217)). However we should draw attention to one philosophical aspect of Böhm-Bawerk's argument. Böhm-Bawerk proceeds from the decisive assumption that the value of the welfare profit — on which the valuation of a good is based — is obtained from the determination of the magnitudes of feelings of pleasure and displeasure. If the strength or intensity of the pleasure or displeasure is to be treated as such a measurable magnitude, then — according to Böhm-Bawerk — a calculation of the welfare maximum is possible just to the extent that intensities of feeling can not only be compared, but also summed and determined arithmetically. Such a pleasure–displeasure calculus doubtless shows strong hedonistic tendencies. Of course Böhm-Bawerk attempted to counter the charge of hedonism that was brought against him by contemporaries and also later (for example, especially strongly by Myrdal (1954, Chapter 4)). But when Böhm-Bawerk says in his defence that he never intended to espouse a hedonistic theory, and further understands under 'welfare' all possible purposes worth pursuing (not merely egoistic ones), this still in one important respect leaves the criticism intact: as long as welfare interest, whatever may be understood by this, can be determined by means of a calculus of pleasure and displeasure whose magnitudes may be compared purely quantitatively, and as long as the estimation of the importance of needs is not qualitatively evaluated, but made dependent only on the strength of the associated pleasure feelings, then a characteristic element of hedonism is retained.

Finally we should like to draw attention to an author whose reputation in the history of Austrian economics does not come up to those of Menger and his immediate followers, but who holds an important position in terms of the reciprocal influence of the two Austrian value theory schools, namely Oskar Engländer (1866–1936). Like Kraus, Engländer studied law at the German University in Prague, where after the First World War he became Professor of Economics and Financial Science. Influences on his scientific work came from two directions. As W. Stark reports ('Biographische Skizze' in *Oskar Engländer. Festschrift zur Feier seines 60. Geburtstages*, Brünn/Leipzig/Vienna: Rohrer 1936, pp. 345–6), Engländer moved from law to economics under the influence of Wieser and Robert Zuckerkandl, but the shape of his work was determined by the influence of Marty and Kraus. It was they who introduced him to the thought of Brentano which was to form the basis and framework for his scientific work. It was, incidentally, a mistake of Emil Kauder (1969, p. 131) to describe Engländer as a student of Meinong. In addition to Marty and Kraus, Engländer also attended lectures given by Ehrenfels, but never by Meinong.

Engländer frequently cites Brentano and uses Brentanian ideas. He accepts the distinction between primary goods, which are desired for their own sake and are always psychic in character, and secondary goods (including services), which are desired for the sake of attaining primary goods. He also distinguishes correspondingly between primary and secondary evils. But he criticises those who would distinguish between primary and secondary *value*. According to Engländer, it is wrong to speak of economic, extrinsic or secondary value, as though it were some special kind of value. He sees all value as primary or intrinsic: one should speak of value in economic action (*Wert beim Wirtschaften*) rather than economic value (*wirtschaftlicher Wert*) (compare Engländer's contribution to *Probleme der Wertlehre*, (Mises and Spiethoff, 1931–3, vol. II, p. 14)). The economic value of a good is the intrinsic value which the possession of the good has for the individual. The distinction between means and ends concerns actions and states, and secondarily goods, but not values as such. Engländer also credits Brentano with the recognition of the independence and importance of the concepts of preference and choice. So psychology is for Engländer essential as a basis for economics to the extent that many of the basic concepts of economics are themselves psychological. In particular, an explanation, as against a mere description, of economic phenomena, demands reference to the motives of the agent: 'We can only penetrate to the inner essence of economic actions through motives' (Engländer 1914, p. 1513).

However, while ready to agree with the Austrian economists on the importance of psychological foundations, and readier than others to accept the findings of philosophical psychologists such as Brentano, Engländer is unwilling — along with Wieser — to see economics as applied or extrapolated psychology. He is prepared only to say that psychology is for economics 'merely an auxiliary science, if an indispensable one' (Engländer 1935, p. 540). The reason is that he does not agree with all the findings of the Austrian economists. For Engländer, the basic phenomenon requiring explanation in economics is price, and psychology is indispensable to the extent that it helps to explain price. The Austrians criticised the classical Ricardian theory of price, which sought to explain it in terms of objective costs, and attempted instead to explain price in terms of subjective values. Engländer finds both the criticism and the positive theory of the Austrians wanting, and contends that there is no direct path from subjective values to prices (ibid.). He introduces the concept of the price one is willing to pay (*Preiswilligkeit*) as distinct from the price that is actually paid, and the value placed on the good, and criticises Wieser and other Austrians for confusing value and *Preiswilligkeit* under the term 'estimation of value' (*Wertschätzung*).

In summary we may say that Engländer is far less critical of Brentano and the philosophical-psychological basis of economic theory than he is of the use to which this basis is put in the theories of the Austrian economists. He is even ready to use Brentano's work on ethics (*Ursprung*) to clarify the relationship between ethics and economics (Engländer 1914). With Menger's conception of economics as a science investigating the *essence* of economic phenomena, and with the conviction of the indispensability of a psychological basis, Engländer is in perfect accord.

A Bibliography of Value Theory with Special Reference to the Austrian Tradition

We wish to thank Wolfgang Grassl for suggestions which have been incorporated into this bibliography.

Bibliographies

Albert, Ethel and Kluckhohn, Clyde (1959). *A Selected Bibliography on Values, Ethics, and Esthetics in the Behavioral Sciences and Philosophy*, Glencoe, Ill.: The Free Press.

Chisholm, Roderick M. (1976). 'Bibliography of the Published Writings of Franz Brentano' in L.L. McAlister (ed.), *The Philosophy of Franz Brentano*, London: Duckworth, 240-7.

Ebeling, Richard M. (1983). 'Austrian Economics — An Annotated Bibliography', *Humane Studies Review*, 2.

Fabian, Reinhard (1983). 'Gesamtverzeichnis der veröffenlichten Schriften und Briefe von Alexius Meinong (1873–1978)' in A. Meinong, *Gesamtausgabe*, ed. R. Haller *et al.*, vol. VII, 325–42.

Gray, John (1984). 'Bibliography [of F.A. von Hayek]' in *Hayek on Liberty*, Oxford: Blackwell, 143–209.

Heyde, Johannes Erich (1928–31). 'Gesamtbibliographie des Wertbegriffes', *Literarische Berichte aus dem Gebiete der Philosophie, 15–16* (1928), 111–19; *17–18* (1928), 66–75; *19–20* (1929), 11–18; *21–22* (1930), 106–8; *25* (1931), 93–4.

Kraus, Oskar (1914). 'Literaturverzeichnis' (in connection with the article 'Die Grundlagen der Werttheorie'), in M. Frischeisen-Köhler (ed.), *Jahrbücher der Philosophie*, vol. II, Berlin: Mittler, 219–25.

Kraus, Oskar (1929). 'Schriftenverzeichnis', in R. Schmidt (ed.), *Die Philosophie der Gegenwart in Selbstdarstellungen*, Leipzig: Meiner, vol. VII, 201–3. (Bibliography of the writings of O. Kraus to 1929, in connection with his autobiography or *Selbstdarstellung*.)

Rescher, Nicholas (1969). 'Bibliography on the Theory of Value' in N. Rescher, *Introduction to Value Theory*, Englewood Cliffs: Prentice-Hall, 149–86.

Rosenstein-Rodan, P.N. (1927). Bibliography on economic theory of value (in connection with the article 'Grenznutzen') L. Elster *et al.* (eds), *Handwörterbuch der Staatswissenschaften*, vol. IV, Jena: Fischer, 1213–23.

Smith, Barry (1981). 'Ehrenfels Bibliography' in B. Smith (ed.), *Structure and Gestalt: Philosophy and Literature in Austria–Hungary and her Successor States*, Amsterdam: Benjamins, 155–9.

Weber, Wilhelm, Albert, Hans and Kade, Gerhard (1961). 'Bibliography' (in connection with the article 'Wert') in E. von Beckerath *et al* (eds), *Handwörterbuch der Sozialwissenschaften*, vol. XI, Stuttgart: Fischer, pp. 654–8.

Philosophy

Acham, Karl (1980). 'Werttheorie' in J. Speck (ed.), *Handbuch wissenschaftstheoretischer Begriffe*, vol. III, Göttingen: Vandenhoeck & Ruprecht, pp. 713–20.

Åkesson, Elof (1930). 'Det "opersonliga" värdet. Ett utvecklingsmotiv i Meinongs värdelära' in G. Aspelin and E. Åkesson (eds), *Studier tillägnade Efraim Liljeqvist*, vol. I, Lund: Skånska Centraltryckeriet, pp. 449–66.

Ameseder Rudolf (1906). 'Über Wertschönheit', *Zeitschrift für Ästhetik und allgemeine Kunstwissenschaft*, 1, pp. 203-15.

Arleth, Emil (1903). *Die metaphysischen Grundlagen der Aristotelischen Ethik*, Prague: Calve.

Bausola, Adriano (1968). *Conoscenza e moralità in Franz Brentano*, Milano: Vita e Pensiero (with bibliography of literature on Brentano).

Bear, Harry (1955). *The Theoretical Ethics of the Brentano School: A Psychoepistemological Approach* (dissertation), Columbia University, N.Y. , Ann Arbor: University Microfilms.

Benndorf, Hans (1951). *Persönliche Erinnerungen an Alexius Meinong*, Graz: Kienreich.

Brentano, Franz (1862). *Von der mannigfachen Bedeutung des Seienden nach Aristoteles*, Freiburg i.B.: Herder, reprint 1960, Darmstadt: Wissenschaftliche Buchgesellschaft; translated as *On the Several Senses of Being in Aristotle*, by R. George, Berkeley: University of California Press, 1975.

Brentano, Franz (1867). *Die Psychologie des Aristoteles, insbesondere seine Lehre vom ΝΟΥΣ ΠΟΙΗΤΙΚΟΣ*, Mainz: Kirchheim; 1867; translated as *The Psychology of Aristotle, in Particular His Doctrine of the Active Intellect*, by R. George and R.M. Chisholm, Berkeley: University of California Press, 1977.

Brentano, Franz (1874). *Psychologie vom empirischen Standpunkt*, vol. I, Leipzig: Duncker & Humblot.

Brentano, Franz (1889). *Vom Ursprung sittlicher Erkenntnis*, Leipzig: Duncker & Humblot; translated as *The Origin of the Knowledge of Right and Wrong*, by C. Hague, London: Constable, 1902.

Brentano, Franz (1893). *Über die Zukunft der Philosophie*, Vienna: Hölder, enlarged edition, ed. O. Kraus, Leipzig: Meiner, 1929; second edition (Hamburg: Meiner), 1968.

Brentano, Franz (1895). *Die vier Phasen der Philosophie und ihr augenblicklicher Stand*, Stuttgart: Cotta, enlarged edition, ed. O. Kraus, Leipzig: Meiner, 1926; second edition (Hamburg: Meiner), 1968.

Brentano, Franz (1907). *Untersuchungen zur Sinnespsychologie*, Leipzig: Duncker & Humblot; second enlarged edition, ed. R.M. Chisholm and R. Fabian, Hamburg: Felix Meiner, 1979.

Brentano, Franz (1911). *Von der Klassifikation der psychischen Phänomene*, Leipzig: Duncker & Humblot (new edition of the second part of Brentano (1894)).

Brentano, Franz (1911). *Aristoteles und seine Weltanschauung*, Leipzig: Quelle & Meyer; reprint (Hamburg: Meiner), 1977; translated as *Aristotle and His World View*, by R. George and R.M. Chisholm, Berkeley: University of California Press, 1978.

Brentano, Franz (1922). *Vom Ursprung sittlicher Erkenntnis*, second edition, ed. O. Kraus, Leipzig: Meiner; third edition 1934; fourth edition (Hamburg: Meiner), 1955; translated as *The Origin of Our Knowledge of Right and Wrong*, by R.M. Chisholm and E. Schneewind, London: Routledge & Kegan Paul, 1969.

Brentano, Franz (1924–5). *Psychologie vom empirischen Standpunkt*, vols I–II, second edition, ed. O. Kraus, Leipzig: Meiner; reprint (Hamburg: Meiner), 1955–9 and 1971–3; translated as *Psychology from an Empirical Standpoint*, by A.C. Rancurello, D.B. Terrell, and L.L. McAlister, London: Routledge & Kegan Paul, 1973.

Brentano, Franz (1925). *Versuch über die Erkenntnis*, ed. A. Kastil, Leipzig: Meiner; second enlarged edition (Hamburg: Meiner), 1970.

Brentano, Franz (1928). *Psychologie vom empirischen Standpunkt*, vol. III: *Vom sinnlichen und noetischen Bewusstsein*, ed. O. Kraus, Leipzig: Meiner; second edition (Hamburg: Meiner), 1968; translated as *Sensory and Noetic Consciousness (Psychology from an Empirical Standpoint III)*, by M. Schättle and L.L. McAlister, London: Routledge & Kegan Paul, 1981.

Brentano, Franz (1929). *Vom Dasein Gottes*, ed. by A. Kastil, Leipzig: Meiner; reprint (Hamburg: Meiner), 1968, 1980.

Brentano, Franz (1930). *Wahrheit und Evidenz*, ed. O. Kraus, Leipzig: Meiner; reprint (Hamburg: Meiner), 1974; translated as *The True and the Evident*, by R.M. Chisholm and E. Politzer, London: Routledge & Kegan Paul, 1966.

Brentano, Franz (1933). *Kategorienlehre*, ed. A. Kastil, Leipzig: Meiner; reprint (Hamburg: Meiner), 1974; translated as *The Theory of Categories*, by R.M. Chisholm and N. Guterman, Den Haag: Nijhoff, 1981.

Brentano, Franz (1952). *Grundlegung und Aufbau der Ethik*, ed. F. Mayer–Hillebrand, Berne: Francke; reprint (Hamburg: Meiner), 1978; translated as *The Foundation and Construction of Ethics*, by E. Schneewind, London: Routledge & Kegan Paul, 1973.

Brentano, Franz (1954). *Religion und Philosophie*, ed. F. Mayer-Hillebrand, Berne: Francke/Hamburg: Meiner.

Brentano, Franz (1956). *Die Lehre vom richtigen Urteil*, ed. F. Mayer-Hillebrand, Berne: Francke/Hamburg: Meiner.

Brentano, Franz (1959). *Grundzüge der Ästhetik*, ed. F. Mayer-Hillebrand, Berne: Francke/Hamburg: Meiner.

Brentano, Franz (1963). *Geschichte der griechischen Philosophie*, ed. F. Mayer-Hillebrand, Berne: Francke/Hamburg: Meiner.

Brentano, Franz (1966). *Die Abkehr vom Nichtrealen*, ed. F. Mayer-Hillebrand, Berne: Francke/Hamburg: Meiner.

Brentano, Franz (1976). *Philosophische Untersuchungen zu Raum, Zeit and Kontinuum*, ed. S. Körner and R.M. Chisholm, Hamburg: Meiner.

Brentano, Franz (1980). *Geschichte der mittelalterlichen Philosophie*, ed. K. Hedwig, Hamburg: Meiner.

Brentano, Franz (1982). *Deskriptive Psychologie*, ed. R.M. Chisholm and W. Baumgartner, Hamburg: Meiner.

Brentano, Franz (1985). *Über Aristoteles. Nachgelassene Aufsätze*, ed. R. George,

Hamburg: Meiner.
Chisholm, Roderick M. (ed.) (1960). *Realism and the Background of Phenomenology*, Glencoe, Ill.: The Free Press.
Chisholm, Roderick M. (1966). 'Brentano's Theory of Correct and Incorrect Emotion', *Revue Internationale de Philosophie*, *78*, 395–415; revised in L.L. McAlister (ed.), *The Philosophy of Brentano*, London: Duckworth, 1976, 160–75.
Chisholm, Roderick M. and Haller, Rudolf (eds) (1978). *Die Philosophie Franz Brentanos*. Beiträge zur Brentano-Konferenz, Amsterdam: Rodopi (also as *Grazer Philosophische Studien*, 5).
Chisholm, Roderick M. (1982). *Brentano and Meinong Studies*, Amsterdam: Rodopi.
Clarke, Mary Evelyn (1929). *A Study in the Logic of Values*, London: University of London Press.
Clarke, Mary Evelyn (1938). 'Cognition and Affection in the Experience of Value', *The Journal of Philosophy*, *35*, 5–18.
Cohn, Aron (1934). *Hauptprobleme der Wertphilosophie*, Vienna: Jahoda und Siegel.
Dürr, E. (1906). 'Zur Frage der Wertbestimmung', *Archiv für die gesamte Psychologie*, 6, 271–88.
Eaton, Howard O. (1930). *The Austrian Philosophy of Values*, Norman: University of Oklahoma Press (with bibliography).
Ehrenfels, Christian von (1890). 'Über "Gestaltqualitäten"', *Vierteljahrsschrift für wissenschaftliche Philosophie*, 14, 249–92; reprinted in F. Weinhandl (1960, 11–43); English translation in Smith (1986).
Ehrenfels, Christian von (1887). 'Über Fühlen und Wollen. Eine psychologische Studie', *Sitzungsberichte der Kaiserlichen Akademie der Wissenschaften* (Wien), Philosophisch-historische Klasse, *114*, 523–636.
Ehrenfels, Christian von (1893–4). 'Werttheorie und Ethik', *Vierteljahrsschrift für wissenschaftliche Philosophie*, *17*, (1893), 76–110, 200–66, 321–63, 413–75; *18* (1894), 77–97; reprinted in Ehrenfels (1983).
Ehrenfels, Christian von (1895). *Allegorische Dramen, für musikalische Composition gedichtet*, Wien: Konegen.
Ehrenfels, Christian von (1896). *Zur Klärung der Wagner-Controverse. Ein Vortrag*, Vienna: Konegan.
Ehrenfels, Christian von (1896). 'The Ethical Theory of Value', *International Journal of Ethics*, 6, 371–84; reprinted in Ehrenfels (1983).
Ehrenfels, Christian von (1896). 'Von der Wertdefinition zum Motivationsgesetze', *Archiv für systematische Philosophie*, 2, 103–22; reprinted in Ehrenfels (1983).
Ehrenfels, Christian von (1897). 'Über ethische Wertgefühle', *Dritter internationaler Congress für Psychologie in München* (1896), München: Lehmann, 231–4; reprinted in Ehrenfels (1983).
Ehrenfels, Christian von (1897a). *System der Werttheorie*, vol. I: *Allgemeine Werttheorie — Psychologie des Begehrens*, Leipzig: Reisland; reprinted in Ehrenfels (1983).
Ehrenfels, Christian von (1898). *System der Werttheorie*, vol. II: *Grundzüge einer Ethik*, Leipzig: Reisland; reprinted in Ehrenfels (1983).
Ehrenfels, Christian von (1898a). 'Die Intensität der Gefühle. Eine Entgegnung auf Franz Brentanos neue Intensitätslehre', *Zeitschrift für Psychologie*, *16*, 49–70.
Ehrenfels, Christian von (1899). 'Entgegnung auf H. Schwarz' Kritik der empiristischen Willenspsychologie und das Gesetz der relativen Glücksförderung', *Vierteljahrsschrift für wissenschaftliche Philosophie*, 23, 261–84.
Ehrenfels, Christian von (1902–3). 'Zuchtwahl und Monogamie', *Politische-Anthropologische Revue*, 1, 611–19, 689–703.

92   *The Second Austrian School of Value Theory*

Ehrenfels, Christian von (1907). *Grundbegriffe der Ethik*, Wiesbaden: Bergmann.
Ehrenfels, Christian von (1907). *Sexualethik*, Wiesbaden: Bergmann.
Ehrenfels, Christian von (1916). *Kosmogonie*, Jena: Diederichs; translated as *Cosmogony*, by M. Focht, New York: The Comet Press, 1948.
Ehrenfels, Christian von (1922). *Das Primzahlengesetz, entwickelt und dargestellt auf Grund der Gestalttheorie*, Leipzig: Reisland.
Ehrenfels, Christian von (1930). 'Die Sexualmoral der Zukunft', *Archiv für Rassen– und Gesellschäftsbiologie*, 22, 292–304.
Ehrenfels, Christian von (1983). *Philosophische Schriften, Band I: Werttheorie*, ed. R. Fabian, with an introduction by W. Grassl, Munich: Philosophia.
Ehrenfels, Christian von (1985). *Philosophische Schriften, Band II: Ästhetik*, ed. R. Fabian, with an introduction by R. Haller, Munich: Philosophia.
Eisler, Robert (1902). *Studien zur Werttheorie*, Leipzig: Duncker & Humblot.
Fabian, R. (ed.) (1985). *Christian von Ehrenfels. Leben und Werk*, Amsterdam: Rodopi.
Findlay, John N. (1963). *Meinong's Theory of Objects and Values*, second edition, Oxford: Clarendon Press.
Findlay, John N. (1970). *Axiological Ethics*, London: Macmillan.
Findlay, John N. (1973). 'Meinong the Phenomenologist', *Revue Internationale de Philosophie*, 27, 161–77.
Finscher, Helmut (1925). 'Das Problem der Existenz objektiver Werte', *Kant-Studien*, 30, 357–80.
Frankena, William K. (1967). 'Value and Valuation', in P. Edwards (ed.), *The Encyclopedia of Philosophy*, vol. VIII, New York: Macmillan, 229–32.
Frondizi, Risieri (1963). *What Is Value? An Introduction to Axiology*, La Salle, Ill.: Open Court; second edition, 1971.
Gómez Nogales, Salvador (1960). 'Critica de Ortega a la teoria de los valores de Christian von Ehrenfels' in Weinhandl (1960, 145–59).
Grassl, Wolfgang (1981). 'Grenznutzenlehre und Ethik' in E. Morscher and R. Stranzinger (eds), *Ethics. Foundations, Problems and Applications* (Proceedings of the Fifth International Wittgenstein Symposium), Vienna: Hölder-Pichler-Tempsky, 219–22.
Grassl, Wolfgang (1983). 'Christian von Ehrenfels als Werttheoretiker' in Ehrenfels (1983, 1–22).
Gregoretti, Paolo (1977). *Etica e temi giuridico-politici nel pensiero di Franz Brentano*. Trieste: CLUET.
Gurvitch, Georges (1937). *Morale théorique et sciences des moeurs*, Paris: Alcan.
Hägerström, Axel (1910). 'Kritiska punkter i värdepsykologien', in *Festskrift tillägnad E. O. Burman på hans 65-års dag*, Uppsala: Almqvist & Wiksell, 16–75.
Hägerström, Axel (1911). 'Om moraliska förestallningars sanning', reprinted in Hägerström (1966).
Hägerström, Axel (1929). 'Axel Hägerström (Selbstdarstellung)', in R. Schmidt (ed.), *Die Philosophie der Gegenwart in Selbstdarstellungen*, Leipzig: Meiner, vol. VII, 111–59.
Hägerström, Axel (1935–6). 'Om primitiva rudimenter i modernt föreställningssätt', reprinted in Martin Fries (ed.), *Socialfilosofiska uppsater*, second edition, Stockholm 1966.
Hägerström, Axel (1952). *Moralpsykologie*, ed. Martin Fries, Stockholm.
Hall, Everett Wesley (1952). *What is Value? An Essay in Philosophical Analysis*, London: Routledge & Kegan Paul, New York: Humanities Press.
Haller, Rudolf (ed.) (1972). *Jenseits von Sein und Nichtsein. Beiträge zur Meinong-Forschung*, Graz: Akademische Druck– und Verlagsanstalt.
Hartlich, Christian (1939). *Die ethischen Theorien Franz Brentanos und N.*

Hartmanns in ihrem Verhältnis zu Aristoteles (dissertation), Würzburg: Triltsch.
Hartmann, Nicolai (1926). *Ethik*, Berlin/Leipzig: de Gruyter; translated as *Ethics* by St. Coit, 3 vols., London: Allen & Unwin/New York: Macmillan, 1932.
Heibel, K. (1939). 'Die Lehre Franz Brentanos vom Ursprung sittlicher Erkenntnis', *Philosophisches Jahrbuch*, 52, 142–59.
Heyde, Johannes Erich (1926). *Wert. Eine philosophische Grundlegung*, Erfuth: Stenger.
Höfler, Alois (1890). *Philosophische Propädeutik: Logik* (written with the assistance of A. Meinong), Vienna-Prague: Tempsky, Leipzig: Freytag.
Höfler, Alois (1897). *Psychologie*, Vienna-Prague: Tempsky; second enlarged edn, ed. A. Wenzl, Vienna-Leipzig: Hölder-Pichler-Tempsky, 1930.
Höfler, Alois (1921). 'Die Philosophie des Alois Höfler' in R. Schmidt (ed.), *Die deutsche Philosophie der Gegenwart in Selbstdarstellungen*, Leipzig: Meiner, vol. II, 121–64, second edition, 1923.
Höfler, Alois (1922). *Logik*, second enlarged edn, Vienna: Hölder-Pichler-Tempsky, Leipzig: Freytag.
Husserl, Edmund (1976). 'Reminiscences of Franz Brentano' in L.L. McAlister (ed.), *The Philosophy of Franz Brentano*, London: Duckworth, 47–55; first published in German, in O. Kraus, *Franz Brentano. Zur Kenntnis seines Lebens und seiner Lehre*, Munich: Beck, 1919, 151–67.
Ingarden, R. (1983). *Man and Value*, trans. A. Szylewicz, Munich: Philosophia.
Johnston, William M. (1972). *The Austrian Mind. An Intellectual and Social History 1848–1938*, Berkeley: University of California Press; revised edition published as *Österreichische Kultur- und Geistesgeschichte. Gesellschaft und Ideen im Donauraum 1848 bis 1938*, Vienna/Cologne/Graz: Böhlau, 1974.
Jonson, Erik (1928). 'En svårighet i Meinongs värdeteori' in *Festskrift tillägnad Axel Hägerström den 6 September 1928 av filosofiska och juridiska föreningarna i Uppsala*, Uppsala: Almqvist and Wiksell.
Kastil, Alfred (1900). 'Die Frage nach der Erkenntnis des Guten bei Aristoteles und Thomas von Aquin', *Sitzungsberichte der Kaiserlichen Akademie der Wissenschaften* (Wien), Philosophisch-historische Klasse, *142*.
Kastil, Alfred (1951). *Die Philosophie Franz Brentanos. Eine Einführung in seine Lehre*, ed. F. Mayer-Hillebrand, Berne: Francke, Munich: Lehnen, Salzburg: Bergland, Hamburg: Meiner.
Katkov, Georg (1937). *Untersuchungen zur Werttheorie und Theodizee*, Brünn: Rohrer (Veröffentlichungen der Brentano-Gesellschaft, III).
Kindinger, Rudolf (ed.) (1965). *Philosophenbriefe. Aus der wissenschaftlichen Korrespondenz von Alexius Meinong*, Graz: Akademische Druck- und Verlagsanstalt.
Kohn, Elizabeth (1925). *Meinongs Wertlehre in ihrer Entwicklung*, Dissertation, Munich.
Kraft Victor (1937). *Die Grundlagen einer wissenschaftlichen Wertlehre*, Vienna: Springer (Schriften zur wissenschaftlichen Weltauffassung, 11); second, revised edition, 1951.
Kraus, Oskar (1894). *Das Bedürfnis. Ein Beitrag zur beschreibenden Psychologie*, Leipzig: Friedrich.
Kraus, Oskar (1901). *Zur Theorie des Wertes. Eine Bentham-Studie*, Halle a.S.: Niemeyer.
Kraus Oskar (1905a). 'Die aristotelische Werttheorie in ihren Beziehungen zu den Lehren der modernen Psychologenschule', *Zeitschrift für die gesamte Staatswissenschaft*, *61*, 573-92.
Kraus Oskar (1905b). *Die Lehre von Lob, Lohn, Tadel und Strafe bei Aristoteles*, Halle a.S.: Niemeyer.
Kraus, Oskar (1908). 'Zur Lehre von den Bedürfnissen', *Zeitschrift für*

Volkswirtschaft, Sozialpolitik und Verwaltung, 17, 499–516 (review of F. Cuhel's book *Zur Lehre von den Bedürfnissen*, 1907).

Kraus, Oskar (1910). 'Gossen, Hermann Heinrich', in *Allgemeine Deutsche Biographie*, Leipzig: Duncker & Humblot, vol. 55, 483–8.

Kraus, Oskar (1914). 'Die Grundlagen der Werttheorie', *Jahrbücher der Philosophie, 2*, 1–48, 219–25 (bibliography).

Kraus, Oskar (1916). *Anton Marty. Sein Leben und seine Werke. Eine Skizze*, Halle a.S.: Niemeyer; published also in A. Marty (1916–20, vol. I, 1–68 (with bibliography of the writings of A. Marty)).

Kraus, Oskar (1918). 'Über Franz Brentanos ethische Prinzipienlehre', *Monatshefte für pädagogische Reform (= Österreichischer Schulbote, 68)*, special issue, Vienna, 499-506.

Kraus, Oskar (1919). *Franz Brentano. Zur Kenntnis seines Lebens und seiner Lehre. Mit Beiträgen von Carl Stumpf und Edmund Husserl*, Munich: Beck; contributions by C. Stumpf and E. Husserl translated as 'Reminiscences of Franz Brentano' in L.L. McAlister (1976, 10–55).

Kraus, Oskar (1926). 'Franz Brentano', in *Neue Österreichische Biographie*, ed. A. Bettelheim, Vienna: Amalthea, vol. III, 102–18; translated as 'Biographical Sketch of Franz Brentano', in L.L. McAlister (1976, 1–9).

Kraus, Oskar (1929). 'Oskar Kraus' *(Selbstdarstellung)*, in R. Schmidt (ed.), *Die Philosophie der Gegenwart in Selbstdarstellungen*, Leipzig: Meiner, vol. VII, 161–203 (with bibliography).

Kraus, Oskar (1937). *Die Werttheorien. Geschichte und Kritik*, Brünn/Vienna/Leipzig: Rohrer (Veröffentlichungen der Brentano-Gesellschaft, II).

Kreibig, Josef Clemens (1896). *Geschichte und Kritik des ethischen Skepticismus*, Vienna: Hölder.

Kreibig, Josef Clemens (1902). *Psychologische Grundlegung eines Systems der Wert-Theorie*, Vienna: Hölder.

Kreibig, Josef Clemens (1912). 'Über den Begriff des "objektiven Wertes"', *Archiv für systematische Philosophie*, 18, 159–66.

Krüger, Felix (1898). *Der Begriff des absolut Wertvollen als Grundbegriff der Moralphilosophie*, Leipzig: Teubner.

Kubát, Daniel (1956). *Bedeutung und Wandel der ethischen Grundbegriffe bei Franz Brentano*, dissertation, University of Munich.

Kubát, Daniel (1958–9). 'Franz Brentano's Axiology. A Revised Conception', *Review of Metaphysics, 12*, 133–41.

Laird, John (1929). *The Idea of Value*, Cambridge: University Press.

Laszlo, Ervin and Wilbur, James B. (eds) (1973). *Value Theory in Philosophy and Social Science*, New York/London/Paris: Gordon and Breach.

Lavelle, Louis (1951). *Traité des valeurs*. Tome I: *Théorie générale de la valeur*, Paris: Presses universitaires de France.

Lawrence, J.M. Wilt (1980). 'Franz Brentano's Epistemology for Ethics', dissertation, Indiana University.

Lenoci, Michele (1972). *La teoria della conoscenza in Alexius Meinong: Oggetto, giudizio, assunzioni*, Milan: Vita e Pensiero (with bibliography of primary and secondary literature on Meinong, to 1970).

Liel, Wilhelmine (1904). 'Gegen eine voluntaristische Begründung der Werttheorie' in A. Meinong (ed.), *Untersuchungen zur Gegenstandstheorie und Psychologie*, Leipzig: Barth, 527–78.

Liljeqvist, Efraim (1904). *Meinongs allmänna värdeteori*, Gothenburg: W. Zachrisson.

Lindenfels, David F. (1980). *The Transformation of Positivism. Alexius Meinong and European Thought*, Berkeley/Los Angeles/London: University of California Press.

McAlister, Linda L. (1969). *The Development of Brentano's Ethics*, dissertation, Cornell University; published Amsterdam: Rodopi, 1982.

McAlister, Linda L. (ed.).) (1976). *The Philosophy of Brentano*, London: Duckworth (with bibliography of primary and secondary literature on Brentano).

Mackenzie, J.S. (1895). 'Notes on the Theory of Value, *Mind, 4*, 425–49.

Mally, Ernst (1912). 'Gegenstandstheoretische Grundlagen der Logik und Logistik', *Zeitschrift für Philosophie und philosophische Kritik, 148*, supplementary volume.

Mally, Ernst (1926). *Grundgesetze des Sollens. Elemente der Logik des Willens*, Graz: Leuschner & Lubensky; reprinted in E. Mally (1971, 227–324).

Mally, Ernst (1935). *Erlebnis und Wirklichkeit. Einleitung zur Philosophie der natürlichen Weltauffassung*, Leipzig: Klinkhardt.

Mally, Ernst (1971). *Logische Schriften: Grosses Logikfragment — Grundgesetze des Sollens*, ed. K. Wolf and P. Weingartner, Dordrecht: Reidel (with a bibliography of the writings of E. Mally).

Margolius, Hans (1929). *Die Ethik Franz Brentanos*, Leipzig: Meiner (with bibliography).

Martinetti, Piero (1927). 'La teoria del valore di F. Brentano', in P. Martinetti, *Saggi filosofici e religiosi*, Turin: Bottega d'Erasmo, 522–30.

Marty, Anton (1908). *Untersuchungen zur Grundlegung der allgemeinen Grammatik und Sprachphilosophie*, vol. I, Halle a.S.: Niemeyer.

Marty, Anton (1916–20). *Gesammelte Schriften*, 4 vols, ed. J. Eisenmeier, A. Kastil and O. Kraus, Halle a.S.: Niemeyer.

Mayer-Hillebrand, Franziska (1963). 'Rückblick auf die bisherigen Bestrebungen zur Erhaltung und Verbreitung von Franz Brentanos philosophischen Lehren und kurze Darstellung dieser Lehren', *Zeitschrift für philosophische Forschung, 17*, 146–69 (with bibliography).

Meinong, Alexius (1894). *Psychologisch-ethische Untersuchungen zur Werth-Theorie*, Graz: Leuschner & Lubensky; reprinted in A. Meinong, *Gesamtausgabe*, vol. III (1968), 1–244.

Meinong, Alexius (1895). 'Über Werthaltung und Wert', *Archiv für systematische Philosophie*, 1, 327–46; reprinted in A. Meinong, *Gesamtausgabe*, vol. III (1968), 245–66.

Meinong, Alexius (1899). 'Über Gegenstände höherer Ordnung und deren Verhältnis zur inneren Wahrnehmung', *Zeitschrift für Psychologie, 21*, 182–272; reprinted in A. Meinong, *Gesamtausgabe*, vol. II (1971), 377–471; translated as 'On Objects of Higher Order and their Relationship to Internal Perception' in M.-L. Schubert Kalsi (1978, 137–208).

Meinong, Alexius (1902). *Über Annahmen*, Leipzig: Barth; second enlarged edition, 1910, reprinted in A. Meinong, *Gesamtausgabe*, vol. IV (1977); translated as *On Assumptions* by J.M. Heanue, Berkeley/Los Angeles/London: University of California Press, 1983.

Meinong, Alexius (ed.) (1904a). *Untersuchungen zur Gegenstandstheorie und Psychologie*, Leipzig: Barth.

Meinong, Alexius (1904b). 'Über Gegenstandstheorie und Psychologie', Leipzig: Barth, 1–50, reprinted in A. Meinong, *Gesamtausgabe*, vol. II (1971), 481–530, translated as 'The Theory of Objects', in R.M. Chisholm (1960, 76–117).

Meinong, Alexius (1912). 'Für die Psychologie und gegen den Psychologismus in der allgemeinen Werttheorie', *Logos, 3*, 1–14; reprinted in A. Meinong, *Gesamtausgabe*, vol. III (1968), 267–82.

Meinong, Alexius (1913–14). *Gesammelte Abhandlungen*, vol. I: *Abhandlungen zur Psychologie*, vol. II: *Abhandlungen zur Erkenntnistheorie und Gegenstandstheorie*, Leipzig: Barth; reprinted in A. Meinong, *Gesamtausgabe*, vol. I–II (1969, 1971).

Meinong, Alexius (1915). *Über Möglichkeit und Wahrscheinlichkeit. Beiträge zur Gegenstandstheorie und Erkenntnistheorie*, Leipzig: Barth; reprinted in A. Meinong, *Gesamtausgabe*, vol. VI (1972).

Meinong, Alexius (1917). 'Über emotionale Präsentation', *Sitzungsberichte der Akademie der Wissenschaften* (Wien), Philosophisch-historische Klasse, *183*, II; reprinted in A. Meinong, *Gesamtausgabe*, vol. III (1968), 283–476; translated as *On Emotional Presentation*, by M.-L. Schubert Kalsi, Evanston, Ill.: Northwestern University Press, 1972.

Meinong, Alexius (1921). 'A. Meinong' *(Selbstdarstellung)*, in R. Schmidt (ed.), *Die deutsche Philosophie der Gegenwart in Selbstdarstellungen*, Leipzig: Meiner, vol. I, 101–60; reprinted in A. Meinong, *Gesamtausgabe*, vol. VII (1978), 1–62.

Meinong, Alexius (1923). *Zur Grundlegung der allgemeinen Werttheorie*, ed. E. Mally, Graz: Leuschner & Lubensky (as a substitute for a second edition of *Psychologisch-thische Untersuchungen zur Werttheorie*); reprinted in A. Meinong, *Gesamtausgabe*, vol. III (1968), 469–656.

Meinong, Alexius (1968). 'Ethische Bausteine' in A. Meinong, *Gesamtausgabe*, vol. III, 657–724.

Meinong, Alexius (1968–78). *Gesamtausgabe*, vol. I–VII, ed. R. Haller, R. Kindinger, and R.M. Chisholm, Graz: Akademische Druck- u. Verlagsanstalt (vol. VII contains a complete bibliography of Meinong's works to 1978).

Meinong, Alexius (1978). *Kolleghefte und Fragmente. Schriften aus dem Nachlass*, ed. R. Fabian and R. Haller, Graz: Akademische Druck- u. Verlagsanstalt (supplementary volume of the *Gesamtausgabe*).

Modenato, Francesca (1968). 'L'evidenza come criterio di valutazione morale nella "Psychologie" di F. Brentano', in C. Giacon (ed.), *La fondazione del giudizio morale*, Padova: Antenore, 97–109.

Modenato, Francesca (1979). *Coscienza ed essere in Franz Brentano*, Bologna: Pàtron.

Moore, G.E. (1903a). *Principia Ethica*, Cambridge: Cambridge University Press.

Moore, G.E. (1903b). 'Review of F. Brentano's *The Origin of the Knowledge of Right and Wrong*', *International Journal of Ethics*, *14*, 115–23; reprinted in L.L. McAlister (1976, 176–81).

Most, Otto (1931). *Die Ethik Franz Brentanos und ihre geschichtlichen Grundlagen. Untersuchungen zum ethischen Wertproblem*, Münster i.W.: Helios (Universitas-Archiv, 43).

Mulligan, Kevin (ed.) (forthcoming). *Mind, Meaning and Metaphysics. The Philosophy and Theory of Language of Anton Marty*, Dordrecht/Boston/Lancaster: Nijhoff.

Mulligan, Kevin and Smith, Barry (1985a). 'Franz Brentano and the Ontology of Mind', *Philosophy and Phenomenological Research*, *45*, 627-44.

Mulligan, Kevin and Smith, Barry (1985b). 'Mach und Ehrenfels: Über Gestaltqualitäten und das Problem der Abhängigkeit' in Fabian, 85–111; expanded English version in Smith (1986).

Orestano, Francesco (1907). *I valori umani: Teoria generale del valore. Saggio di una teoria dei valori morali*, Turin: Bocca (Bibliotèca di scienze moderne, 29); second edition, Milan: Bocca, 1942 (2 vols).

Ortega y Gasset, José (1923). 'Introducción a una estimativa', *Revista de Occidente I*; reprinted in *Obras Completas*, vol. VI, Madrid: Revista de Occidente, 1947 (5th edition, 1961), 315–35.

Parris, Marion (1909). 'Total Utility and the Economic Judgement Compared with their Ethical Counterparts' (dissertation), Bryn College, Philadelphia: Winston.

Perry, Ralph Barton (1926). *General Theory of Value: Its Meaning and Basic Principles Construed in Terms of Interest*, New York: Longmans; reissue 1950, Cambridge, Mass.: Harvard University Press.

Pichler, Hans (1919). *Grundzüge einer Ethik*, Graz/Vienna/Leipzig: Leuschner & Lubensky.

Puglisi, Mario (1938). 'La teoria del valore di Fr. Brentano', *Rivista di filosofia, 29*, 175–82.

Radaković, Konstantin, Silva-Tarouca, Amadeo and Weinhandl, Ferdinand (eds) (1952). *Meinong-Gedenkschrift*, Graz: Styria (Schriften der Universität Graz, I).

Rashdall, Hastings (1907). *The Theory of Good and Evil. A Treatise on Moral Philosophy*, vol. I–II, Oxford: Clarendon; second edition, London: Milford, 1924.

Reibenschuh, Gernot (1970). 'Der absolute Wert. Eine kritische Untersuchung zu Alexius v. Meinong's Werttheorie' (dissertation), University of Graz, Graz.

Rescher, Nicholas (1969). *Introduction to Value Theory*, Englewood Cliffs NJ: Prentice-Hall (with bibliography).

Rodhe, Sven Edvard (1937). *Über die Möglichkeit einer Werteinteilung*, Lund: Gleerup, Leipzig: Meiner (with bibliography).

Rosso, Corrado (1973). *Figure e dottrine della filosofia dei valori*, Naples: Guida (with bibliography).

Roth, Alois (1960). *Edmund Husserls ethische Untersuchungen. Dargestellt anhand seiner Vorlesungsmanuskripte*, The Hague: Nijhoff (Phaenomenologica, VII).

Rutte, Heiner (1978). 'Bemerkungen zu Brentanos antinaturalistischer Grundlegung der Ethik', *Grazer Philosophische Studien, 5*, 149–68.

Scharwath, Alfred G. (1967). *Tradition, Aufbau und Fortbildung der Tugendlehre Franz Brentanos innerhalb seines gesamten philosophischen Schaffens*, Meisenheim a.G.: Hain (containing four posthumous articles by Brentano on Aristotelian ethics, and also bibliographies of primary and secondary literature on Brentano).

Scheler, Max (1913–16). *Der Formalismus in der Ethik und die materiale Wertethik*, vol. I–II, in *Jahrbuch für Philosophie und phänomenologische Forschung*, 1 (1913), 2 (1916); fourth edition in M. Scheler, *Gesammelte Werke*, vol. II, Berne: Francke, 1954.

Schubert Kalsi, Marie-Luise (1978). *Alexius Meinong on Objects of Higher Order and Husserl's Phenomenology*, The Hague/Boston/London: Nijhoff (containing the translation of four articles by Meinong).

Schuhmann, Karl (1977). *Husserl-Chronik. Denk- und Lebensweg Edmund Husserls*, The Hague: Nijhoff (Husserliana-Dokumente, I).

Schwarz, Ernst (1934). *Über den Wert, das Soll und das richtige Werthalten*, Graz: Leykam (Meinong-Studien, II).

Shaw, Charles G. (1900–1). 'The Theory of Value and its Place in the History of Ethics', *International Journal of Ethics, 11*, 306–20.

Simons, P.M (ed.) (forthcoming). *Essays on Meinong*, Munich: Philosophia.

Smith, B. (1985). 'The Theory of Value of Christian von Ehrenfels', in Fabian (1985), 150–71.

Smith, B. (ed.) (1986). *Foundations of Gestalt Theory*, Munich: Philosophia.

Smith, B. (forthcoming (a)). 'Pleasure and its Modifications: Witasek, Meinong and the Aesthetics of the Grazer Schule' in Simons (forthcoming).

Smith B. (forthcoming (b)). 'Brentano and Marty: An Inquiry into Being and Truth', in Mulligan (forthcoming).

Spang, Alfons (1939). *Die Gnoseologie der sittlichen Werte bei Franz Brentano* (dissertation), University of Bonn; Düsseldorf: Nolte.

Stern, Alfred (1938–9). 'Le problème de l'absolutisme et du relativisme axiologique et la philosophie allemande', *Revue Internationale de Philosophie, 1*, 703–42.

Strich, Walter (1909). 'Das Wertproblem in der Philosophie der Gegenwart' (dissertation), Berlin: Schade.

Stumpf, Carl (1873). *Über den psychologischen Ursprung der Raumvorstellungen*, Leipzig: Hirzel.

Stumpf, Carl (1883–90). *Tonpsychologie*, vol. I–II, Leipzig: Hirzel, reprint 1965, Amsterdam: Bonset.

Stumpf, Carl (1876). 'Reminiscences of Franz Brentano' in L.L. McAlister (ed.) 1976, 10–46; first published in German, in O. Kraus, *Franz Brentano. Zur Kenntnis seines Lebens und seiner Lehre*, Munich: Beck 1919, 85–149.

Terstenjak, Anton (ed.) (1972). *Vom Gegenstand zum Sein — Von Meinong zu Weber. In honorem Francisci Weber octogenarii*, Munich: Trofenik, containing also three articles by Franz Weber (155–367): 'Meine Beziehungen zu Meinong', 'Vorlesungen über die Philosophie der Persönlichkeit', 'Zusammenfassende Gedanken zur Frage der Wirklichkeit'.

Twardowski, Kasimir (1894). *Zur Lehre vom Inhalt und Gegenstand der Vorstellungen. Eine psychologische Untersuchung*, Vienna: Hölder; reprint, Munich: Philosophia, 1982.

Urban, Wilbur Marshall (1909). *Valuation: Its Nature and Laws, Being an Introduction to the General Theory of Value*, London: Sonnenschein, New York: Macmillan.

Weber, Franz (1921). *Sistem filozofije*, Ljubljana: Kleinmayr & Bamberg ('System of Philosophy', published in Slovenian under the name France Veber).

Weber, Franz (1932). *Etika. Prvi poizkus eksaktne logike nagonske pameti*, Ljubljana: Učiteljska tiskarna ('Ethics', published in Slovenian under the name France Veber).

Weber, Franz (1972). 'Meine Beziehungen zu Meinong', 'Vorlesungen über die Philosophie der Persönlichkeit', 'Zusammenfassende Gedanken zur Frage der Wirklichkeit' in R. Trofenik (1972), 155–367.

Weinhandl, Ferdinand (ed.) (1960). *Gestalthaftes Sehen. Ergebnisse und Aufgaben der Morphologie. Zum hundertjährigen Geburtstag von Christian von Ehrenfels*, Darmstadt: Wissenschaftliche Buchgesellschaft.

Weltsch, Felix (1932). 'Christian Ehrenfels', *Ceská mysl*, 28, 265–73 (in Czech).

Werkmeister, William Henry (1970–3). *Historical Spectrum of Value Theories*, vol. I: *The German-Language Group*, vol. II: *The Anglo-American Group*, Lincoln, Nebr.: Johnsen.

Witasek, Stephan (1902). 'Wert und Schönheit', *Archiv für systematische Philosophie, 8*, 164–93.

Witasek, Stephan (1908). *Grundlinien der Psychologie*, Leipzig: Meiner.

Wolf, Karl (1968). 'Die Grazer Schule: Gegenstandstheorie und Wertlehre', *Wissenschaft und Weltbild, 21*, 31–56.

Wolf, Karl (1952). 'Die Entwicklung der Wertphilosophie in der Schule Meinongs', in K. Radaković (1952), 157–71.

Economics

Bayer, Hans (1930). 'Behaviorismus und die psychologischen Grundlagen der österreichischen Schule', *Zeitschrift für Nationalökonomie*, 1, 250–65.

Birck, L.V. (1922). *The Theory of Marginal Value*, London: Routledge.

Bloch, Henri S. (1937). *La théorie des besoins de Carl Menger*, Paris: Librairie Générale de Droit et de Jurisprudence.

Böhm-Bawerk, Eugen von (1886). 'Grundzüge der Theorie des wirtschaftlichen Güterwerts', *Jahrbücher für Nationalökonomie und Statistik, 13*, 1–82, 477–541; reprint 1932, London.

Böhm-Bawerk, Eugen von (1909–14). *Kapital und Kapitalzins*, volume I: *Geschichte und Kritik der Kapitalzins-Theorien*; volume II: *Positive Theorie des Kapitales*; suppl. volume: *Exkurse zur 'Positiven Theorie des Kapitales'*, third edition, Innsbruck: Wagner; reprint 1961, Meisenheim/G.: Hain, translated as *Capital and Interest*, vol. I–III, by G.D. Huncke and H.F. Sennholz, South Holland, Ill.:

Libertarian Press, 1959.

Böhm-Bawerk, Eugen von (1911). 'Wert', in *Handwörterbuch der Staatswissenschaften*, third edition, ed. J. Conrad *et al.*, Jena: Fischer, vol. VIII, 756–74; fourth edition, ed. L. Elster *et al.*, vol. VIII (1928), 988–1007, 'Nachträge' by F.X. Weiss, 1007–1017.

Böhm-Bawerk, Eugen von (1886). *Gesammelte Schriften*, vol. I–II, ed. F.X. Weiss, Vienna: Hölder.

Brentano, Lujo (1908). 'Die Entwickelung der Wertlehre', *Sitzungsberichte der Königlich Bayerischen Akademie der Wissenschaften zu München*, Philosophisch-philologische und historische. Klasse, III; reprinted in L. Brentano, *Konkrete Grundbedingungen der Volkswirtschaft*, Leipzig: Meiner, 1924, 339–435.

Cohn, Heinrich (1899). *Die subjektive Natur des Werthes*, Berlin: Guttentag.

Čuhel, Franz (1907). *Zur Lehre von den Bedürfnissen. Theoretische Untersuchungen über das Grenzgebiet der Ökonomie und der Psychologie*, Innsbruck: Wagner.

Diehl, Karl (1933). 'Wert und Werttheorie', in *Wörterbuch der Volkswirtschaft*, fourth edition, ed. L. Elster, Jena: Fischer, vol. III, 995–1006.

Dolan, Edwin G. (ed.) (1976). *The Foundations of Modern Austrian Economics*, Kansas City: Sheed & Ward.

Engländer, Oskar (1914). 'Die Erkenntnis des Sittlich-Richtigen und die Nationalökonomie', *Schmollers Jahrbuch für Gesetzgebung, Verwaltung und Volkswirtschaft im Deutschen Reiche*, 38, 1509–64, 1737–1802.

Engländer, Oskar (1927). 'Karl Mengers Grundsätze der Volkswirtschaftslehre', *Schmollers Jahrbuch für Gesetzgebung, Verwaltung und Volkswirtschaft im Deutschen Reiche*, 51, 371–401 (review of C. Menger's *Grundsätze der Volkswirtschaftslehre*, second edition, 1923).

Engländer, Oskar (1932). 'Wertlehre' in H. Mayer (ed.), *Die Wirtschaftstheorie der Gegenwart*, vol. II: *Wert, Preis, Produktion, Geld und Kredit*, Vienna: Springer, 1–26.

Engländer, Oskar (1929–30). *Theorie der Volkswirtschaft*, vol. I–II, Vienna, Springer.

Engländer, Oskar (1935). 'Das Seelische und die Volkswirtschaftslehre', *Jahrbücher für Nationalökonomie und Statistik*, 142, 513–40.

Gossen, Hermann Heinrich (1894). *Entwicklung der Gesetze des menschlichen Verkehrs und der daraus fliessenden Regeln für menschliches Handeln*, Braunschweig: Vieweg; third edition, Berlin: Prager, 1927.

Hayek, Friedrich A. von (1968). 'Economic Thought: The Austrian School' in David L. Sills (ed.), *International Encyclopedia of the Social Sciences*, vol. IV, New York, Macmillan and The Free Press, 458–62 (with bibliography).

Hayek, Friedrich A. von (1979). 'The Three Sources of Human Values', the Hobhouse Lecture given at the London School of Economics, 17 May 1978, publ. in the Epilogue to Hayek, *Law, Legislation and Liberty*, vol. III, London: Routledge and Kegan Paul.

Hicks, J.R. and Weber, W. (eds) (1973). *Carl Menger and the Austrian School of Economics*, Oxford: Clarendon.

Howey, R.S. (1960). *The Rise of the Marginal Utility School 1870–1889*, Lawrence, Kans.: University of Kansas Press.

Hutchison, Terence W. (1981). *The Politics and Philosophy of Economics. Marxians, Keynesians and Austrians*, Oxford: Blackwell.

Illy (Schönfeld), Leo (1948). *Das Gesetz des Grenznutzens*, Vienna: Springer.

Kauder, Emil (1953). 'Genesis of the Marginal Utility Theory. From Aristotle to the End of the Eighteenth Century', *The Economic Journal*, 63, 638–50.

Kauder, Emil (1957). 'Intellectual and Political Roots of the Older Austrian School', *Zeitschrift für Nationalökonomie*, 17, 411–25.

Kauder, Emil (1965). *A History of Marginal Utility Theory*, Princeton: Princeton

University Press.
Kaulla, Rudolf (1906). *Die geschichtliche Entwicklung der modernen Werttheorien*, Tübingen: Laupp.
Lachmann, Ludwig M. (1966). 'Die geistesgeschichtliche Bedeutung der österreichischen Schule in der Volkswirtschaftslehre', *Zeitschrift für Nationalökonomie, 26,* 152–67; translated as 'The Significance of the Austrian School of Economics in the History of Ideas', in L.M. Lachmann, *Capital, Expectations, and the Market Process*, ed. W.E. Grinder, Kansas City: Sheed Andrews and McMeel, 1977, 45–64.
Lifschitz, F. (1908). *Zur Kritik der Böhm-Bawerkschen Werttheorie*, Leipzig: Engelmann.
Mayer, Hans (1924). 'Bedürfnis', in *Handwörterbuch der Staatswissenschaften*, fourth edition, ed. by L. Elster *et al.*, Jena: Fischer, vol. II, 450–6.
Menger, Carl (1871). *Grundsätze der Volkswirtschaftslehre. Erster, allgemeiner Teil*, Vienna: Braumüller; reprinted in *The Collected Works of Carl Menger*, vol. I, ed. F. A. v. Hayek, London, 1933 and in C. Menger, *Gesammelte Werke*, vol. I, ed. F.A. v. Hayek, Tübingen: Mohr, 1970; translated as *Principles of Economics, First General Part*, ed. J. Dingwall and B.F. Hoselitz, Glencoe, Ill.: Free Press, 1950.
Menger, Carl (1923). *Grundsätze der Volkswirtschaftslehre*, second enlarged edition, ed. K. Menger, (Jr.), Vienna: Hölder-Pichler-Tempsky/Leipzig: Freytag.
Menger, Carl (1933–6). *The Collected Works*, vols I–IV, ed. F.A. von Hayek, London: London School of Economics.
Menger, Carl (1968–70). *Gesammelte Werke*, vols I–IV, second edition, ed. F.A. von Hayek, Tübingen: Mohr.
Mises, Ludwig von and Spiethoff, Arthur (eds) (1931–3). *Probleme der Wertlehre*, vols I–II, München/Leipzig: Duncker & Humblot (*Schriften des Vereines für Sozialpolitik*, 183/I–II).
Müller, Max, Halder, Alois, Müller, J. Heinz, Stavenhagen, Gerhard, Hommes, Ulrich (1963). 'Wert' in *Staatslexikon*, sixth edition, ed. Görres-Gesellschaft, Freiburg: Herder, vol. VIII, col. 596–618 (with bibliography).
Myrdal, Gunnar (1954). *The Political Element in the Development of Economic Theory*, translated by P. Streeten, Cambridge, Mass.: Harvard University Press.
Naumann, Moriz (1893). *Die Lehre vom Wert* (dissertation), Leipzig: Duncker & Humblot.
Perlmutter, Salomea (1902). *Karl Menger und die österreichische Schule der Nationalökonomie* (dissertation), Bern: Sturzenegger.
Podbielski, Giselle (1985). 'Die österreichische Schule der Nationalökonomie' in Paul Kruntorad (ed.), *A.E.I.O.U.*, Vienna: Österreichischer Bundesverlag, 131–143.
Rosenstein-Rodan, P.N. (1927). 'Grenznutzen', in L. Elster (ed.), *Handwörterbuch der Staatswissenschaften*, fourth edition, Jena: Fischer, (1927) 1190–1223 (with bibliography); translated as 'Marginal Utility', *International Economic Papers, 10*, (1960), 71–106 (translation published without bibliography).
Ruppe-Streissler, Monika (1962–3). 'Zum Begriff der Wertung in der älteren österreichischen Grenznutzenlehre', *Zeitschrift für Nationalökonomie, 22,* 377–419.
Sax, Emil (1930). 'Bedürfnis, Wert und Vorzug', *Zeitschrift für Nationalökonomie,* 1, 356–67 (published posthumously by O. Kraus).
Schönfeld-Illy, Leo (1924). *Grenznutzen und Wirtschaftsrechnung*, Vienna; reprinted with a preface by Kurt R. Leube, Munich: Philosophia, 1983.
Schumpeter, Joseph A. (1954). *History of Economic Analysis*, ed. E.B. Schumpeter, New York: Oxford University Press.
Shand, Alexander (1984). *The Capitalist Alternative. An Introduction to Neo-Austrian Economics*, Brighton: Wheatsheaf.

Slutsky, Eugen (1927). 'Zur Kritik des Böhm-Bawerkschen Wertbegriffs und seiner Lehre von der Messbarkeit des Wertes', *Schmollers Jahrbuch für Gesetzgebung, Verwaltung und Volkswirtschaft im Deutschen Reiche*, 51, 545–60.

Smart, William (1891). *An Introduction to the Theory of Value on the Lines of Menger, Wieser and Böhm-Bawerk*, London: Macmillan; fourth edition 1920.

Stigler, George J. (1950). 'The Development of Utility Theory', *The Journal of Political Economy*, 58, 307–27.

Streissler, Erich (1972). 'To What Extent Was the Austrian School Marginalist?', *History of Political Economy*, 4, 426–41.

Strigl, Richard von (1934). *Kapital und Produktion*, Vienna; reprinted with a preface by Ludwig M. Lachmann, Munich: Philosophia, 1983.

Sweezy, Alan R. (1935). 'The Interpretation of Subjective Value Theory in the Writings of the Austrian Economists', *The Review of Economic Studies*, 1, 176–85.

Weber, Max (1908). 'Die Grenznutzenlehre und das "psychologische Grundgesetz"', *Archiv für Sozialwissenschaft und Sozialpolitik*, 27, 546–58; reprinted in M. Weber, *Gesammelte Aufsätze zur Wissenschaftslehre*, 4th edn, ed. J. Winckelmann, Tübingen: Mohr, 1973, 384–99.

Weber, Wilhelm, Albert, Hans and Kade, Gerhard (1961). 'Wert' in E. Beckerath *et al.*, *Handwörterbuch der Sozialwissenschaften*, Stuttgart: Fischer, vol. XI, 637–58 (with bibliography).

Weinberger, Otto (1926). *Die Grenznutzenschule*, Halberstadt: Meyer.

White, Lawrence H. (1977). *Methodology of the Austrian School* (Occasional Papers, 1), New York: Center for Libertarian Studies.

Wieser, Friedrich von (1884). *Über den Ursprung und die Hauptgesetze des wirthschaftlichen Werthes*, Vienna: Hölder.

Wieser, Friedrich von (1889). *Der natürliche Werth*, Vienna: Hölder; translated as *Natural Value*, ed. W. Smart, translated by Ch.A. Malloch, London/New York: Macmillan, 1893; reprint 1956, New York: Kelly & Millman.

Wieser, Friedrich von (1891). 'The Austrian School and the Theory of Value', *Economic Journal*, 1, 108–21.

Wieser, Friedrich von (1911). 'Das Wesen und der Hauptinhalt der theoretischen Nationalökonomie. Kritische Glossen', *Jahrbuch für Gesetzgebung, Verwaltung und Volkswirtschaft im Deutschen Reich*, 35, 909–13; reprinted in F. von Wieser, *Gesammelte Abhandlungen*, ed. F.A. v. Hayek, Tübingen: Mohr, 1929, 10–34.

Wieser, Friedrich von (1914). 'Theorie der gesellschaftlichen Wirtschaft' in *Grundriss der Sozialökonomik*, vol. I: *Wirtschaft und Wirtschaftswissenschaft*, Tübingen: Mohr, 125–444; translated as *Social Economics*, by F. A. Hinrichs, New York: Greenberg, 1927.

Wieser, Friedrich von (1929). *Gesammelte Abhandlungen*, ed. F.A. von Hayek, Tübingen: Mohr.

3 INTELLECTUAL FOUNDATIONS OF AUSTRIAN LIBERALISM[1]

J.C. Nyíri

1. Introduction

The theoretical achievements of nineteenth-century Austrian liberalism are seldom referred to in contemporary discussions of liberal theory. Indeed what Karl Eder pointed out in his *Der Liberalismus in Altösterreich* (1955), namely that works dealing with the history of European liberalism in general, and German liberalism in particular, do not even mention, let alone analyse, the independent development of liberalism in Austria,[2] can still today be maintained. It is not as though treatises on the subject were simply non-existent. The literature on Austrian liberalism as a whole, or on its various aspects, is vast. But this literature does not set Austrian liberalism within the context of the problems and arguments of present-day liberal theory. Carl E. Schorske, in the introduction to his recently published *Fin-de-Siècle Vienna* (several essays of which have, since their first appearance in the 1960s, exerted a considerable influence), does indeed establish some connection between his interest in Austrian intellectual history and the American sociol-political climate of his own times.[3] And Janik and Toulmin, in their *Wittgenstein's Vienna* (1973), actually point to certain conclusions which, they suggest, are derivable from a study of 'the Kakanian syndrome' and are of relevance to the present day. The sheer linguistic incomprehension, for example, between certain American minorities and the official authorities poses 'problems of communication that bear examination in the light of the Austro-Hungarian experience'.[4] But even in these works no attempt is made to enrich, or criticise, present-day liberal theory through an evaluation of the insights or failures of Austrian liberals.

Analyses within contemporary liberalism, on the other hand, hardly ever take into account the theoretical work done by nineteenth-century Austrian liberals — notwithstanding the fact that, especially in America, these analyses address problems rather similar to those faced (and in some respects solved) by Austrian *Altliberalismus*, and that the work of Austrian-born scholars (Hayek, Mises, Voegelin) is so manifestly present in modern liberal, market-oriented theory, today increasingly associated with the term 'neo-conservatism'.

George H. Nash (1979), for example, points out that post-war American conservatism is constituted, as is well known, by two distinct currents, the classical liberal (or, in its various more extreme forms, *libertarian*) and the traditionalist (or neo-conservative). The tension between these two trends presents one of the most fundamental intellectual challenges to American conservative theory. Three distinct elements can be discerned in the response to this challenge: (i) the insight that democracy and liberalism are concerned with two entirely different problems, the former with the legitimation of government, the latter with the intrinsic limitations of the power of the state; (ii) a move toward greater application of the concept of a *natural law* as opposed to that of natural 'rights'; and (iii) a recognition of the significance for American conservatives of 'the anti-majoritarian, states' rights, limited government, decentralist philosophy'.[5]

Yet despite all this, he does not even mention the nineteenth-century Austrian liberal tradition even though the joint acceptance of both liberal and traditionalist notions was a striking tenet of this tradition; even though the concept of limited government was a basic idea of leading Austrian liberal theorists; and even though post-war American 'classical liberalism' itself has certain markedly Austrian roots.

Naturally Nash does indeed mention that Hayek, Mises, and a number of other initiators of post-war American liberalism, are natives of Austria. But he does not refer to the parallels that hold, for example, between Hayek's position and Austrian *Altliberalismus*. Even Hayek himself, however, seems to be unaware of these parallels. Apart from a casual reference to the fact that Carl Menger — an author who otherwise of course is very much at the centre of his interest — was inclined to conservatism, that is, to 'liberalism of the old type',[6] Hayek apparently never mentions the theories, or even the existence, of nineteenth-century Austrian liberalism as such. It is precisely this current, however, from which he naturally and so obviously seems to be descended.

When discussing the history and main tenets of liberalism, Hayek always stresses that this movement derives from two distinct sources, two distinct traditions which co-existed only uneasily. The first is epitomised by the political doctrine of the English Whigs, a doctrine of *evolutionism*. The second made itself felt where the individual liberty secured to the citizens of Britain inspired continental liberal movements in countries where most of the medieval liberties preserved in Britain had been destroyed. The institutions of liberty then came to be interpreted

> in the light of a philosophical tradition very different from the evolutionary conceptions predominant in Britain, namely of a rationalist or constructivist view which demanded a deliberate reconstruction of the whole of society in accordance with the principles of reason.[7]

Now Hayek explicitly identifies his own position, *true* liberalism as he sometimes calls it, with the *first* of these traditions, and emphasises that this position is distrustful of the power of individual reason but places great value on the interpersonal process of discussion.[8] It is a position that does not take literally the concept of 'natural rights of the individual', but is concerned, rather, with the principle of limiting coercion to the enforcement of general rules of just conduct.[9] It does not deny 'the value of grown institutions' and is not disinclined 'to seek assistance from whatever nonrational institutions or habits have proved their worth'.[10] Indeed Hayek stresses that 'there can be no excuse or pardon for a systematic disregard of accepted moral rules because these rules have no understood justification'.[11] He holds that 'the imposition of egalitarianism' must stop cultural evolution and that

> the most widely held ideas which dominate . . . the twentieth century, a just distribution, a freeing ourselves from repressions and conventional morals, of permissive education as a way to freedom, and the replacement of the market with a rational arrangement by a body with coercive powers

are all superstitions in the strict sense of the word.[12]

There is thus a haunting traditionalism, or conservatism, in Hayek's position,[13] and indeed he has again and again found it necessary to defend himself against the label 'conservative'. But surely, as he himself admits, the present-day American trend of calling 'conservative' what once in Europe was called 'liberal' is not entirely without justification.[14] In the old Whig tradition 'liberal' and 'conservative' ideas did not merely co-exist. They formed, rather, an organic whole; and precisely the same holds of Austrian *Altliberalismus*, the old liberalism of the pre-1848 or pre-1867 era.

Now there can surely be no doubt as to the classification of, for example, Carl Menger as a representative of Austrian liberalism. His middle-class background, his specific political affiliations, and of course the methodological individualism permeating his subjectivist theory of economic needs (Menger, 1871) make up a coherent liberal pattern. But at the same time — as has been stressed by Jeremy Shearmur[15] — Menger definitely displays strong sympathies towards traditionalist, counter-enlightenment views such as those of Burke and Savigny. As Menger writes:

> Burke was probably the first, who, trained for it by the spirit of English jurisprudence, emphasized with full awareness the significance of the organic structures of social life and the partly unintended origin of these.[16]

Burke taught that numerous institutions of his country

> were not the result of positive legislation or of the conscious common will of society directed toward establishing this, but the unintended result of historical development. He first taught that what existed and had stood the test, what had developed historically, was again to be respected, in contrast to the projects of immature desire for innovation. Herewith he made the first breach in the one-sided rationalism and pragmatism of the Anglo-French Age of Enlightenment.[17]

Menger comes close to agreeing with the Savigny school also when they maintain that the universal desire for reform brought about by the Revolution in France rested on a failure to recognise the 'organic origin' of law, the state and of political institutions, that there is a 'subconscious wisdom' manifested in those institutions that come about organically, that the meddlesome advocates of reform 'would do well less to trust their own insight and energy than to leave the reshaping of society to the "historical process of development" '.[18] And he criticises the German economists for their failure to work out the idea of a conservative position, analogous to that of the Savigny school, in the sphere of economics, a position 'which would have defended existing economic institutions and interests against the exaggerations of reform ideas, and especially against socialism . . . '[19]

Not only Menger, however, but all prominent liberals in nineteenth-century Austria had strong conservative leanings. 'Austria' here, of course, includes both Austria and Hungary. Count István Széchenyi, for example, initiator of the Hungarian liberal reform movement in the

1830s, published in 1830 an important book entitled *Hitel* ('Credit'), which is the first concentrated attack on Hungary's feudal economy and a call for national awakening. This is a book 'full of Bentham and Adam Smith' and general 'Anglomania',[20] yet Széchenyi can at the same time properly be said to be a representative of early nineteenth-century German conservatism. He belongs to that wing sometimes referred to as *reform conservatism*.[21] Thus Iványi-Grünwald calls Széchenyi a 'progressive conservative',[22] someone whose belief in material and historical progress is inseparable from the belief in Christian perfectibility. Széchenyi did not share the characteristic liberal faith in the powers of autonomous reason. Indeed there is a characteristic passage in *Hitel* where he forcefully rejects the abstract concept of reason.[23] Thus he did not believe in following abstract plans or blueprints. 'When cooking', he tells us, 'it is the experience of the cook that is of first importance; only he who is experienced can usefully employ recipes.'[24] And he was definitely adverse to unrestricted social mobility.

It is customary to speak of Széchenyi's 'conservative turn' in the 1840s, 'motivated by his growing abhorrence of the possibility of a revolutionary explosion in Hungary';[25] but this is only partially correct. There was in fact always, in his liberalism, a conservative streak. The same holds of Baron József Eötvös, a leading Hungarian liberal politician, recently referred to as the most important political theorist of nineteenth-century Austria-Hungary.[26] For despite the fact that Eötvös was overtly a liberal, his major work, *The Influence of the Ruling Ideas of the 19th Century on the State* (1851–4), is in fact a conservative manifesto, promulgating Christian values, organic historical evolution, and the values of aristocracy. The ideas of liberty and equality are, according to Eötvös, 'luminous ideals': they lead people only to disaster.[27]

Eötvös played a substantial role in preparing the way for the *Ausgleich* (constitutional compromise between Austria and Hungary leading to the establishment of the dual monarchy) of 1867. One of his Austrian counterparts in that process was the Styrian liberal leader Moritz von Kaiserfeld. Kaiserfeld's biographer characterises his views as exhibiting a 'conservative liberalism',[28] tracing in great detail the evolution of these views during and after the events of 1848.

Kaiserfeld was of Slovenian origin. His grandfather was ennobled in 1817. In 1847 he played a minor role in the Styrian *Landtag* and was subsequently sent to the new German National Parliament in Frankfurt. While still in Styria, he wrote a series of articles in the

Grazer Zeitung analysing current political developments. These analyses are strongly critical of the 'Austrian democrats', whose 'exultations of freedom' would, Kaiserfeld suggests, surely be ridiculed by the 'sober North American'. 'Revolutions are evils', writes Kaiserfeld; 'like hurricanes in the physical world; only their necessity can justify them'. And of Vienna in the last few months of 1848 he writes: 'the insanity of radicalism has done more harm there than the existence of reactionary tendencies'.[29] His subsequent reactions to the political scene in Frankfurt are concisely reflected in a letter he wrote to his wife in March 1849:

> I am not a democrat in the sense in which this word has now become discredited, and had I come here with such impractical ideas, to a place where I see and hear how these kinds of democrats manipulate people, I would have ceased to be one of them. You know my character, and that dishonourable means (applied, incidentally, also by conservatives) are repugnant to me. . . . . Console yourself, I am not at all a man of extremes, and the club to which I belong (Pariser Hof, Hotel Schröder) is itself more conservative than I would wish.[30]

Liberty, Kaiserfeld maintained, has its boundaries, and these are constituted by the law.[31]

It was constitutional government, then, not democracy or the individual's 'natural rights' with which Austrian liberals were generally concerned. Even where, as for example in the case of Thomas G. Masaryk, the problem of individual autonomy becomes central, an unmistakable streak of conservatism remains present. Although Masaryk (subsequently the founder of Czechoslovakia) was of Slovakian-Moravian origin, it is certainly proper to regard him, at least until about the mid-1880s, as an Austrian. And he was undoubtedly a liberal of sorts; indeed Karl Popper calls him 'one of the greatest of all fighters for the open society'. Thus on the one hand his book *Der Selbstmord als sociale Massenerscheinung der modernen Civilisation* (1881)[32] is intent on demonstrating the possibility of a 'religious-ethical individualism'. Yet on the other hand Masaryk is repelled by the idea of a society where every norm is open to criticism, where no institution is viewed with a feeling of its ultimate necessity: 'What one calls European morals, social relations, progress, presuppose conditions that many fulfil only by their mental health becoming destroyed. . . . . What we call civilisation, enlightenment, liberal education, progress, brings forward a widely spread public psychosis.'[33] Not reason, but only *religion* can guide man.

> If the practice of religion and the power of the church disappears, along with it disappear consolation, hope and joy in life. Individual spirits may well be able, as they believe, to live the true, the good, and yet that is really mere deception the beautiful without any religion . . . We find the bread-ovens of mental derangement among peoples who throw off the yoke of authority, among peoples who form associations, seek to make their own laws, and have a literary calling, in nations where an incessant impulse drives men to flee the sphere circumscribed by their birth.[34]

The specific conceptual ways in which 'liberal' and 'conservative' ideas were linked together in the theory of Austrian *Altliberalismus* will, then, form the principal subject-matter of the present paper. I shall divide my discussion of this subject into the following sections: section 2 will analyse the ideas of the *Vormärz* period of 1830–48, i.e. the sources, elements and initial aspirations of Austrian — and in section 3 Hungarian — liberalism. Sections 4 and 5 will concentrate on the period from revolution to *Ausgleich*, on the theoretical reaction to the March events and on the political fate of liberal ideas up to 1867 and 1873 generally, with special stress on Eötvös, Kaiserfeld, and the poet Grillparzer. A final section will be devoted to Austrian liberalism on the decline, in particular to *fin-de-siècle* intellectual responses to a liberalism spiritually distorted, morally bankrupt, and politically defeated.

2. Vormärz: 1830–48

The year 1830 marks an evident turning-point in the history of Austrian liberalism. In a sense, indeed, it marks the beginning of that history. As Georg Franz puts it in his fundamental work *Liberalismus: Die deutschliberale Bewegung in der Habsburgischen Monarchie* (1955): 'up until the time when influences of the July revolution in France became perceptible, liberal tendencies in Austria were almost exclusively of a Josephinist type'.[35] The July revolution however, as Franz emphasises, was not so much a cause as rather an outward symptom of a general change in the political and intellectual climate of Europe. In his characterisation of this upsurge, Franz refers particularly to basic changes in Britain's foreign policy. England had so closely identified its trading interests with the interests of political liberalism, that it came to appear as the protector of constitutional and national efforts, both in Europe and overseas, and thus it was in England that that which was decisive in the regeneration of the movement for progress was rooted.

And once again, as in 1789, France dramatised this development with the application of violence. The consequences of the July Revolution in France were to be felt, with varying intensity, in the whole of continental Europe. . . . . These effects were, from the outside, least apparent in Prussia and Austria. Yet even in these bastions of conservatism we can discern a subterranean strengthening of liberal influences — making themselves felt principally in the realm of literature and in the ever-increasing activity of newly founded liberal movements of every kind.[36]

In Hungary, 1830 was the year when Széchenyi's *Hitel* was published. The book received immediate attention, and it had by December 1832, when the Diet of that year assembled, exerted considerable political influence. The significance of this Diet for the Hungarian liberal reform movement is analysed thoroughly by C.A. Macartney in his magnificent *The Habsburg Empire 1790–1918* (1971), which also contains an account[37] of the new impetus gained by the liberal movement in Austria around 1840. He points in particular to the founding in 1842 of the *Juridisch-Politischer Leseverein*, a body which included such men as Count Leo Thun, the future Ministers Bach, Schmerling, Doblhoff, Hornbostl and indeed almost all leading representatives of the 'bourgeois opposition'.[38]

Macartney, incidentally, has some reservations about applying without qualification the term 'liberal' to the *Vormärz* reform movement in Austria. He would rather distinguish two separate trains of thought amongst the would-be reformers: the one Josephinist — corresponding to a desire for efficiency, for the perfection of the bureaucratic state; the other 'liberal' in the more usual sense, constituted by the desire for

intellectual freedom, including freedom of the Press and the abolition of the censorship (these were very strong demands) and freedom of conscience, although since the Jewish element among them was still small, the anti-clericalism which later obsessed

Austrian Liberalism was still embryonic.

They also wanted 'the relaxation of bureaucratic control over business life, a small and cheaper Civil Service, and above all, control by the tax-payer over the public purse'.[39]

That Josephinism cannot be equated with liberalism or construed as some specific early version of it is of course clear. Nor can it be considered simply as the Austrian form of Enlightenment. It comprehends a whole series of attitudes and political tendencies emanating from different aspects of the Theresian–Josephian reforms.[40] It is however certainly correct to recognise Josephinism as one of the *elements* of early Austrian liberalism. As Franz puts it: '*Vormärz* liberalism is at bottom characterised by three tendencies: a Josephinist, a feudal or conservative *(ständisch-konservative)* and a bourgeois-liberal tendency.'[41] Thus since Austrian liberalism itself is already of a peculiarly conservative bent, Josephinism should definitely be regarded as a trend inherent in and retained by the Austrian liberal tradition, a trend with which the dynastic loyalty of Austrian liberals can also be associated.[42]

How is the conservatism of Austrian liberals to be made compatible with the constantly recurring 'glorification by Austrian authors of English constitutional conditions'?[43] Consider, for example, Viktor Freiherr von Andrian-Werburg's *Österreich und dessen Zukunft* of 1841. Here England is referred to as the ideal of a constitutional state, as 'the motherland of freedom and enlightenment — the model, the archetype, the pride of Germanic institutions and of the Germanic spirit!'[44] Paradoxically one can discern in this Anglomania an element of *romanticism* within the Austrian liberal movement. Another romantic element — absent from Austrian *Altliberalismus* proper, but conspicuous in Hungarian liberal theory — was the *national idea*. Regarded as conservative by Hayek[45] and as incompatible with conservatism by Oakeshott (1971) (or, in his singularly unperceptive book, by Kedourie (1960)), the national idea is in fact susceptible of both conservative and liberal incarnations. It is liberal, even radical, when directed against the *ancien régime* — against the feudal order — but becomes conservative when directed against, say, uprooting cosmopolitanism. It is indeed at one and the same, time both liberal and conservative when directed, in a multinational state or federation, against the uncontrolled centralising forces of bureaucracy.

3. Hungarian Liberal Conservatism

An organic unity of liberal, conservative and national ideas is represented by the work of Count István Széchenyi. Széchenyi, as Macartney puts it in his excellent summary, is

> one of the most important figures in the modern history of the Monarchy, one of the most admirable and of the most tragic, because the waters which he released, out of the deepest conviction and with the purest intention, turned within a few years into a raging torrent which menaced the very foundations of what he still held to be essential to their useful operation.[46]

Széchenyi did not succeed, politically, in diverting Hungary from the disastrous course on which the interaction of short-sighted absolutism and blind radicalism had set her in the 1840s. But during and after 1848 his views, prophecies and admonitions proved themselves right and were, in retrospect, almost unanimously accepted.[47]

Széchenyi came from a noble family whose loyalty to the Habsburg dynasty had been total. He began his adult life in the service of the Monarch as an officer of the Hussars: loyalty to the Monarch was something to be accepted without question. For him 'devotion to God was so mingled with an intense and compassionate love of Hungary and of the Magyar people that the elements defy separation'.[48] When, from 1815 on, he travelled in Western Europe, especially England, he was shocked

> by the contrast between the progress, wealth and civil liberty which he found there and the backwardness, poverty and degradation of the 'great fallow-land', as he termed his own country, and had immediately set himself to diagnosing the ills which he found there, and to seeking remedy for them. . . . .[49]

Despite the moral and religious passion which dominated his personality, Széchenyi 'was in fact the only Hungarian of his age to occupy himself seriously with questions of the national economy'.[50]

The Hungarian-language literature on Széchenyi is, naturally, vast. In the English language however George Barany's *Stephen Széchenyi and the Awakening of Hungarian Nationalism* (1968) is the only extensive study. There is an early summary of *Hitel* in John Paget's *Hungary and Transylvania*,[51] as also in Knatchbull-Hugessen's *The*

Political Evolution of the Hungarian Nation (1908). Charles
Dickens' journal *All the Year Round* published in 1870 a long unsigned
essay (actually written by Lord Lytton[52]) on Széchenyi, and there are
some more recent studies listed in the bibliographical essay of Barany's
book.[53]

Széchenyi's diaries, written in German, the complete edition of
which was published in 1925–39, are particularly fascinating to read.
And although in no way constituting a complete personal or intellectual
autobiography they do reveal — by a process sometimes
approximating to free association — much that is important in the
background of Széchenyi's treatises. A much-cited entry, notable from
the personal, psychological point of view, but also simultaneously
reflecting some significant convictions which Széchenyi never
thereafter abandoned, is the following:

> The 19th of April 1819 was a remarkable day in my life. After
> brooding, for so long, like most people, about God, the soul,
> immortality, etc., etc., etc., and after having forced my way through
> works about these things with a fire of youth, something which
> normally carries us away from that which we have learned into the
> realms of the eccentric, I finally and after a lot of toing and froing
> came to an understanding with myself that every religion is good as
> long as we are conscious that we know nothing, if we only do not
> allow ourselves to be misled in our actions and principles by
> illusions, false axioms and sophisms, but rather follow that voice
> which never hides from us the truth and never speaks to us with
> flattery, and if the heart and mind of a man do not become confused
> and degenerate through education and example — which is of course
> hardly possible — then he becomes the child abandoned to nature, of
> himself always conscious of whether he has acted well or badly. All
> honest people are, in the religion of their hearts and souls, at one; the
> forms are different in which they pray to their God or show their
> compassion or seek to save their souls for the other world. . . . And I
> have learned to recognise that in every circumstance of life if one is to
> be happy one should be a good companion, a good friend and a good
> citizen, and that beside that which is dictated by the inner voice one
> should also observe the forms of that religion which is his own. I have
> failed, in my life, in respect of all of this, unforgivably and
> unforgettably, the memory of this is enough to allow me not a single
> completely happy hour in my life. I am convinced that I shall no
> longer err against these laws, for there is no longer any distraction

which could allow me to become unconscious of them.

My religion commands that at least once a year I confess my sins and partake of the sacrament of holy communion. I shall never again neglect it and will from now on observe everything precisely, but without scruple and exaggerations. I would do the same in whatever religion I had been born and educated under, for I hold the ceremonies of the peoples who pray to the sun as just as worthy as our own. They have to pray to something. They feel, in their blindness and stupidity, that something is above them giving life and order to the world; but they do not see it and they must choose a symbol for themselves since their powers of imagination can go no further . . .

I find in my own religion the feeling of having become totally humble, sublime — and of having attained the glory of this victory over myself, the purest and most welcome moral joy that a man can experience! And can a man humble himself more than when he reveals all his failings to another, of lesser value, suppressing all vanity and showing himself as bad and as weak as a man in fact is, in a light in which he would never wish to be considered. I have been able to win this victory over myself, and even in front of the most abject Italian priest I was not ashamed to break into the bitterest of tears and to reveal to him the strangest events of my life.[54]

A recurrent early theme in Széchenyi's diaries is England — and America. In 1815, during his first visit to England, he refers to 'three things that one must learn in England: the constitution, the machines, and the breeding of horses', and reflects upon the inferiority of Austria as compared to England.[55] He regularly mentions British journals such as the *Quarterly Review*, the *Edinburgh Review*, and *Blackwoods Magazine*, books like De Lolme's *Constitution of England* (which he went so far as to begin translating in 1824), authors like Gibbon, Arthur Young, Adam Smith, Bentham, John Bowring, and Macaulay. America he calls '*das werdende Land*'[56], and he is fascinated by the 'health' and 'freshness' of Americans — '*was werden die einst für ein Volk bilden!*'[57]

But the nation most often reflected upon and compared to other nations is of course Hungary. Széchenyi points out that human beings everywhere tacitly assume that their customs and habits, their modes of living, will be held in a certain veneration, even imitated. Thus a Hungarian who travels to England or France cannot expect to bring about improvements in the French or English way of life. But even a

Hungarian who has travelled widely is not in a position to introduce changes into his own society. The Hungarian is just as proud, just as set in his ways, as is the Englishman. The difference between the two peoples, he holds, is this: that the English have brought the life of *society* to the highest possible degree of perfection. The Hungarians, in contrast, do not even understand the word 'society'.[58]

The Hungarian people, furthermore, have no concept of comfort. The peasant house is as it is not because of any proud disdain for that which is easy and commodious, but because of pure ignorance. Certainly there are many with a great deal of knowledge, but this knowledge is not fundamental: it does not penetrate to the roots. For what could it be to which a Hungarian could turn with all his heart and mind? Not to agriculture, for Hungary is a land in which there is almost no organised market, where the circumstances of production mean that a great proportion of effort is frittered away. Nor, either, to the service of the law and to the administration of his country. For this is a monarchy within which the Hungarian was conceived always as a rebel, as a seditious disturber of the peace — and treated as such. The laws of Hungary, sanctioned by the King, are holy. It is he who must concern himself with their application; he who must protect their purity. And it is his toadies who can alone lay down what is allowed to appear as a just claim to employment, to honour and to reward, whilst the law-abiding remnant of society is subject to every kind of persecution. And with what should the Hungarian concern himself, if the study of the land, of the economy and of the law remain closed to him? Because these trying and honourable occupations are closed off, Hungary is struck by an effervescence of dilettantism in the humanistic sciences, in the arts, and in metaphysics — and it is not at all clear to Széchenyi whether this is or is not to the good of his country.[59]

Széchenyi's comparisons of different nations are not selected at random. They are designed to illustrate the general theory or philosophy of nationhood, indeed of history, against the background of which they should be viewed. The source of this philosophy was German Romanticism, in particular Herder, which was transmitted to Széchenyi mainly through the writings of Madame de Staël, fashionable in Vienna in the early years of the century.[60] Among the very first entries in his diaries are dozens of quotations from *De l'Allemagne*, many of them centred around the problem of national spirit and of the natural character of a country.

Thus the idea of comparing the development of a nation to the life of an individual, so extremely important in Széchenyi's thinking, was taken over by him from Mme Staël . . . Even when he disagreed with her, as in the case of the suggestion that a nation's 'character' shows only when it is free, Széchenyi's reaction was characteristic for both Hungarian conditions and for the trend of development in his own thinking: 'It seems to me that peoples reveal their [true] character mostly when they are about to lose their freedom or have already lost it and seek to regain it!'[61]

The arguments and main ideas of Széchenyi's treatises are not, as a rule, coherently represented in the diaries. Of some aspects of *Hitel*, Széchenyi's own best summary is perhaps contained in a letter he wrote to his niece on 28 November 1829:

> God created man not for a negative, but for a positive happiness. Just as a stone, because it does not know suffering, is cut off from happiness, so a peasant, because he does not know so many of the pleasures of life that we enjoy, is therefore not to be envied, but to be pitied. And the greatest happiness lies in the development of the mind. Man, in contrast to the beast, has been created for thinking; and for the man who has greatness of soul, a good book or good company are more intense needs than beef or *pilaf*. Thus it is a duty to carry forward true civilisation, in particular for the Hungarian, for that is the post to which he has been assigned . . .
> Hungary is our cradle! We must improve it, raise it upward, fill it with happiness. Our family has in its hands a significant part of the means to achieve this feat.[62]

These means consist in what Széchenyi calls an *'edle Aufklärung'*, a noble or patrician Enlightenment, an idea which captures perfectly the Austrian synthesis of liberalism and conservatism. Through this Enlightenment the peasant, on the one hand, will learn that he must work industriously and efficiently, that he should behave with moderation (*'genügsam und gehorsam'*). The prince, on the other hand, must learn that he must live his life as an example, and that he must honour the rights of the poorest peasant. 'We have to attempt to educate and to ennoble our nationality, for it is on this that every improvement, every movement forward, rests: we must expand our knowledge, improve our language, refine our customs.'[63]
The book *Hitel* itself is an only partially synthesised amalgam of

liberal economic doctrines adapted from the works of English classical economists, of reflections by Benjamin Franklin, of whole passages taken over from Bentham (with Christian values, however, taking the place of utilitarian ones), and of the organic-romantic philosophy of nationhood and national development. Its main line of argument can be summed up as follows. The Hungarian land-owners' economic impotence stems primarily from a lack of capital and credit due to an antiquated legal system, which gives no security to the creditor. However, *credit*, in the strict, economic sense, cannot be introduced without first establishing a system or order of 'credit in the broader sense'. By this Széchenyi meant mutual trust and the sanctity of one's word. Moreover, mutual trust and honesty, while intimately bound up with the ability to believe in God, presuppose 'civic virtue', which in turn rests on the firm foundations of nationality. In Széchenyi's words, 'one has first to exist (as a Hungarian, an Englishman, a Roman, etc), and only afterwards can one develop into a good, honest and virtuous man' — the implication being that nationality is a moral category and an a priori pre-condition for a country's development. Nationality, when examined closely, 'is a human being's natural property, present in his veins and in the secret recesses of his soul, which cannot be annihilated without annihilating his self-respect'. However, side by side with this romantic approach, he proposed, as a means of strengthening national bonds, the concentration of social forces arising through free association — a concentration which must, however, be founded upon human wisdom, upon 'the educated head'. This, then, is the ultimate foundation of credit in the broad sense, and thus in the strict sense as well. The sequence of values may, and of course should, be reversed also — since in practice economic credit forms the pre-condition of civic virtue, nationality and general intelligence. Thus the whole edifice may be visualised as a circle, as a structure of mutual dependence.[64]

Széchenyi's next two books, *Világ* ('Light', 1831) and *Stádium* ('Stage', published in 1833 and generally regarded as his most radical work) in essence continue the argument and reiterate the conclusions of *Hitel*. But in 'The People of the Orient' (*A' Kelet Népe*, 1841), which was written in rather different political circumstances, the more conservative aspects of Széchenyi's thinking come to the fore. He still sees himself in this work as a *liberal*. Thus he derides the atrocities of the 'anti-liberal anthropophagi' who mistakenly think that the word 'liberal' denotes one specific type of doctrine, and comprehends a specific class of evil men, 'yearning for other people's property, especially their wives, subverting everything, trampling every accepted principle and custom underfoot, scorning every religion, defiling every authority, and perhaps stealing now and then a silver spoon out of carelessness or natural instinct'.[65] Yet there is one type of liberalism from which Széchenyi does quite deliberately distance himself, the type of liberalism which consists in enlightened proposals, superficially of the highest possible moral worth, which are yet incapable of becoming effective in practice.

> To indulge in rhetoric and endless writing is fine in itself — if it *is* fine. It is not, however, a *deed*, and it increases the spiritual and material wealth, and thus the power of the nation, only insofar as it induces useful deeds and prevents useless and harmful ones, since words and letters are but *tools*, by themselves *nothing*. They become useful or harmful only by their application; and so often the most applauded speech and declamation, or a book in the greatest vogue, if it is not usefully translated into deed and life, is of lesser value than an hour's unwitnessed and unapplauded ploughing by a ploughman.[66]

Széchenyi actually suggests that further liberalisation — of the press, of speech — would at that juncture be tantamount to revolutionary radicalism and would lead to the eventual disintegration and perishing of the nation. And even though Széchenyi is the very opposite of an aggressive nationalist, the value of the nation yet remains supreme throughout the book.

Thus consider his attitude to the process of Magyarisation. Here Széchenyi wished to rely exclusively on the intrinsic attraction of Magyardom itself — that which his work was precisely intended to bring about. As Barany points out, *The People of the Orient* contains an explicit declaration that 'true patriotism was incompatible with forcible Magyarizing campaigns'.[67]

By 1842, however, both Széchenyi's conservative liberalism and his liberal nationalism had ceased to exert any decisive influence on the Hungarian political climate, while Kossuth and his more radical type of liberalism had gained increasing popularity. 'There are moments', he wrote in his diary in September 1841, 'when I have my doubts . . . whether it was a good thing to come out with *Hitel* and *Kelet Népe*. And when doubt has once taken power over our souls . . . then all is done with happiness upon this earth.'[68] Certainly his prophecies of doom proved correct, as is made clear by the following description of his position, provided by Lord Lytton in 1848:

[Széchenyi] knew that Austria was as necessary to Hungary as Hungary to her; and he had the common sense to perceive that Austria had the additional advantage of being necessary to the equilibrium of Europe, and that Europe would not passively assent to the annihilation of the Austrian Empire. He foresaw that the war with Austria could have but one result for Hungary: utter defeat and prostration. He knew that such a defeat would involve the loss, perhaps for ever, of all he had lived, and laboured, and hoped for. It was in the bitterness of this knowledge that he exclaimed to many, by whom his words will never be forgotten: 'My life is defeated, my work is destroyed, this nation is doomed, and all is lost!'[69]

It is often asserted that Széchenyi came to realise in the 1850s that it had been his own views and politics in the 1840s that had been wrong, and that those of his radical opponent Kossuth had been right. This assertion is entirely false. Thus there are in Széchenyi's *Nachlass* drafts which suggest that in the second half of 1859 he sent altogether seven letters to the London *Times*, signing them Ignotus. These drafts display an obvious continuity in Széchenyi's thinking before and after 1848, and anticipate to a remarkable extent the ideas that eventually led to the 1867 *Ausgleich* or 'compromise' with Austria.[70] Incidentally, it seems that these letters were — contrary to the generally held view — never published.[71]

The significance of Széchenyi's work to present-day political theory seems to be twofold. First, he has provided, from a conservative point of view, plausible arguments for a *market-oriented* or laissez-faire economy, achieving a conceptual synthesis by placing emphasis not on the rights of individuals but on personal initiative, self-reliance and responsibility and on the nation-building effects of free commercial communication and exchange. This stands in conflict with the now increasingly accepted view that mutual aid and other values associated with traditional communities depend upon local rootedness, and that since the market rests on labour mobility it has to be curtailed or supplemented by bureaucratic intervention if the fragmentation of a society is to be avoided.[72] Széchenyi has provided the rudiments of a conceptual framework within which this position appears to be quite without substance. Secondly, he has convincingly shown that national prejudice is neither a prerequisite nor a characteristic feature of nationalism — if this latter term is interpreted as meaning the acute consciousness of the individual's psychological need for, or dependence on, some historico-cultural linguistic community.

4. Eötvös: The Influence of the Ruling Ideas of the 19th Century on the State

A recent, extensive and well-researched monograph on Eötvös is Paul Bödy's 'Joseph Eötvös and the Modernization of Hungary, 1840–1870. A Study of Ideas of Individuality and Social Pluralism in Modern Politics' (1972), which also contains a useful bibliography of the Hungarian literature on the subject. In 1966 Gerald Stourzh published a perceptive essay under the title 'Die politischen Ideen Joseph von Eötvös und das österreichische Staatsproblem', and in their works on Austrian political history both Robert Kann and Josef Redlich have written at some length on Eötvös. It is his views concerning the nationalities question and the reconstruction of the Monarchy after 1848 that mainly interest these authors. But they certainly do acknowledge the importance of Eötvös's general political theory as formulated in his principal work *The Influence of the Ruling Ideas of the 19th Century on the State*. This work, Stourzh writes, 'presents one of the most significant and original achievements of the European liberal theory of the state — if at the same time one which is today forgotten'.[73] Redlich describes Eötvös as a man who, even by Western European standards, 'was able to combine the highest political and literary scholarship of his age with a deeply rooted Magyar patriotism in the single, wholly original and creative personality of a modern political thinker and statesman'. *The Ruling Ideas* made its author 'one of the most respected proponents of European liberalism at its height, and even today it is still to be described as one of the most singular and intellectually richest writings on the modern state'.[74] Bödy characterises the book as an attempt to explain 'why the Western European revolutions had failed in their quest to establish individual liberty in modern society'.[75]

Eötvös locates the sources of the European tradition of freedom first of all in the English liberal (as contrasted with the French democratic) tradition — but then ultimately in Christianity. His treatise begins with an explanation of the failure of liberal idealism in 1848. Liberty, equality and nationality he saw as the three 'ruling ideas' on which the revolutions of that year had been based. And they had failed, as Bödy expresses it in his summary, because of a 'contradiction between two interpretations of these political ideas'[76] — loosely: the French, and the English. The French interpretation rests on the notion of an absolute sovereignty of the people: equality therefore signifies an equal entitlement to participate in the exercise of sovereignty. The English interpretation sees the possibility of a plurality of sovereign powers — King, parliament, the courts, cabinet, even the church and private associations – each limited by the others in such a way that there is no absolute power within the state and in such a way that the rights of individuals are clearly guaranteed.

> This concept of liberty also defined the English understanding of equality. Its meaning was that each citizen enjoyed the equal protection of the laws, all citizens were entitled to the same freedoms, and all citizens were equal before the law.[77]

Thus Eötvös saw the principal motivating force behind the French Revolution as being that of augmenting the power of the state: 'In his view, the theory of popular sovereignty negated individual freedom because it extended to the state unlimited power over the rights of its citizens.'[78]

There are important affinities between Eötvös on the one hand, and Guizot and Tocqueville on the other. He was greatly influenced by both of them, and after the publication of *The Ruling Ideas* briefly corresponded with the latter. Bödy cites a letter from Toqueville to Eötvös in which the former expresses his reaction to *The Ruling Ideas*, which he read in the German version through the mediation of Montalembert, the noted French liberal Catholic publicist who also corresponded with Eötvös.[79] Bödy specifically refers to the impact Western European liberal Catholics had on 'Eötvös's distinction between the spiritual and temporal power as a guarantee of civil liberties in the liberal state',[80] and he points out that Lord Acton held a historical and political position strikingly parallel to that of Eötvös, though no direct contact between them can be established. What Bödy does not emphasise, however, is that these affinities would today be classified as conservative rather than liberal, and indeed he seems to ignore all the more directly conservative trends in Eötvös's thought. Thus even at the level of methodological foundations, Eötvös displays a characteristically conservative aversion to philosophy. Pre-conceived ideas, he suggests in the first draft of *The Ruling Ideas*, cannot serve as a basis for sound political action: 'Man can derive pleasure from absolute theories and his poetic inclinations can never be satisfied more than when confronted by poetic ideals under the cover of philosophy.'[81] In *The Ruling Ideas* he stresses that 'instead of philosophising about the opinion of the people in general', one should rather 'turn one's attention to the desires and prospects of the individuals out of which "the people" are constituted'.[82] It will then turn out that the striving for, say, absolute freedom, exists only in philosophical speculation — and in the minds of those who, as Eötvös says, belong in a mental asylum.[83] Society cannot be changed in accordance with abstract ideals.

> A society in which — in order to set it up anew in a preconceived form — all the mortar holding together the individual parts has been dissolved away, in which everything that had seemed too large has been diminished and everything that had seemed too firm and not amenable to every realignment has been broken into pieces, can just as little achieve durability through its form alone, as a heap of gravel — whether heaped up like ninepins or as a pyramid — can withstand the storms and the rains.[84]

It is clear, further, that liberal and conservative elements coalesce in Eötvös's main idea, that of regionalism or territorial self-government. Not only individual liberty but also historical continuity are threatened by centralised government. A system of territorial pluralism, of municipalities, on the other hand, will defend the freedoms of minorities (and ultimately those of the individual) against centralist absolutism. The 'autonomous township', as Bödy puts it, will replace the lost communal relationships of the feudal system and provide for a sense of community in the modern state.[85] So, too, social and institutional pluralism will defend the organic continuity of historically given institutions against radical-utopian alterations, whether brought about by the central government itself, or by a radical movement against which such a government is, in the long run, defenceless.

> There are many who believe that that which exists can only be preserved through the influence of a powerful central political force, and the fact that the system of centralisation finds so many defenders amongst statesmen is for the greater part attributable to this belief. Yet it is a point of view which rests on an error. That which exists cannot be protected against changes by the state; it is much rather the immutability of a host of other relationships through which the state itself must be protected against upheavals. Every comfortably appointed house which a citizen erects on the territory of the state is not only a channel through which a whole series of citizens will step up to superior habits. It is at the same time a protective bastion for civil society. Every right whose possession is guaranteed to the individual by the state is a guarantee of civil society. And every

securely organised municipality is a stone by means of which the
larger structure will be secured. The better one understands how to
insert these stones into the building, the more will one understand
how to use the particular as an essential part of the whole, the more
unshakeable will stand the state.[86]

Of the various elements whose autonomy and permanence —
according to Eötvös — specifically guarantee the organic continuity of
the whole, two — the municipalities and an independent church — have
already been mentioned:

> the independence of the church in relation to the state is at one and
> the same time the guarantee of every independence which is granted
> by the constitution to the individual parts of the state. The freedom of
> the church and of the municipalities mutually support each other,
> since both rest upon the same principles, i.e. that the power of the
> state can be an absolute one only in certain spheres, and not
> everywhere.[87]

The third element singled out by Eötvös is an Upper House, for
which both the English House of Lords, its members naturally linked to
the history of the state by birth and family traditions, and the American
Senate, whose natural task is to defend, as a historic right, the autonomy
of the individual states, might serve as models: 'The task of the Upper
House in the constitutional states is . . . none other than that of
defending the right of history in the rough-and-tumble of real and
imagined needs of the moment.'[88]

Finally, Eötvös mentions the different nationalities of a
multinational state or federation. Indeed, his critique of the national
idea — as something whose effects may be destructive — very marked
in Part I of *The Ruling Ideas*, is almost totally withdrawn in Part II.

> Since the principle of self-government is nothing other than the
> application of the principle of individual freedom to individual legal
> objects, so also the claims of the individual nationalities — which
> become moral persons through the consciousness of their peculiarity
> — can be satisfied only through the application of this principle . . .
> The fascination of the concept of nationality is nothing other than a
> celebratory protestation of all peoples, in the name of the Christian
> principle of individual freedom, against the absolute power of the
> state.[89]

Thus the national idea is a conservative element and, Eötvös writes, it is 'quite certainly one of the greatest dangers of our time that the conservative elements in this idea are too weak in comparison with those elements that push forward'.[90] The awakening of this idea is indeed 'a wonderful dispensation of divine foresight', an awakening which might indeed have the power to curb or to reverse 'that sequence of massive upheavals set in train by France, in which not only thrones, but even the concept of law and everything which man had held holy have been made unsteady', and moreover to change those artificial political institutions with which we are familiar, through which 'the rabble of the capital city has been allowed to dispose over the form of government of a great nation'.[91]

In the 1860s Eötvös had the opportunity of putting many of his theoretical ideas into practice. Of course political theories, as Eötvös knew only too well, are more often the offspring of frustrated political practice than the source from which successful policy will flow. Ideas, as Eötvös himself pointed out, 'will be realised. . . . not with strict logical consistency but in accordance with possibilities'.[92] Still, the Hungarian Elementary Education Act of 1868, a major political achievement in Eötvös's career, certainly reflected the views elaborated in *The Ruling Ideas*. As Bödy puts it:

> the most distinctive feature of this act was the attempt to protect the variety and freedom of education in the broadest sense by acknowledging the right of each individual, township, association, nationality, and church to sponsor and exercise control over the schools.[93]

The Nationality Act of 1868, on the other hand, scarcely reflects Eötvös's views on safeguards for the minorities. His original draft of 1867 *did* fully, or almost fully, embody his former theoretical position. But this draft was rejected by the Hungarian Parliament. However, the most important political achievement with which Eötvös's name should be associated — even if he cannot be said to have played the lead in engineering it — was the Austro-Hungarian Compromise of 1867 itself, a settlement which, for all its shortcomings, was a definite victory over centralist absolutism.

5. Altliberalismus in Austria: 1848–67

It is interesting to note, in the light of the above, that it was precisely a lack of understanding of political regionalism which prevented Anton von Schmerling, the Austrian Minister of State in the early 1860s, from reaching an agreement with the Hungarians. Schmerling[94] played a substantial role in the already mentioned *Juridisch-Politischer Leseverein*, and in the Lower Austrian estates. In 1848 he made his appearance in Frankfurt as the most German-minded of Austria's public servants, becoming Minister of the Interior, and subsequently Minister President of the new German Reich Ministry. In 1849 he became Minister of Justice in the Austrian government, carrying out important legal reforms. He was a constitutionalist in principle, without having real faith in the workings of a parliament, a German centralist sensitive to and impatient of opposition. In 1861 he was instrumental in the issuing of the so-called February Patent, a German liberal-centralist constitution. Not being able to solve the Hungarian problem, he was sharply attacked in parliament by Kaiserfeld in 1864, and dismissed in the following year. Schmerling's political views and sentiments on the one hand, and his politics and ultimate fate on the other, certainly form a coherent pattern.

The same holds for Moritz von Kaiserfeld who, as has already been mentioned, was one of Eötvös's counterparts in preparing the way for the *Ausgleich*. Kaiserfeld's early views can be conveniently reconstructed from his diaries, which Krones, in his excellent biography, quotes extensively. During his journey through Germany in 1844 Kaiserfeld asks himself

> why, when our neighbours the Saxons and the Bavarians enjoy the blessings of a constitution, should we be incapable even of. ... lending our voice where such supreme goods as freedom and property are at stake? No, it will not remain so, however much a narrow-minded politics may make it its task to prolong the status quo.[95]

In describing Kaiserfeld's general outlook and attitudes on the eve of the 1848 upheavals Krones emphasises specifically that Kaiserfeld

> knew his homeland and what was due to it: the needs of the estates and of the peasants. ... [he had a] rigorous feeling for the rule of law and a repugnance for violent and destructive innovations, as well as for aggressive busybodying. He had learnt from the English, from English history and English writings. On the other hand the history and the works of thinkers and poets of the recent past confirmed his

belief in the justification of progress and the ideal of civic freedom.[96]

In the debates of the Styrian *Landtag* during June and July of 1848 Kaiserfeld opposed excessive independence of small municipalities. His fundamental belief, however, was that it would be absolutely necessary to maintain against the centralising tendencies of the *Reichsrat* the territorial autonomy of greater historical units such as the Austrian *Länder*.[97] And in 1861 he appeared on the Austrian political scene as the leader of one of the three wings of the German liberals, the 'German Autonomists',[98] for whom (as opposed to the other liberal factions) the 1861 constitution — the February Patent — was much too centralist. Consequently it was they who first reached an agreement with the Hungarians.[99]

The specific character of Austrian *Altliberalismus*, both in its *Vormärz* period and in the phase following 1848, has found a remarkable expression in the work of that most Austrian of all Austrian poets, Franz Grillparzer. As another celebrated Austrian literary figure, Hugo von Hofmannsthal, put it in 1915,

> the thinking Austrian will, in hard-pressed times, always return to Grillparzer . . . Where everyone else was a 'Young German', a Saint-Simonian, a liberal, a republican or whatever fantastic kind of pan-European, he remained an Austrian and also something of a practitioner of *Realpolitik*. Where all the others went in for what was general, he saw the specific; he grasped that which was to endure, even where it was not apparent.[100]

Grillparzer was of low middle-class origin and a civil servant from his early youth until his retirement. His liberalism was of a markedly Josephinian bent, the conservative elements inherent in it becoming dominant in and after 1848.[101] His mental outlook, as Eder correctly stresses, 'remained a model for countless civil servants, officers and representatives of the professions, right up until the dissolution of the Monarchy'.[102]

The best source on Grillparzer is his own diaries, in which one of the most frequently recurring themes is his critique of Germans as contrasted with Austrians, a critique clearly expressing the moderate liberal's disgust with the more radical varieties of his own creed. The basic fault of 'German thinking', he writes in 1834, is that there is a 'weak personality' underlying it. The German mind can hold on to nothing that is ultimate, for there is nothing makes so strong an impression upon him that he becomes convinced of it for its own sake. Thus German philosophy is to all intents and purposes atheistic, and if in recent times there has been much talk of God, that is merely an arbitrarily imposed thought-barrier, that he should not completely fall into the bottomless chasm which threatens to open up beneath him. The Germans adopt a God — as a substitute for being convinced of His existence. He has no reality for them; and they respect Him as their own work, not themselves as His.[103]

The German, he says, 'is accustomed from his school days onwards to show disdain for healthy human understanding by being satisfied with words that have been raised up to the noble standing of concepts'.[104] And with an obvious allusion to Protestant Germany he says that 'the Catholic faith has something of foolishness about it; Protestantism, in contrast, something impertinent'.[105]

Grillparzer's concept of individual freedom is, then, not a rationalistic one: 'It is remarkable that antiquity [*die Alten*] conceived what the new Germany characterises as the highest end of man: the *free spirit*, as a sign of idiocy.'[106] He agrees, rather, with the ancient view:

Wer seine Schranken kennt, der ist der Freie,
Wer frei sich wähnt, ist seines Wahnes Knecht

(He who knows his limitations is free/he who fancies himself to be free, is the slave of his madness), two oft-quoted lines of his play *Libussa*.

Grillparzer specifically criticises the notion of liberty as a 'natural right' of man:

It is of course ridiculous to speak of natural (inborn) rights. A right is nothing other than this, that I am not allowed to be hindered by others in one or other expression of my power. How, then, should there belong to the nature of man that which lies not in him, but in others.[107]

His disillusionment after 1848 is concisely expressed in the following remark:

What is most sad about the events of recent times is not the cloud which they have cast over the present, but that the belief in the perfectibility of man, in the so-called education of mankind, has become to the highest degree unstable.[108]

Not perfection, but decay is what Grillparzer is able to discern in the age in which he lived.

Some months earlier he had written:

> These days one hears nothing more often than expressions like 'the new age', 'the new time', whereby it is our own time which is meant. This expression has from the very beginning something cock-eyed about it. For since nature remains the same, and so also the foundations of human nature, so also nothing wholly new should be allowed to escape the suspicion of being to a large extent also false. The proposition that that which is old does not return again is of unquestioned validity, yet its opposite, *nihil novi in mundo*, can be recognised as being just as true; there is nothing new under the sun. Continual change on the basis of the old foundations is the law of all existence. And this implies the rejection not of the new, but of the taking of leaps, and above all of the incoherent and the sudden.[109]

Slow modification instead of sudden change. Not revolution but organic evolution. As Grillparzer's views exemplify, this was the ideal upheld by Austrian *Altliberalismus*.

6. The End of Austrian Liberalism: 1867–1903

Between 1961 and 1973 Carl E. Schorske, the distinguished American historian, published a series of essays on late nineteenth-century Austrian intellectual history. These essays, now constituting four of the seven chapters of his book *Fin-de-Siècle Vienna* (1980), have a common thesis, that the remarkable cultural vigour of late nineteenth-century and turn of the century Austria can fruitfully be explained in terms of the political decline of Austrian liberalism and the unique circumstances of that decline. After the heroic age of struggle against absolutism and the interregnum after 1848 the liberals

> came to power and established a constitutional régime in the 1860s almost by default. Not their own integral strength, but the defeats of the old order at the hands of foreign enemies brought the liberals to the helm of the state. From the first, they had to share their power

with the aristocracy and the imperial bureaucracy. Even during their two decades of rule, the liberals' social base remained weak, confined to the middle-class Germans and German Jews of the urban centres. . . . Soon new social groups raised claims to political participation: the peasantry, the urban artisans and workers, and the Slavic peoples.[110]

Such groups were soon forming mass parties whose rapid success is seen in the fact that by 1895 Vienna itself, the centre of liberalism, was under the control of the Christian Socialists, and the liberals were never to regain their parliamentary political power. Thus

the program which the liberals devised against the upper classes occasioned the explosion of the lower. . . . Far from rallying the masses against the old ruling class above, then, the liberals unwittingly summoned from the social deeps the forces of a general disintegration. . . . The new anti-liberal mass movements — Czech nationalism, Pan-Germanism, Christian Socialism, Social Democracy, and Zionism — rose from below to challenge the trusteeship of the educated middle class, to paralyze its political system, and to undermine its confidence in the rational structure of history.[111]

Schorske emphasises that 'the era of political ascendency of the liberal middle class in Austria, begun later than elsewhere in western Europe, entered earlier than elsewhere into deep crisis'.[112] Failure in four different areas — national unity, social justice, economic prosperity and public morality — 'converged in the early seventies to produce a deep crisis of confidence in liberalism before it had had the chance to stabilise its newly won power'.[113]

One of the centres of this revolt against liberal values was the *Leseverein der deutschen Studenten Wiens*. William J. McGrath in his book on this circle gives a concise characterisation of Austrian *Altliberalismus*, [114] contrasting it with the less subtle, more aggressive, rationalistic and doctrinaire 'high liberalism' of the post-1867 period. The latter was seen as embodying 'an expression of individualism which eschewed concern for the social question, an emphasis on cosmopolitanism which neglected the issue of German nationalism, and a preference for the scholarly intellectual style which ignored the passions of the heart'.[115] Gustav Mahler and Victor Adler were among the members of the circle, as also was Sigmund Freud. Indeed in his fascinating essay, 'Politics and Patricide in Freud's Interpretation of Dreams', Schorske shows how the victory and subsequent early defeat of this form of liberalism in Austria and Freud's own political ambitions and frustrations form an underlying theme of *Die Traumdeutung* (1900). Freudian psychoanalysis is in fact seen by Schorske as part of the anti-liberal reaction:

> By reducing his own political past and present to an epiphenomenal status in relation to the primal conflict between father and son, Freud gave his fellow liberals an a-historical theory of man and society that could make bearable a political world spun out of orbit and beyond control.[116]

In fact psychoanalysis did not just make the world of the post-liberal collapse bearable. It also *explained* it, by pointing out that liberal politics could not possibly have triumphed since they were based on a false anthropology. Freud showed that the concept of the rational, intellectually autonomous individual was illusionary. As he put it in an essay, written as late as 1917 but still in full harmony with the views he expressed in *Die Traumdeutung:*

> The human being, even when of a lowly status in the outside world, feels himself sovereign in his own soul ... But the two-fold recognition, that the life of sexual drives in ourselves is not fully to be brought under control, and that psychic processes are as such unconscious and accessible to and capable of coming under the dominion of the self only through an incomplete and unreliable perception, becomes equivalent to the assertion that *the ego is not master in his own house.*[117]

A work that displays the influence of the Schorske thesis is *Wittgenstein's Vienna* by Allan Janik and Stephen Toulmin. 'If any single factor can be singled out to account for the special character of Vienna's borgeois society,' they write, referring to Schorske, 'it is the failure of liberalism in the political sphere.'[118] Ultimately the failure of liberalism was responsible for the decay of moral values which served as the historical background to Wittgenstein's *Tractatus Logico-Philosophicus*, and the central thesis of Janik and Toulmin is, perhaps, 'that to be a *fin-de-siècle* artist or intellectual, conscious of the social realities of [Austria-Hungary], one had to face the problem of *the nature and limits of language, expression and communication*'.[119]

And this is precisely what Wittgenstein did, on an abstract-logical level.

Schorske's influence is acknowledged also in the present writer's 'Philosophy and Suicide-Statistics in Austria-Hungary' (Nyíri, 1978) as well as in his 'From Eötvös to Musil: Philosophy and Its Negation in Austria and Hungary' (Nyíri, 1981a). Further, the decline of liberalism — in particular the impact of German nationalism upon Austrian liberal culture — serves as the natural basis of investigation of a number of other recent works. In J.T. Blackmore's dissertation *Ernst Mach — His Life, Work and Influence* (1971),[120] the tension between Czechs and Germans in Prague and Mach's reaction to that tension are presented as the background against which the *Beiträge zur Analyse der Empfindungen* of 1886 gains socio-psychological and politico-historical significance. Also Gershon Weiler's book *Mauthner's Critique of Language* (1970) shows how, in the work of Fritz Mauthner, rising German nationalism among Bohemian Jews is one factor leading to the adoption of a specific, nominalist linguistic philosophy.[121] Likewise Tibor Hanák, in his *Lukács war anders* (1973), presents a picture of the turn-of-the-century Viennese culture — the absence of accepted unquestioned moral values, of valid social and ethical norms in Austrian (and Hugarian) upper middle-class life —a picture of the impressionistic world against which the young Lukács — as much a citizen of Vienna as of Budapest — revolted, for example in his *The Soul and the Forms*. It must be added here that in Hungary itself one cannot speak of a fundamental crisis of liberalism before 1918. There liberal values still had a certain validity at the turn of the century, even if they were charged, as always in the history of Hungarian liberalism, with strong nationalist overtones. In the first parts of Franz Alexander's *The Western Mind in Transition* (1960) there is described the life-style and world-view of an upper middle-class Budapest intellectual of Jewish origin who is at one and the same time an enlightened liberal and a Hungarian nationalist. It is perhaps worth also remarking here the extent to which, in nineteenth- and early twentieth-century Hungary, ennoblement was — especially for a Jew — the most obvious sign and the crowning step of bourgeois success, whether economic or intellectual,[122] a phenomenon clearly connected with the fact that in Hungary it was precisely the nobility which, in the absence of a middle class, initiated and put into effect the modernisation of society.[123]

One major work which does not regard the decline of Austrian liberalism from the mid-1870s onwards as a fact relevant to intellectual history, or indeed as a fact at all, is W.M Johnston's *The Austrian Mind* (1972). This is not the place to dwell on the merits and relative shortcomings of Johnston's extremely informative book. His critical attitude to the Schorske thesis must, however, be registered, especially since he has explicitly rearticulated it in a review of recent books on Austrian cultural history (Johnston, 1981). Johnston here refers, in particular, to Ingrid Belke's book on Popper-Lynkeus, the first chapter of which 'presents a pioneering survey of reform movements in Vienna between 1880 and 1930'. This chapter, writes Johnston, offers material

> for a major reappraisal of the Schorske thesis. The 'late liberals' of 1900 were less relentlessly apolitical and less resigned to their political demise than many of us have acknowledged. It is time to hold a symposium entitled 'Vienna 1900: Reform Movements in the Capital of Aestheticism'.[124]

Johnston does not, however, emphasis a point repeatedly mentioned by Belke herself, namely that the 'late liberals' formed but a dwindling minority, cherishing values not shared by the majority of the middle class. They were regarded as eccentrics of the kind memorably subjected to irony in Musil's *Mann ohne Eigenschaften*.

To select 1903 as the year which closes the period here surveyed is to some degree arbitrary. But it was in 1903 that there was published Otto Weininger's famous book *Sex and Character*, and it would be difficult to point to a work in which the self-mutilation of Austrian liberalism is (even if in an abstract philosophical manner) more vehemently, more brutally expressed. Macartney also regards 1903 as a year in which a new absolutist phase in Austrian history began.[125] Austrian liberalism had by then — and for a long time to come — lost not only its political power, but also its intellectual attraction and spiritual force.

Notes

1. I should like to thank Barry Smith for his unfailing help, both theoretical and practical, in preparing this essay. A companion piece, with special reference to Bohemian developments, has now appeared as Nyíri (1985).

2. Eder (1955, p. 7).

3. 'The political and intellectual life of post-war America,' Schorske writes, 'suggested the crisis of a liberal polity as a unifying context for simultaneous transformation in the separate branches of culture. . . . Where America between the wars found interest in Austria before 1918 as a multinational state that failed, it now found

"worthy of note" the intellectual products of the same period of Austria's history'. Schorske (1980, p. xxv).

4. Janik and Toulmin go on to suggest that the successive massive expansions of the American Republic threaten the constitutional arrangements of 1776, which must be made more adaptable 'if they are to serve adequately the legitimate human purposes of all individuals and groups that now play a part in the life of the Republic. Otherwise, one may be in danger of creating and intensifying artificialities and false values of the kind that were eventually endemic in the Habsburg Empire' (Janik and Toulmin (1973, p. 270)).

5. Compare Nash (1979, pp. 64, 166, 208).

6. Hayek (1934, p. xxxiii).

7. Hayek (1973, p. 119).He goes on to point out the 'early association and almost identification of the Continental movement with the movement for democracy, which is concerned with a different problem from that which was the chief concern of the liberal tradition of the British type' (p. 120).

8. Hayek (1973, p. 148).

9. Hayek (1973, p. 137). Compare also Gray (1984, Chapter 3).

10. Hayek (1960, pp. 399, 406).

11. Hayek (1978, p. 25).

12. Hayek (1978, pp. 25, 30).

13. 'All progress', he tells us, 'must be based on tradition' (Hayek, 1978, p. 19).

14. Hayek (1973, p. 121).

15. J.F.G. Shearmur, 'Hayek and the Invisible Hand' read at the symposium of the Seminar for Austro-German Philosophy on Austrian Philosophy and Austrian Politics held in London in April 1980.

16. Menger (1934, p. 173).

17. Ibid.

18. Menger (1934, p. 91).

19. Menger (1934, pp. 84, 91). Indeed Menger suggests that even Adam Smith and his school 'did not know how to value the significance or "organic" social structures for society in general and economy in particular and therefore was nowhere concerned to *preserve* them. What characterizes the theories of Smith and his followers is the one-sided economic rationalistic liberalism, the not infrequently impetuous effort to do away with what exists, with what is not always sufficiently understood, the just as impetuous urge to create something new in the realm of political institutions — often enough without sufficient knowledge and experience' (p. 177).

20. Knatchbull-Hugessen (1908, vol. I, p. 279).

21. Compare Epstein (1966, p. 8ff).

22. Iványi-Grünwald (1930, p. 141).

23. Széchenyi (1830, p. 335).

24. Széchenyi (1830, p. 388).

25. Barany (1968, 396).

26. Stourzh (1966, p. 205).

27. Eötvös (1848, section 16).

28. Krones (1888, p. 64).

29. Articles of 3–4 October and 1 November, quoted in Krones (1888, p. 68).

30. Quoted in Krones (1888, p. 93).

31. Krones (1888, p. 61).

32. One must agree with Machovec (1969, p. 66) according to whom Masaryk never abandoned the views elaborated in this early work.

33. Masaryk (1881, p. 115). See also Nyíri (1985).

34. Masaryk (1881, pp. 84, 111).

35. Franz (1955, p. 19).

36. Franz (1955, p. 21).

37. This is based in part upon the description given by Franz.
38. Macartney (1971, p. 302).
39. Macartney (1971, p. 301).
40. Compare Franz (1955, p. 13).
41. Franz (1955, p. 37); compare Johnston (1972, p. 15), where Josephinism is characterised as 'a fount of both liberalism and conservatism'.
42. The *ständisch-konservativ* element of Austrian liberalism consisted in the demand to revitalise and extend the semi-feudal system of estates, a system in which, as Franz (1955, p. 38) writes, 'the corporate freedoms of the pre-absolutist era, the ancient heritage of Germanic freedoms, still in part lived on'. Compare also Franz (1955, p. 31), where this strand of liberalism is referred to as '*bodenständig-deutsch*'.
43. Franz (1955, p. 32).
44. Andrian-Werburg (1843, p. 143, 199).
45. Hayek (1960, p. 405).
46. Macartney (1971, pp. 243).
47. The single exception was constituted by Kossuth and his circle of emigrés.
48. Macartney (1971 p. 244). Macartney goes on to point out that his consistent view of Hungary in terms of the *Gesammtmonarchie* was partly also a matter of calculation: 'just before his suicide he said to an Austrian [Crenneville]: "Hungary can exist only in Austria. In German arms she may feel herself squeezed, but in Slav arms, she would certainly be crushed" [Corti, *Mensch und Herrscher*, p. 253]. He also had a realistic appreciation of Hungary's weaknesses, political, national and financial, and was convinced that the help, protection and financial resources of Vienna were essential to her.'
49. Macartney (1971, p. 244).
50. Ibid.
51. Paget (1839, vol. I, pp. 209–16).
52. Compare Gál (1973, p. 205).
53. Barany (1968, pp. 470ff). Széchenyi's major works have been — with the exception of *Kelet Népe* — translated into German. There exist, however, no English translations. Barany translates a number of passages which he calls 'meager efforts to convey the original pathos and flavour of Széchenyi's unique style, impossible to imitate even in Hungarian' (p. 14).
54. Széchenyi (1925–39, vol. I, pp. 591, 594).
55. Széchenyi (1925–39, vol. I, pp. 165–8).
56. Széchenyi (1925–39, vol. I, p. 162).
57. Széchenyi (1925–39, vol. I, p. 550).
58. Széchenyi (1925–39, vol. I, p. 107).
59. Széchenyi (1925–39, vol. I, pp. 361ff).
60. Széchenyi met her in person in 1810.
61. Barany (1968, p. 61). Although in 1821 Széchenyi called the 'woman writer' 'exceptionally superficial', 'he continued reading her books immediately after they had been published: in February 1823 he read *De l'Amour*; in May 1824 he reread all four parts of *De l'Allemagne*, copying new citations into his diary; and in August 1825 he finished reading the *Lettres sur l'Angleterre*' (Barany (1968)).
62. Széchenyi (1889, vol. I, pp. 131ff).
63. Ibid.
64. Compare Baranyi (1968, pp. 204–12).
65. Széchenyi (1841, p. 391).
66. Ibid.
67. Barany (1968, p. 411). In the same spirit, in his address to the Academy in 1842, 'Széchenyi still contended that a country should assign priority to the cultivation of the national idiom even over the sciences and applied technology, because this was the foremost guarantee of national life. But he gave no quarter to those whose patriotism was

exhausted by indulging in the propagation of the outward signs of Magyardom and in the provocation of peoples of different ethnic backgrounds' (p. 412).
68. Széchenyi (1925–39, vol. V, p. 496).
69. Lytton (1870, p. 480).
70. Compare Károlyi (1921, pp. 201ff).
71. Dávid Angyal (1971, p. 142) has not been able to locate them in *The Times* and neither has the present writer.
72. This view is expressed, e.g. by Walzer (1979, p. 6).'The more people move about, the more they depend upon officials'.
73. Stourzh (1966, p. 207).
74. Redlich (1920, p. 547).
75. Bödy (1972, p. 66).
76. Ibid.
77. Ibid.
78. Ibid.
79. Bödy (1972, p. 67). Incidentally, the German text of *The Ruling Ideas* was not, as is normally suggested, a translation. The book was in fact composed in that language. Compare Nyíri (1980a, n. 19).
80. Bödy (1972, p. 80).
81. Eötvös (1848, section 16).
82. Eötvös (1854, p. 33).
83. Eötvös (1854, p. 274).
84. Eötvös (1851, p. 244).
85. Compare Bödy (1872, p. 72).
86. Eötvös (1854, p. 505).
87. Eötvös (1854, p. 409).
88. Eötvös (1854, p. 166).
89. Eötvös (1854, pp. 518, 520).
90. Eötvös (1854, p. 520).
91. Eötvös (1854, p. 519).
92. Eötvös (1848, section 16).
93. Bödy (1972, p. 101).
94. Here a basic work is Paul Molisch (1944).
95. Krones (1888, p. 23).
96. Krones (1888, p. 38).
97. This was expressed, e.g., in an article entitled 'Die Integrität der Provinzen', *Grazer Zeitung*, 29 September 1848.
98. The main strength of this wing lay in Styria where they could rely on strong local traditions.
99. A detailed account of the theoretical and political differences between the various formations within the German liberal group is given in Eva Somogyi (1976).
100. Hofmannsthal (1952, p. 252).
101. On certain perhaps crucial affinities between Grillparzer's thought and the later philosophy of Wittgenstein see Nyíri (1980; 1982a).
102. Eder (1955, p. 94). The characteristic features of Grillparzer's attitude, as discernible both in his poetry and in his quasi-theoretical writings, are especially well analysed in Seitter (1968) and in Politzer (1972).
103. Grillparzer (1872, vol. IV, p. 207).
104. Grillparzer (1872, vol. V, p. 103).
105. Grillparzer (1872, vol. V, p. 237).
106. Grillparzer (1872, vol. V, p. 68).
107. Grillparzer (1872, vol. V, p. 120).
108. Grillparzer (1872, vol. V, p. 216).
109. Grillparzer (1872, vol. V, p. 210).

110. Schorske (1980, p. 5).
111. Schorske (1980, p. 117).
112. Schorske (1980, p. xxvi).
113. Schorske (1978, p. 112).
114. McGrath (1974). Compare McGrath (1965) which further describes the intellectual atmosphere of the *Leseverein* and the activities and careers of its most prominent members, as also McGrath (1967). McGrath (1974), which is dedicated to Schorske, traces in particular the history of the Pernerstorfer circle, a group formed in 1867 which later played an important role within the *Leseverein*.
115. McGrath (1974, p. 12). 'Moreover, the subsequent crises that beset the liberal governments of the 1870s — the Franco-Prussian War, the economic collapse of 1873, the Ofenheim scandal — all served to deepen their disillusionment. Increasingly they, and students like them, felt impelled to count themselves amongst the opponents rather than the supporters of the liberal movement.'
116. Schorske (1980, p. 203).
117. Freud (1947, pp. 8, 11).
118. Janik and Toulmin (1973, p. 48).
119. Ibid.
120. An abridged version of this work was published under the same title in 1972.
121. A useful memoir in which the relevant developments in Vienna and Prague are described from a contemporary liberal leader's point of view is Ernst von Plener's *Erinnerungen*, see especially the first two volumes, 1911, 1921.
122. Compare McCagg (1972) in which typical features in the family histories of successful Hungarian Jews are traced.
123. This fact is classically stated and analysed in Gyula Szekfü's brilliant and notorious *Három nemzedék: Egy hanyatló kor története* (1920), a conservative liberal's retrospective survey of Hungarian history between 1830 and 1918.
124. Johnston (1981, section IV). Another, more radical, reappraisal of the Schorske thesis is presented in Grassl and Smith (1986)
125. Macartney (1971, p. 749).

Bibliography

Alexander, Franz (1960).   *The Western Mind in Transition. An Eyewitness Story*, New York: Random House.
Andrian-Werburg, Viktor, Freiherr von (1843).   *Österreich und dessen Zukunft*, 3rd edn, Vienna: Hoffmann.
Angyal, Dávid (1971).   *Emlékezések*, London.
Barany, George (1968).   *Stephen Széchenyi and the Awakening of Hungarian Nationalism*, Princeton: Princeton University Press.
Belke, Ingrid (1978).   *Die sozialreformerischen Ideen von Josef Popper-Lynkeus (1838–1921), im Zusammenhang mit allgemeinen Reformbestrebungen des Wiener Bürgertums um die Jahrhundertwende*, Tübingen: Mohr.
Blackmore, J.T. (1971). *Ernst Mach — His Life, Work, and Influence* (dissertation), Ann Arbor: University Microfilms.
Blackmore, J.T. (1972).   *Ernst Mach — His Life, Work, and Influence*, Berkeley: University of California Press.
Bödy, Paul (1972).   'Joseph Eötvös and the Modernization of Hungary, 1840–1870. A Study of Ideas of Individuality and Social Pluralism in Modern Politics', *Transactions of the American Philosophical Society*, new series, *62*.
Eder, Karl (1955).   *Der Liberalismus in Altösterreich. Geisteshaltung, Politik und Kultur*, Vienna/Munich: Herold.
Eötvös, József (1848).   'Munich Sketch' in J.C. Nyíri (ed.), *Austrian Philosophy*.

Studies and Texts, Munich: Philosophia Verlag, 1980, 153–72.
Eötvös, József (1851).   *Der Einfluss der herrschenden Ideen des 19. Jahrhunderts auf den Staat*, Part I, Vienna: Manz; also published Leipzig: Brockhaus (1854).
Eötvös, József (1854).   *Der Einfluss des herrschenden Ideen des 19. Jahrhunderts auf den Staat*, Part II, Leipzig: Brockhaus.
Epstein, Klaus (1966).   *The Genesis of German Conservatism*, Princeton: Princeton University Press.
Franz, Georg (1955).   *Liberalismus. Die deutschliberale Bewegung in der habsburgischen Monarchie*, Munich: Georg D.W. Callwey.
Freud, Sigmund (1900).   *Die Traumdeutung*, Leipzig and Vienna: Deuticke.
Freud, Sigmund (1947).   'Eine Schwierigkeit der Psychoanalyse' in *Gesammelte Werke*, vol. XII, London: Imago.
Gál, István (1970).   'Dickens és folyóirata Kossuthról és Széchenyiről', *Filológiai Közlöny*, 1–2.
Grassl, W. and Smith, B. (1986) 'A Theory of Austria' in J.C. Nyíri (ed.), *The Tradition of Austrian Philosophy*, Vienna: Hölder-Pichler-Tempsky.
Gray, John (1984).   *Hayek on Liberty*, Oxford: Blackwell.
Grillparzer, Franz (1872).   *Sämtliche Werke*, ed. by A. Sauer, Stuttgart: Cotta.
Hanák, Tibor (1973).   *Lukács war anders*, Maisenheim am Glan: Anton Hain.
Hayek, F.A. von (1934).   'Carl Menger' in *The Collected Works of Carl Menger*, vol. 1, London: London School of Economics.
Hayek, F.A. von (1960).   'Why I Am Not a Conservative' in Hayek, *The Constitution of Liberty*, London: Routledge & Kegan Paul.
Hayek, F.A. von (1973).   'Liberalism' in Hayek, *New Studies in Philosophy, Politics, Economics and the History of Ideas*, London: Routledge & Kegan Paul (1978).
Hayek, F.A. von (1978). 'The Three Sources of Human Values', London: London School of Economics and Political Science; repr. in *Law, Legislation and Liberty*, vol. III, London: Routledge and Kegan Paul (1979).
Hofmannsthal, Hugo von (1952). 'Grillparzers politisches Vermächtnis' in *Gesammelte Werke, Prosa III*. Frankfurt/M.: Fischer.
Iványi-Grünwald, Béla (1930). 'Gróf Széchenyi István *Hitel* cimü munkája. Történeti bevezetés' in *Gróf Széchenyi István Összes Munkái*, vol. 2, Budapest.
Janik, Allan and Stephen Toulmin (1973).   *Wittgenstein's Vienna*, New York: Simon and Schuster.
Johnston, W.M. (1972).   *The Austrian Mind. An Intellectual and Social History 1848–1938*, Berkeley: University of California Press.
Johnston, W.M. (1981).   'Recent Books in Austrian Cultural History', *Modern Austrian Literature, 14*.
Kann, R.A. (1964).   *Das Nationalitätenproblem der Habsburgermonarchie*, 2 vols, 2nd edn, Graz and Cologne: Styria.
Karolyi Árpád (1921).   'Történeti bevezetés' in *Gróf Széchenyi István döblingi irodalmi hagyatéka*, vol. I (*Gróf Széchenyi István Összes Munkái*, vol. 7), Budapest.
Kedourie, Elie (1960).   *Nationalism*, London: Hutchinson.
Knatchbull-Hugessen, C.M. (1908).   *The Political Evolution of the Hungarian Nation*, 2 vols, London: National Review Office.
Krones, F. von (1888).   *Moritz von Kaiserfeld. Sein Leben und Wirken als Beitrag zur Staatsgeschichte Österreichs in den Jahren 1848 bis 1884*, Leipzig: Duncker and Humblot.
Lytton, E.R. (1870).   'The Great Magyar', *All the Year Round*, April.
Macartney, C.A. (1971).   *The Habsburg Empire 1790–1918*, London: Weidenfeld and Nicolson.
Mach, Ernst (1886).   *Beiträge zur Analyse der Empfindungen*, Jena: Fischer.
Machovec, Milan (1969).   *Thomas G. Masaryk*, Graz: Styria.
Masaryk, T.G. (1881).   *Der Selbstmord als sociale Massenerscheinung der*

modernen Civilisation, Vienna: Konegen; repr. Munich: Philosophia, 1982. Page references are to the original edition; use has, however, been made of the recent American translation (Chicago: University of Chicago Press, 1970).

McCagg, Jr, W.O. (1972). *Jewish Nobles and Geniuses in Modern Hungary* (East European Monographs III), Boulder: East European Quarterly.

McGrath, W.J. (1965). *Wagnerianism in Austria: The Regeneration of Culture through the Spirit of Music*, dissertation, Ann Arbor: University Microfilms (1967).

McGrath, W.J. (1967). 'Student Radicalism in Vienna', *The Journal of Contemporary History*, Vol. 2, no. 3, July.

McGrath, W.J. (1974). *Dionysian Art and Populist Politics in Austria*, New Haven: Yale University Press.

Menger, Carl (1871). *Grundsätze der Volkswirtschaftslehre*, Vienna: Braumüller,

Menger, Carl (1934). *Untersuchungen über die Methode der Sozialwissenschaften, und der politischen Ökonomie insbesondere* in *Collected Works of Carl Menger*, ed. F.A. von Hayek, London: London School of Economics.

Molisch, Paul (1944). 'Anton v. Schmerling und der Liberalismus in Österreich', *Archiv für Osterreichische Geschichtsforschung, 116*, Vienna.

Morton, Frederic (1980). *A Nervous Splendour. Vienna 1888/1889*, London: Weidenfeld and Nicolson.

Musil, Robert (1930). *Der Mann ohne Eigenschaften*, Berlin: Rowohlt.

Nash, G.H. (1979). *The Conservative Intellectual Movement in America. Since 1945*, 2nd edn, New York: Basic Books.

Nyíri, J.C. (1978). 'Philosophy and Suicide-Statistics in Austria-Hungary', *East Central Europe, 5*, 69–89.

Nyíri, J.C. (1979). 'Wittgensteins Spätwerk im Kontext des Konservatismus', in M. Nedo and H.-J. Heringer (eds), *Wittgensteins geistige Erscheinung*, Frankfurt: Suhrkamp, 83–101; English translation 'Wittgenstein's Later Work in Relation to Conservatism' in B.F. McGuinness (ed), *Wittgenstein and his Times*, Oxford: Blackwell, 44–68.

Nyíri, J.C. (1980). 'Grillparzer and Wittgenstein' in R. Haller and W. Grassl (eds), *Language, Logic and Philosophy*, Vienna: Hölder-Pichler-Tempsky, 189–91.

Nyíri, J.C. (1981a). 'From Eötvös to Musil. Philosophy and its Negation in Austria and Hungary', in J.C. Nyíri (ed.), *Austrian Philosophy, Studies and Texts*, Munich: Philosophia, 9-30.

Nyíri, J.C. (1981b). 'Philosophy and National Consciousness in Austria and Hungary. A Comparative Socio-psychological Sketch' in B. Smith (ed.), *Structure and Gestalt: Philosophy and Literature in Austria-Hungary and Her Successor States*, Amsterdam: Benjamins, 235–62.

Nyíri, J.C. (1982a). 'Wittgenstein 1929–31: Die Rückkehr', *Kodikas/Code, 4–5*, 115–36; abridged English translation 'Wittgenstein as a Conservative Philosopher', *Continuity, 8* (1984), 1–23.

Nyíri, J.C. (1982b). 'Introduction' to the reprint of Masaryk (1881), 5–42.

Nyíri, J.C. (with B.F. McGuinness) (1984). 'Introduction' to J.C. Nyíri (ed.), Karl Wittgenstein, *Politico-economic Writings*, Amsterdam: Benjamins, i–xl.

Nyíri, J.C. (1985). 'Geschichtstypologische Bemerkungen zur böhmischen Frage' in R. Fabian (ed.), *Christian von Ehrenfels: Leben und Werk*, Amsterdam: Rodopi, 247-80; repr. in Nyíri (1986a).

Nyíri, J.C. (1986a). *Am Rande Europas. Ideengeschichtliche Entwürfe*, Vienna: Böhlau.

Nyíri, J.C. (1986b). 'Liberale Ökonomie: der Vater Wittgenstein', ch. 3 of Nyíri, (1986a).

Oakeshott, Michael (1971). *On Human Conduct*, Oxford: Oxford University Press.

Paget, John (1839). *Hungary and Transylvania*, 2 vols, London: J. Murray.

Politzer, Heinz (1972).   *Franz Grillparzer oder das abgründige Biedermeier*, Vienna: Molden.
Redlich, Josef (1920).   *Das österreichische Staats- und Reichsproblem*, vol. I, Leipzig: Der Neue Geist.
Redlich, Josef (1926).   *Das österreichische Staats- und Reichsproblem*, vol. II, Leipzig: Der Neue Geist.
Schorske, Carl E. (1978).   'Generational Tension and Cultural Change: Reflections on the Case of Vienna', *Daedalus, 107*.
Schorske, Carl E. (1980).   *Fin-de-Siècle Vienna. Politics and Culture*, New York: Alfred A. Knopf.
Seitter, Walter (1968).   *Franz Grillparzers Philosophie*, München.
Somogyi, Éva (1976).   *A birodalmi centralizációtól a dualizmusig. Az osztrák-német liberálisok utja a kiegyezéshez*, Budapest: Akadémiai Kiadó.
Stourzh, Gerald (1966).   'Die politischen Ideen Josef von Eötvös' und das österreichische Staatsproblem', *Der Donauraum, 11*.
Szekfü, Gyula (1920).   *Három nemzedék. Egy hanyatló kör története*, Budapest.
Széchenyi, Gróf István (1830).   *Hitel*. Page references are to the *Összes Munkái* edition, Budapest (1930).
Széchenyi, Gróf István (1841).   *A' Kelet Népe*. Page references are to the *Összes Munkái* edition, Budapest (1930).
Széchenyi, Gróf István (1825–39).   *Naplói* (Diaries), 6 vols, ed. Gyula Viszota, Budapest.
Széchenyi, Gróf István (1889).   *Levelei* (Letters), vol. 1, ed. Béla Majláth, Budapest.
Walzer, Michael (1979).   *Mauthner's Critique of Language*, Cambridge: Cambridge University Press.
Weininger, Otto (1903).   *Geschlecht und Charakter*, Vienna: Braumüller.
Wittgenstein, Karl (1985).   *Politico-Economic Writings. An Annotated Reprint of 'Zeitungsartikel Und Vortage'*, ed. by J.C. Nyíri, Amsterdam: John Benjamins.

4 MARKETS AND MORALITY: AUSTRIAN PERSPECTIVES ON THE ECONOMIC APPROACH TO HUMAN BEHAVIOUR

Wolfgang Grassl

Der höchste Ausdruck aller
Moral ist: *Sei!*
Der Mensch handle so, dass in
jedem Momente seine *ganze*
Individualität liege.

Otto Weininger[1]

1. The Utilitarian Background of Descriptive Ethics

Scarcity of means to satisfy particular ends is a ubiquitous condition of life. It requires agents not only to economise, that is, to choose the appropriate means for achieving individual ends, but also to enter into relations of exchange with those other agents who dispose of desired goods. We may need or desire not only material but also immaterial resources, and agents are at times willing to trade material goods or services for ideas, psychic recompensation, or even purely moral reward. All interpersonal exchange may therefore assume an economic character. Social behaviour in general may be interpreted as a trade-off which takes place at various levels, ranging from the lowest level of the individual with his needs and dispositions to higher levels constituted by aggregates such as groups and societies. At all levels the essential problem consists in matching means with ends, and man as a rational agent calculating his interests will try to achieve a relation most conducive to his personal satisfaction conceived in the broadest possible sense.

Description of the conditions under which maximisation of individual utility comes about has traditionally been the task of economic theory. But if all human conduct may be regarded as involving economising agents, this must pertain also, *a fortiori*, to what may be called moral conduct. Individual moral decisions are subject to the same principles and constraints that govern other species of behaviour which do not clearly have a moral aspect. And moral values

139

can to this extent be conceived as abstractions from considerations of rationality and utility. These are reflected in the rationale of the price-system, as individual economisers enter into it and exchange in a market-place of physical and psychic goods.

Market assumptions entered moral philosophy with the competitive model of society envisaged by Thomas Hobbes. Society was constituted by the sum of market relations holding between its members, and the moral norms prevailing in a society were interpreted as a resultant of these relations. Hobbes saw the distribution of power between men in terms of the market and equated the value which is attributed to an individual with the 'price' this individual achieves in the esteem of his competitors:

> The *Value*, or WORTH of a man, is as of all other things, his Price; that is to say, so much as would be given for the use of his Power: and therefore is not absolute; but a thing dependent on the need and judgement of another.[2]

This conception went along with a decidedly subjectivist theory of value which was based on the psychological premiss that 'the value of all things contracted for, is measured by the Appetite of the Contractors: and therefore the just value, is that which they be contented to give'.[3] It is obvious that Hobbes had parted with the labour theory of value that had predominated in most medieval expositions of these matters and that in anticipation of neoclassical economics he identified demand as the true determinant of value:

> As in other things, so in men, not the seller, but the buyer determines the Price. For let a man (as most men do,) rate themselves as the highest Value they can; yet their true Value is no more than it is esteemed by others.[4]

The system of market incentives and market morality (which includes the right of unlimited individual appropriation) is regarded as the only distributive mechanism in a society based on the division of labour. The mechanisms of price-formation are generalised so as to apply to all goods, including moral values.[5]

This conception, however, gives rise to a serious dilemma. While on the one hand the principle of supply and demand is supposed to determine the distribution of all resources, this presupposes that every individual competing for a better position in the market observes certain rules which exclude the use of force and other illicit means. Hobbes's market model, however, supplies neither such rules nor the justification of a particular moral code. It refers instead to a coercive state as the only institution charged with sanctioning any infringement of the rules upon which the free market is based. Hobbes's thought does not yet reflect the idea of a *self-regulation* of the market economy: the market in terms of which he sees society does not manifest the workings of an invisible hand; it requires state interference to coordinate the multitude of individual wills and actions, just as, according to Locke, human beings require 'a common Power to keep them in awe'.

A liberal solution of Hobbes's dilemma became possible as a consequence of the new belief in a natural order of society. As an alternative to étatist paternalism, John Locke proposed to leave it to the market to solve the problems which it had itself created. If it can indeed be demonstrated that the new market system represents an economic order rooted in the nature of man, capable, like other natural systems, of achieving its own equilibrium, then efforts to control it may be viewed as either futile or pernicious. According to Locke, individuals seek to maximise their own interest as determined by the market; it is not the task of legislation to change the equilibrium to which this process inevitably gives rise. Society thus appears as an organism which — leaving aside external shocks — satisfies the needs of individuals increasingly successfully as a result of an internal process of improvement impelled by the forces of the market. Each person, taken separately, is ruled by market values, while the market values are in their turn the product of the manifold of their separate decisions.

With Locke, the market model of society and of moral conduct already assumes a distinctively utilitarian aspect. It is the merit of classical utilitarianism to have recognised clearly that an economic aspect inheres in all human activity. The goal of all conduct, in the moral, political, economic, or legal sphere, is seen as that of maximising utility. The essence of rational conduct consists in economising or, in Jeremy Bentham's formulation, in the maximisation of happiness at minimum cost. But this descriptive principle is also given a moral force; it is to determine 'what we do as well as to determine what we shall do'.[6] Because all action is motivated by desire for pleasure and aversion to pain, pleasure is the only thing which is intrinsically good, pain the only thing which is intrinsically evil. Actions which promote the greatest happiness of the greatest number are therefore to be approved of just because they promote what is intrinsically good.

Bentham derives the principle of utilitarian morality from the assumption of psychological hedonism: that men are governed in all their actions by the desire for pleasure and for the avoidance of pain. Psychological hedonism, however, must not be equated with psychological egoism. Bentham does not claim that all human action is selfish in the ordinary sense. In a list of different kinds of pleasure, he includes the pleasures of amity, benevolence, and of association, attainment of which will require altruistic conduct. The individual cannot satisfy all his needs except in collaboration and competition with others, and the basic rules of this social process acquire the status of moral rules.

In his explanation of the relation between the individual and society, Bentham relies on the same model of exchange that had inspired the thought of Hobbes and Locke. But his ideas are affected also by classical political economy, particularly by Adam Smith's thesis of the natural harmony of interests. By the mechanism of exchange and the division of labour individuals, without desiring it or even being aware of it, and while pursuing each his own interest, are contributing towards the realisation of the common good. An individual interested in maximising his own happiness can be relied upon to accept just those forms of conduct (or 'moral rules') that are also in the interest of other individuals, because he can be relied upon to realise that his own happiness is to a certain degree dependent upon theirs. The fundamental moral notion is thus no longer that of obligation or duty as *a priori* postulates, but that of exchange. Bentham's ethics provides a psychological foundation of what was described above as Locke's solution of the dilemma of market morality. It reflects the same confidence in a natural equilibrium that had motivated classical economic thought. It is appropriate, therefore, to observe that 'the morality of the Utilitarians is their economic psychology put into the imperative'.[7]

Utilitarianism is an economic theory of morals: morality is treated as a process of exchange and distribution in which moral value and moral obligation are determined by the workings of the market-place. When a utilitarian regards honesty as on the whole the best policy, he means that it will tend to bring larger returns, in terms of pleasure, than dishonesty. When he rejects the principle of 'honour for honour's sake', he applies to honour the same method of valuation that the economist applies to a painting or a bushel of wheat; that is to say, for the subjective value of honour as measured by this or that personal point of view he substitutes 'value in exchange' as measured by an objective mathematical standard. And thus, in the utilitarian ethics, pleasure or happiness becomes a kind of moral currency, which plays the same part in moral valuation as is played by money in the valuations of commodity markets. And personal obligation becomes a matter of *quid pro quo*. The moral man, like the *homo oeconomicus*, is one who buys cheap and sells dear; the neighbour to whom he owes the greatest obligation is the one from whom he may in turn expect the greatest consideration. And it was still an economic point of view that guided Bentham when he laid down the formula of 'the greatest happiness of the greatest number' — in which 'everybody is to count for one and nobody for more than one' — as a rule for the administration of law and the distribution of public benefits. For in the last analysis the greatest happiness principle is a principle neither of distributive justice nor of humanitarian sympathy. It is simply a convenient rule for the distribution of goods based upon a typically economic estimate of what is conducive to the highest average of welfare or prosperity.

Bentham's utilitarianism is an example of what has come to be called *act-utilitarianism*. It holds that morality requires the individual to act, on every occasion, so as to maximise the sum of human happiness. This means that moral rules, such as the rules of justice and promise-keeping, are provisional only and may be breached if strict adherence to them would diminish the sum of human happiness. As a moral doctrine, act-utilitarianism licenses individuals to determine for themselves the likely consequences of actions; yet no individual can ever *know* these consequences. It is because of this ignorance that men develop *rules* to guide their conduct so that they do not have to estimate the probable consequences of various courses of action on every occasion.[8]

Rule-utilitarianism evaluates not the consequences of particular actions but the consequences of following rules. General rules, such as promise-keeping, telling the truth, and the rules of justice, are justified on utilitarian grounds.

This is the kind of utilitarianism that David Hume had in mind. While emphasising the importance of rules, it does not found them upon 'intention' or on any abstract metaphysic not related to human wants and social survival. In the Humean model, rules are not so much planned and designed but develop almost *spontaneously*, and men adopt and retain those rules that prove to be useful. The rules of justice, for example, were not rationally demonstrated from an abstract notion of a 'social contract' but emerged as devices by which individuals could make their relationships predictable.[9] Thus rules acquire a validity which is independent of immediate consequences but is linked with utility and welfare *in the long run*.

The basic conception inherent in this form of rule-utilitarianism is that of rules forming in a market envisaged as a self-propelled evolutionary process. Hume and the 'British moralists' realised that human actions have non-intended consequences; competition and limited altruism constituted the determinant influences on the market of human valuation. Society at large was — in the words of Adam Ferguson — regarded as 'the result of human action, but not of human design'.

Within the 'economic theory of morals' we can thus distinguish two different versions. The first goes back to Hobbes and is based on a mechanicist view of man as a pleasure-maximiser. It recognised the boundlessness of desires that motivate human beings, but it could not explain the spontaneous coordination of these desires on a market. The second version views rule-formation as a process in which continual adjustment to continual change occurs. Men do not consciously set out to create the practices and values that define their society; rather, these things grow out of people's experiences in dealing with one another. That is, they evolve *spontaneously*.

Whatever their differences may be, these divergent versions of utilitarianism also share a number of common features. Perhaps the most striking feature of the tradition that originated with Hobbes and led to Locke, Bentham, Mill, Spencer and beyond, is the common engagement in what may be called *descriptive ethics*. This can be understood as an attempt to explicate the principles underlying the observed activity of making moral judgements with the intention of displaying its rationale or motivation. Already Hobbes derived the system of moral requirements from the operation of a motivational factor which can be independently understood, together with certain highly general assumptions about the human condition. The basic motive was taken as given and was conceived as something prior to ethics. It is surely not an ethical principle that all men should want to preserve their own lives; so in that sense judgements about motivation are at the most fundamental level, and ethical judgements are essentially dependent upon these. Claims about what we *should* do are on this view claims about what we have a certain sort of *motivation* for doing.

Bentham did not everywhere follow Hobbes' lead. Yet he did share this psychological approach to ethics. And even utilitarians like Hume, who clearly realised the logical problems connected with naturalistic foundations of ethics, could agree that if anything is good, it is so by reference to people's desires, inclinations, and approvals. If reason merely informs, whilst the passions rule our actions, then the possibility of justifying particular moral precepts is of course strictly limited. On this view too, descriptive ethics is but an elaboration of psychological assumptions about people's dispositions to approve or disapprove of given actions. To the extent that utilitarian ethics is prescriptive at all, it is a consequentialist, not a deontological, ethical theory: the principle of utility requires people to judge actions and moral rules solely according to their consequences, but does not provide them with any absolute standard of rightness or moral value.

2. The Shortcomings of Classical Utilitarianism

In spite of the indubitable merits of the descriptive approach — not the least of which is that it opened up the possibility of conceiving of morality in quantitative terms — Bentham's economic theory of ethics poses a number of philosophical problems that seriously call into question its acceptability:

(i) Notwithstanding his praise for Hume's remark about the separate realms of 'is' and 'ought', Bentham's derivation of moral from psychological hedonism is open to the criticism of constituting a particularly instructive example of the 'naturalistic fallacy', that is, the derivation of a prescriptive statement from a purely descriptive one.

(ii) The hedonistic psychology on which classical utilitarianism rested seems not only philosophically untenable; it has also been empirically discredited as a valid theory of motivation. As a matter of fact, many things other than pleasure are also desired as primary goods. Human action in general, and presumably therefore also in the market-place, is not under the constant and detailed guidance of careful and accurate hedonic calculations, but is to a great extent the product of an unstable and non-rational complex of reflex actions, impulses, instincts, habits, customs, fashions, and expectations.

(iii) Bentham's observation that the assumption of economic rationality is at one and the same time a universal descriptive principle and a norm signifies an unwelcome intrusion of normative ethical considerations into economic science.

(iv) Utilitarian ethics lacks any foundation in a theory of human nature that could distinguish men from other creatures and that would account for our intuition that it is only persons, or rational agents, who are properly to be regarded as moral agents.

(v) Bentham's dictum 'quantity of pleasure being equal, pushpin is as good as poetry' seems to imply an untenable moral theory. As a matter of fact, however, we are not free to adopt or reject any moral principle *ad libitum*, but are always bound to relate personal utilities to a surrounding social framework.

(vi) If the principle of utility is to provide standards of conduct for particular cases, individuals would have to be credited with perfect knowledge of what is — or what is likely to be — conducive to the enhancement of general welfare. But a market-model which takes moral norms to be determined, like prices, by the relations of supply and demand constituting the market, seems to clash with a moral principle which presupposes that individuals have a good knowledge of the consequences of their actions even *before* they have offered these actions for valuation on the market.

(vii) The individualist foundation on which utilitarian social philosophy is usually held to be based comes therefore into a strange conflict with the conception of morality as a self-regulating mechanism.

The confusion in the Benthamist theory of society — between the assumption of a natural harmony and the need for an external arbitrator to create an artificial harmony between conflicting self-interests — seems to derive from Bentham's failure to resolve into a consistent theory the two views of man and society, one inherited from Hobbes, the other from Locke and the classical economists. To this extent at least, utilitarianism has not succeeded in providing a satisfactory solution to the dilemma of market-morality which could both account for the empirical facts of moral valuations and remain consistent with the attitude of liberal individualism.

3. Varieties of Marginalism

These difficulties of utilitarian philosophy were highlighted by the so-called 'marginalist revolution' in economics which set the seal upon the development of descriptive ethics in a distinctive and decisive way. Though they agreed that the starting-point of economic science ought to be not the socio-economic relations between men as producers but the psychological relations between men and goods in process of production, the three principal founders of marginalism came to take quite divergent views on how to resolve the problems inherent in classical utilitarianism. More than anything else, it was the relation between economics and ethics — between the study of markets and of morality — that needed to be redefined. It was the school of William Jevons which was least prone to abandon the use of ethical concepts in economic theory. Jevons attempted to rehabilitate the hedonistic psychology of utilitarian ethics and to develop a calculus of pleasure and pain modelled on Bentham's 'felicific calculus', founding a tradition that has remained influential in economics until recent times: modern welfare economics remained resolutely utilitarian until at least the 1930s.

In opposition to this revival of a substantially naturalistic position the Continental schools of marginalist economics agreed on the necessity of freeing economics from any reliance upon psychological and ethical assumptions and of rejecting the view that economics as such could have practical policy-implications. Both Carl Menger and Léon Walras endeavoured to redefine economics as a self-sufficient science, but with this difference: in Vienna the economic agent, in Lausanne the equilibrium-system, was made the pivot of economic theory.

Walras regarded pure or theoretical economics as a value-free science, attributing to its objects of investigation the physico-mathematical character of an equilibrium-system. Economic phenomena were thus to be studied by the methods of rational mechanics.

The Austrians, on the other hand, whilst they shared with Walras the conception of economics as a value-free science, rejected the assumptions by means of which he had arrived at this conception. And they shared with Jevons the use of psychological arguments in justifying economic assumptions; but they forcefully repudiated his still utilitarian reliance on ethical premises imported from elsewhere. Indeed few economists have been more radical than Menger in their insistence on the disjunction of the spheres of ethics and economics.

The Austrian approach rests upon an image of man in complete opposition to the anthropology of the utilitarians. Man's essence is seen as residing in *purposeful activity* rather than merely in his status as a consumer of utilities. Man is no longer a more or less passive recipient interested only in maximising his pleasure; he is seen, rather, as a rational agent engaged in the complicated business of making means meet ends.

The most characteristic features of the Austrian school are its resolute individualism and the emphasis it puts on the view of the market as a process, rather than as a mere configuration of prices, quantities, and qualities that are in harmony with each other in the sense that they produce some kind of equilibrium. This new viewpoint, which centres on the study of human preference and choice, requires a break with the simplistic associationist psychology that had been used by the utilitarians to underpin their hedonistic theory of motivation. For the older Austrian school — for Menger and his disciples — a turn towards a cognitive psychology was the consequence of the shortcomings perceived in psychological hedonism. The rudiments of this new view of mental life had already been prepared by a group of Austrian philosophers upon whose discoveries the economists could rely in advancing their own theories.

Where the representatives of the older Austrian school had formulated their theories in psychological terms, or in such a way as to involve reference to the mental activity of economic agents, the later Austrians took up a different position on the relation between psychology and ethics.[10] Ludwig von Mises, the most thorough-going advocate of subjectivism among modern economists, denied that there is the slightest connection between economic theory and psychology, holding that pure economics or 'praxeology' is not concerned with the specific motives behind actually existing human actions but only with the implications of the concept of action itself. Praxeology in this sense is an *a priori* science of human action, independent of experience and expressible with absolute deductive certainty, while its objects of description are at the same time encountered within empirical reality. Since praxeology deals with the formal implications of the concept of action rather than with the contents of actions themselves, it follows that economic theory cannot itself establish ethical judgements. Their refusal to advocate any specific ends, and their willingness to investigate only the relationship that holds between means and ends generally conceived, might still put Misesian praxeologists into the utilitarian tradition *sensu lato*. But their rigid exclusion of ethics from the realm of economics and their conception of economic theory as an *a priori* science independent of psychological assumptions makes their methodology seem too far removed from Benthamite utilitarianism to warrant its inclusion within this tradition.

The emphasis on the *Wertfreiheit* of economic science which is common to all generations of the Austrian school does not, however, rule out the possibility of linking ethics and economics on the level of their respective subject-matters. Within the Austrian framework, it is possible to generalise economic value-theory so as to make it applicable to all species of human conduct, including moral behaviour. (The fundamentals of such a theory will be outlined in section 8 below.) But in order to steer clear of the difficulties encountered by utilitarian market-conceptions of morality, a general theory along Austrian lines requires a new psychology that conceives of man not simply as a 'pleasure machine', but as a rational agent consciously appraising means and ends and trying to maximise what he regards as conducive to his happiness. This is the first task to be approached, and here recourse can be made to some conceptions developed by Austrian philosophers.

4. The Austrian Philosophy of Value

It has become customary to distinguish between two schools of Austrian value theory.[11] The first school is that of the marginalist economists and consists principally of Menger, Eugen von Böhm-Bawerk, Friedrich von Wieser and their followers. The second school includes the philosophers Alexius von Meinong, Christian von Ehrenfels, Oskar Kraus and Josef Clemens Kreibig. All members of the second school trace their philosophical ancestry back to Franz Brentano, in whose work one may see the inception of value theory as an independent branch of philosophical enquiry. The influences between the two groups were reciprocal. Though it is certainly true that the members of the second school relied more heavily on the ideas of the economists, it should not be forgotten that there was also a flow of ideas in the other direction: the marginalists looked to the Brentanians for certain psychological underpinnings of their subjective value theory. What made Brentanian descriptive psychology appear a particularly suitable model for the economists was the fact that Brentano's philosophical theory of value, like the economic theory of the first Austrian school, was subjectivist. Value, for Brentano, was in every case an inseparable moment of an act of an individual subject. Brentano maintained that there is a faculty of 'love' and 'hate' in the human mind as real as that of theoretical judgement. Values, then, are not properties of objects, but rather products of the emotions, i.e. of the acts of right love and right hate. Value is founded in the attitude of the subject which qualifies a given presentational content as pleasant.[12]

Similarly, the members of the first school confined themselves strictly to the study of valuation as a mental act, to the complete exclusion of metaphysical questions as to the nature of the objects of valuation. Value thus assumed a psychological dimension. According to one source, Menger himself turned to the writings of Brentano, Meinong, Ehrenfels and Kraus, in an attempt to add a psychological basis to his system.[13] His modifications of classical economics, and specifically of the labour-cost theory of value, resembled Brentano's own criticisms and modifications of the psychology of stimulus and response.

Menger effected a radical break with the older tradition of economics by reorientating the concept of economic value about the economising subject. Thus he saw value not as something residing in physical objects themselves, but as resting on or ensuing from conscious judgements about the significance of such objects for the satisfaction of subjective needs.[14] Value is thus not an inherent quality of goods, but is *imputed* to those goods from which the satisfaction of given needs may be expected. By considering value to be a relation between a state of consciousness and an object in the world, Menger conceived of it in terms very similar to Brentano's definition of intentionality. Value is expressed by a judgement; it exists merely in subjective meaning-bestowing mental acts (where, for Brentano, a mental act is but the manner in which a mind is related to an object). Precisely as one does not, according to Menger, judge that to have value which has value in itself, but rather in contrast, that has value which our mind judges to be valuable, so, according to Brentano, the value of (for instance) the true or the good is ascribed to those objects which we — with our subjective powers (which are in no way arbitrary, but are rather guided by our experiences of evidence) — judge to be true or good. Among those acts which Brentano locates as belonging to the affective-conative level of experience, he refers particularly to acts of preference. Preference as the act of choosing between alternatives thus assumes an emotional dimension.

Austrian economists have variously made use of the idea that preference so construed is a psychological phenomenon *sui generis* and that no choice between commodities could come about if the agent had not experienced what Brentano called 'love and hate' and what his pupil Anton Marty referred to as the 'phenomena of interest'.[15] Feelings of love and hate are at the very roots of human preferences and rejections. More generally, Austrian economists have profitably usurped the Brentanian conception of mental acts. Böhm-Bawerk, to take just one example, became interested in discovering which *'psychische Akte'* were basic (and causally relevant) to economic decision. And for Wieser it was not the 'scientific' psychology of the behaviourists, but the introspectionist and common-sense psychology of the realist, Brentanian type which became the pivot of economic theory: the economist's data, he claimed, come from within his own consciousness and from such external facts as he may observe in his ordinary day-to-day existence.[16]

For Meinong, too, an initial psychological orientation served as the starting-point of his value theory. The latter in fact is linked to his psychology of feeling — as in Brentano. An object has value only for an individual person, and the index of this value is his emotional attachment to it. Since all our experiences may affect our emotions, a value theory keyed to our emotional responses is capable of encompassing the whole range of human experience. It is limited neither to problems of ethics nor to those of economics but, in principle, involves all aspects of our interests and actions. It is in these considerations that we may see the beginnings of the attempt to develop a general theory of value on psychological foundations.

While Brentano assumed a fusion of the affective and the conative aspects of experience as constituting the basis of valuation, his disciples agreed that experience suggests a more or less complete distinction between feeling and desire. They differed, however, as to which aspect should be taken as basic.[17] Though Meinong's views underwent considerable changes in the course of his writings, and later evolved into an objectivist account, he never abandoned his essential contention that we attribute value to objects in accordance with the 'emotional significance' they have for us.[18] Valuation, for him, is primarily a matter of feeling, and only secondarily and derivatively a matter of desire. Ehrenfels was quick to point out that Meinong's thesis suffers from one serious weakness. If an object is valuable to the extent that it is capable of producing in us a feeling of pleasure, then only existing objects can be valuable. But the truth is that we value also what does not exist: perfect justice, universal peace, the moral good which is never realised. For this reason, Ehrenfels reversed Meinong's order of precedence and considered value to be more directly connected with desire than with feeling.

Following the Aristotelian interest theory of value, Ehrenfels defined value as 'the relation, erroneously objectified by the language we use, of a thing to a human desire directed towards it'.[19] Meinong objected that on this basis we could desire only what we knew or believed to be non-existent, and that therefore nothing that exists could be valuable. Ehrenfels consequently modified his theory by claiming that existing things are valued just because we think that if they did not exist, or if we did not possess them, we would desire them. He thus came to conceive of value as the relation between an object and the subject's desire for it, which would make the subject covet it if he were not convinced of its existence.[20] Ehrenfels also realised that the simple fact of an object's actually being desired does not yet constitute its value. Value should rather be seen as deriving from the 'desirability' of the object.[21] It is itself not a property of objects, but rather is dependent on the fact that certain objects have the aptitude for producing in us a desire directed towards them, where the magnitude of the value possessed by an object is directly proportional to its desirability. It follows as a necessary consequence that the value of things is essentially subjective, i.e. dependent on individual estimations of their desirability.[22]

This conception obviously raises the question of the validity of psychological hedonism: is it legitimate — as, for instance, Mill supposed in his 'proof' of the principle of utility — to identify the experiences of desiring a thing and of finding it pleasant? The controversy between Meinong and Ehrenfels may be seen as a debate about logical (and perhaps also causal) precedence: whether we desire things because they have value, or whether things have value because we desire them. Although his position was not always consistent, Meinong seems to have inclined to the first view (which, incidentally, he shares with Aquinas: *'appetitur aliquid quia bonum est'*). By interpreting value in terms of feeling, a thing whose existence gives pleasure is taken to have value and as therefore being capable of eliciting a desire.[23] In this sense, 'every object of desire must be an object of value for the desiring person'.[24]

This position reminds one of the principal tenet of psychological hedonism, according to which people always take that action from which they anticipate that they will derive the greatest pleasure. Critics of this tenet have pointed out that, as a matter of fact, many things other than pleasure are also desired. And Joseph Butler added that even if it were true that, whenever one acts, one acts from a desire, and true that pleasure is the natural or even essential consequence of the satisfaction of desire, it does not follow that one's desire is always for pleasure.[25] The main flaw of hedonism is thus held to consist in an implicit *hysteron–proteron* fallacy, a reversal of the true order of logical dependence. It is not the pleasure we expect from something that creates the desire for it, but this pleasure owes its existence entirely to the satisfaction of the desire directed towards it.[26] The pleasure of drinking wine comes from the satisfaction of the desire for wine, not vice versa.

Ehrenfels takes a similar point of view, urging that 'we do not desire things because we perceive a mystical and intangible essence called "value" in them, but on the contrary, we ascribe "value" to things because we desire them'.[27] Desire, rather than pleasure, is to be regarded as the one touchstone of value, thus falling in line with

Hobbes' conviction that what men desire is what they call good, and that happiness is success in getting what is desired: 'Felicity is a continuall progresse of the desire, from one object to another; the attaining of the former, being still but the way to the latter.'[28] Pleasure in this sense does play an important but secondary role in valuation. Desire may not only be for pleasure, but also for objects for their own sake, or for the sake of something else — which brings us to the distinction between intrinsic and instrumental value (see section 6 below).

It appears that Ehrenfels's conception is no longer entrenched in a clearly hedonistic psychology. His view has obvious advantages over hedonism. It avoids the identification of the valuable and the merely pleasurable, holding that we may desire that which may bring no pleasure, and it is thus able to account for the value we may ascribe to actions — such as that of the martyr — in which the costs incurred appear to outweigh the expected benefits. Such an action is good because it is preferred, not because it is pleasurably anticipated. This view also does justice to the facts of relativity of values: value standards vary with the varying preferences and desires of different individuals and groups.

For Ehrenfels the controlling factors in determining the direction and strength of our desires are not the actual feelings, but rather our feeling-dispositions: the implicit and pre-established tendencies to some sort of emotional or volitional reaction. The moral evaluation of an action pertains to the presence or absence of feeling-dispositions of a specific kind — a presence or absence that is revealed only through the actions themselves. A hedonistic tone seems to underly Ehrenfels's claim that

> all acts of desire are determined both in their goal and in their strength by the relative enhancement of pleasure which they, in view of the feeling-dispositions of the individual concerned, bring with themselves by their entrance into and duration in conscious-ness.[29]

The formulation of this 'universal law' does not, however, rely on any notion of teleology or of a causal connection between the enhancement of pleasure following upon an act of desire and this act itself. By making feeling-dispositions, rather than actual feelings, the determinant of desire, this law accounts for the fact that what is desired is often the existence of an object not yet realised, or the non-existence of a realised object. For surely the hedonic accompaniment of a not yet existent object, itself therefore not existent, cannot in any causal sense be the determinant of desire. If psychological hedonism is taken to mean the recognition of a direct causal relation between a cause or occasion of pleasure and the corresponding value, then Ehrenfels cannot properly be classified as a hedonist.[30]

Neither did the members of the second Austrian school subscribe to hedonism in the ethical sense. They assumed that human actions are generally guided by the expectation of attaining happiness or pleasure, but they refrained from defending the normative claim that pleasure *should* be the goal of every action. Moreover, psychological hedonism does not necessarily involve the assumption of psychological (or even ethical) egoism, that is, the view that human conduct is motivated exclusively by self-interest (or even that it *should* be so motivated). All members of the second school conceived of egoism as an unnecessary assumption and, indeed, as something which has been refuted by psychological theory.[31]

5. The Psychology of the First Austrian School

The Austrian economists concurred with the philosophers in the rejection of both hedonism and egoism. Their conception of *homo oeconomicus* is not that of the naturalistic 'pleasure machine', working automatically by the motive power of its sensations of pleasure and pain, but that of a rational agent consciously appraising the 'life and welfare purposes which goods serve to achieve'.[32] To constitute a good, four things, according to Menger, are required: (i) a human want; (ii) certain properties in an object which make it capable of satisfying a want; (iii) the knowledge of — or belief in — this capability; and (iv) the power to dispose of this object in the satisfaction of the want.[33] While desirous of satisfying his wants, the individual is not driven by them, but must still act on the basis of his choice. All that economics presupposes of the factual world, according to Menger, is that tastes differ, that each agent has his scale of preferences, and that the means to satisfy these are scarce. Menger's scale of wants rests on Gossen's laws of diminishing utility: individual desires vary in intensity, and the desire for a further unit of a good diminishes with the increase in the number of goods already acquired or consumed.

The Austrians regarded the satisfaction of wants as the key concept in economic activity, the actions of individual economisers being taken to be intelligible in terms of the idea that they seek to maximise their satisfaction. The proponents of the marginalist doctrine, however, claimed that it is not that increment of a stock of goods which yields the first or most intense satisfaction which determines the value this stock has for an individual, but rather the least urgent want satisfied, the last in a series of wants to receive consideration:

> The magnitude of the value of a good is determined by the importance of that concrete want or partial want which has the lowest degree of urgency among the wants that can be covered by the available supply of goods of the same kind.[34]

From this principle one can derive the main tenets of the theory of marginal utility: (i) that value is determined by subjective utility; (ii) that the utility of successive units of a given commodity gradually decreases, since the intensity of a want diminishes as the number of units possessed increases; and (iii) that it is the utility of the last unit possessed (the least useful, since it corresponds to the least intense desire) which determines and limits the utility of all the others.

Contrary to all earlier formulations of these ideas, however, the Austrian theory of value did not invoke hedonistic postulates.[35] The Austrians naturally made use of the concepts of 'pleasure', 'pain', 'desire', 'happiness', and so on. But they repeatedly emphasised that these need not be understood in a hedonistic sense.[36] Things other than pleasure and the avoidance of pain can be the objects of our desires. Böhm-Bawerk repudiated the doctrine that all desires must necessarily emanate from the emotions in the sense of being teleologically directed towards the attainment of pleasure; but he granted that the emotional qualities of pleasure and pain do generally accompany human wants.[37] When agents choose well, and act efficiently, pleasure ensues; but pleasure may arise in other ways than merely from the fulfilment of desire. This position concurs with Ehrenfels's 'law of the relative enhancement of happiness' in assuming a relation between desire and emotion while eschewing a reduction of the one to the other. Taking his bearing from Ehrenfels's psychology, Böhm-Bawerk pointed to the existence of sensations of pleasure without desires directed at them and, conversely, to desires without corresponding emotions.[38]

This latter insight became crucial for Böhm-Bawerk's theory of capital, which emphasised the significance of time in the economic process and defined capital as the produced factors of production. The basic idea in Böhm-Bawerk's analysis is that roundabout means of production enable humans to increase their productivity, both in terms of increased quantities of goods producible without equipment and in terms of goods producible only through capital goods. The period of waiting resulting from the use of indirect processes provides the basis for his explanation of the phenomenon of interest: the interest accruing on invested capital is regarded as the reward for accepting future remunerations in place of present ones. This willingness to accept future remunerations runs counter to the psychological law that people generally value present goods more highly than future goods with similar characteristics, other things being equal.

For this reason, hedonists would find no easy explanation of the actions of investors: they would have to make the highly problematic assumption that future pleasure, that is, emotions not yet felt, can motivate present actions. Taking his bearing from Ehrenfels's claim that desires can exist without corresponding emotions, Böhm-Bawerk rejected any notion of presentience whilst admitting that we may cognitively anticipate future emotions. Such anticipation constitutes a mental act which is no longer explicable within the sensualist framework of hedonist psychology. In the wake of the Austrian philosophers, and by directly disclaiming any reliance on hedonism, Böhm-Bawerk realised that 'on the basis of conceptions of feeling *we make judgements on the intensity of future feelings of pleasure and pain'*.[39] It is a mental act of this kind that is involved in an individual's decision to invest capital and so to prefer future remunerations to present ones.

Böhm-Bawerk assumed the commensurability of desires and emotions in terms of the intensity of pleasure and pain connected with them. These sensations, however, are not the immediate basis of valuation; as for Ehrenfels, they serve to underpin our valuations only indirectly. The interpretation of subjective value in terms of marginal utility, was therefore, for the Austrians, not reducible to any laws of physiology.[40] The root of every valuation has to be seen not just in the attainment of pleasure, but in the satisfaction of purposeful desires. Valuation consists in a judgement which — in Brentanian terms — asserts that the existence (or possession) of a good recognised to be both useful and scarce (in light of the demand for goods of this kind) affords an advantage to the subject over its non-existence (or non-possession).[41]

It follows from their arguments against hedonism that the members of the first school also repudiated psychological egoism. The motives of economic valuations are not limited to purely selfish considerations of the economising subject's own individual pleasure and pain:

For the economist, and for the theory of the economic value of goods, it is a matter of complete indifference *what* people love and hate, *what* they seek and *what* they avoid, and what, with greater or lesser intensity, they try to attain or attempt to escape from.[42]

The principles of marginal utility theory are independent of the kind of considerations — whether physiological or psychological, religious or secular, altruistic or selfish — that motivate human decisions. Yet even when people act altruistically rather than selfishly they have good reasons to take marginal utility into account, that is, the marginal utility which the goods to be given away will have for their recipients. Donations and alms are given when their significance in promoting welfare, as measured by their marginal utility, is greater for the recipient than for the doner.[43]

It can be seen that Austrian economic value theory heavily relied on psychological premises, though these were hardly ever made explicit. It is the distinguishing methodological mark of the first school that it took its departure 'from within, from the mind of economic man'.[44] Yet most of its members were agreed that the correctness of their explanations of economic phenomena 'will be entirely unaffected by the interpretation of certain psychological premises'.[45] The psychology on which the first school relied was not of the experimental, but of the introspective type, its data being derived from the economist's inner experience and from certain observations shaped by the use of 'idealising assumptions'.[46] Apart from such factual considerations, it may have been this methodological position which made the 'rational' psychology of the second school seem such a fruitful model to the economists. The 'new empiricism' of the Brentanians, with its insistence that the inner perceptions of the individual are just as much data needing explanation as are his sense impressions, reflected the economists' attitude towards psychology. And even Austrian economists of a later generation — who were less inclined to make material psychological assumptions — could benefit from the philosophers' theories.[47] Mises' praxeology, for that matter, closely resembles what Brentano called 'descriptive psychology', though the strict separation of psychology and economic theory implied in Misesian methodology was less sensitive to ideas derived from the material psychology of feeling and desire of the kind developed by Meinong and Ehrenfels.[48]

6. Origins of the Marginalist Analysis of Moral Behaviour

The philosophers of the second Austrian school went about their analyses with an attempt to define value following the accepted marginalist conceptions. The centre of their considerations was the disproportionality of value and utility as it is most vividly exemplified by Adam Smith's puzzlement at the fact that water generally has a great utility and a small value (in exchange) whilst diamonds have a small utility and yet achieve a great value on the market as measured by their price. Meinong's analysis of this paradox involves the distinction between the total and the dependent or marginal utility of a commodity and is substantially in line with that of the Austrian economists: the value of a commodity is not to be identified with its total, but with its marginal utility.[49] He came to realise that value is a function both of the utility and of the scarcity of a commodity and is thus relative to the market conditions in which a person finds himself. Not only must the value and usefulness of a commodity not be identified; usefulness neither constitutes nor defines value but always presupposes it. Value, furthermore, has to be distinguished from price. In a simple purchase transaction the buyer values the desired commodity more than he does the money he has to pay for it, whereas it is the opposite for the seller. Without such a divergence in valuation no purchase could come about. The price agreed upon is then but an index of the respective valuations and in this sense presupposes them.

It is clear that his adoption of this position led Meinong to the rejection both of a definition of value in terms of sacrifices made, and of the 'labour-cost' theory.[50] Not only is the latter held to be incapable of accounting for the value of economic goods; it is also incapable of explaining the value we attach to such intangibles as friendship, love, or honour. Thus Meinong was aiming at a broader application of his ideas on value. Both he and Ehrenfels regarded their value theories as generalisations of the conceptions developed by the Austrian economists.[51] They employed ideas of opportunity cost, marginal product and complementarity derived from the writings of the marginalists. Meinong's only reproach to the economists was that they had sometimes insisted that their subject was the only field of value and had therefore not realised the necessity of extending the value concept to other fields, including ethics (and even aesthetics).[52] But he himself did not further illustrate the applicability of economic conceptions in ethics.

The credit for taking up Meinong's challenge must go to Ehrenfels, who was the first to apply the notion of marginal utility to value theory in general, including the theory of moral value. Working within what would today be called a framework of methodological individualism, he presented the philosophical foundations for a subjectivist theory of value along Mengerian lines, and for an associated theory of ethics.[53] Echoing Aristotle, with his distinction between that which is good 'for itself' and that which is good 'for the sake of something else', Ehrenfels proposed to distinguish between two classes of value: we attribute *intrinsic* value to those objects which we desire for themselves, whilst we attribute *instrumental* value to objects which we value as means of producing other valuable objects. Everything can potentially become an intrinsic value for some person, the magnitude of the intrinsic value we attribute to an object being determined by the intensity of the desire we direct at its attainment. Economic value, however, belongs to the sphere of instrumental values, since we typically do not value commodities for themselves but rather 'in the degree in which we believe intrinsic values to be dependent upon their existence'.[54]

Still Ehrenfels dissociated himself from any hedonistic interpretation of a marginal utility theory which — by regarding conduciveness to pleasure as the only criterion of intrinsic value — would introduce the notion of utility for the sole purpose of reducing instrumental value to the amount of resulting pleasure. Those value objects which are desired for their own sake, yet not for their power of contributing to individual pleasure, are not characterised by the utility they possess, but by the *avail* or *advantage* (*'Frommen'*) which they afford us. By generalising the theory of marginal utility so as to apply it also to objects whose instrumental value is not founded in their utility, Ehrenfels came to formulate the *law of marginal advantage (Gesetz des Grenzfrommens)*: 'The magnitude of the instrumental value of objects is proportional to the marginal advantage attributed to them'.[55]

Ehrenfels thus introduced a quantitative element into his account by making the value which a good (that is, in this context, a particular action) achieves on the moral 'market' contingent upon the quantity or 'supply' of such goods in relation to the demand for further goods of the same species. In the footsteps of Menger and the subjectivist economists he realised that mutual marginal adjustments of individual desires and actions in the everyday world give rise to different kinds of order in society, of which the system of moral values perceived in any given period is the most perspicuous example.

It is a consequence of this empirical approach to the study of morality that the idea of an absolute good-in-itself comes to be conceived as no more than an invalid generalisation of that which is good-under-given-conditions. This is illustrated by the fallacy of testing the value of conduct by conceiving it as universalised. But for Ehrenfels, moral conduct is good just because it is *not* general, but scarce in relation to the social demand for it. Hence the assumption of a single ideal of moral value is shown to be groundless.

The opposition to Kant's moral philosophy could not be more radical. Where Kant had exempted human beings from the realm of *value* ('*Wert*'), and had isolated man by speaking of him as possessing *dignity* ('*Würde*'), Ehrenfels considered such views as a kind of 'metaphysical-mystical dogmatism'.[56] Man was to be seen as a being subject to the laws of the natural world as well as to those of the social sphere, that is, the laws of the market. Furthermore, in contrast to Kantian moral philosophy, Ehrenfels did not make the universalisability of an action a criterion of its value or goodness. Specific norms cannot be understood as categorical but merely as hypothetical imperatives. Their validity — like that of commodity prices on a market — is dependent on a number of contingent and quantifiable factors. The only 'primary moral law' was seen in the respect which is due to the social whole itself. The notion of the duty — the corner-stone of Kantian ethics — was thus relativised to a social context, or more precisely to the particular relation between a given 'supply' of certain feeling-dispositions and that 'supply' which would be desirable for the greatest benefit of society. Which action is morally required in particular cases is therefore dependent upon which feeling-dispositions need to be added to or substracted from the actual supply in the moral market-place at any given time.

The emphasis that Ehrenfels put on acting in accordance with the greatest benefit for the social whole may make us inclined to view him as an exponent of utilitarian ethics. But while admitting to the 'basic tendency' of utilitarianism, Ehrenfels came to criticise this view on grounds of empirical inadequacy.[57] Firstly, utilitarianism had made external actions, rather than the feeling-dispositions whose presence or absence is only indicated by actions, the determinants of moral value-feelings. Secondly, it had assumed a causal nexus between the knowledge people have of the social significance of a given feeling-disposition and the value-feeling directed towards it. The high esteem that altruism achieves in our culture is certainly *dependent* on the recognition of its social usefulness; our value-feeling, however, need not have been *caused* by this recognition; it might just as well have developed spontaneously, perhaps even before we had ever realised the social usefulness of altruism.

But the most serious defect of utilitarianism consists, for Ehrenfels, in its assumption that all actions possessing universal utility are *ipso facto* highly valued (are morally good). This involves a neglect of the fact that it is utility *and* scarcity together which determine the value attributed to goods. Thus the urge to self-preservation is to a certain extent necessarily present in and useful to all societies in order that they may survive; benevolence, on the other hand, is not, in the same way, a condition for the survival of society. The latter is, nevertheless, precisely because of its relative scarcity, of higher moral value. If, however, the supply of benevolent feeling-dispositions should exceed the attention given to self-preservation, benevolence may become a danger for the survival of society: any further act of benevolence will diminish the utility of benevolence for the social whole and will consequently come to be valued as morally objectionable. Social sanctions of various kinds will take effect: blame, loss of public esteem, and juridical penalties — those phenomena which Ehrenfels called 'regulators of social behaviour' — will tend to restore a relation between egoistic and altruistic feeling-dispositions which is more beneficial to society.

More radical still, however, was Ehrenfels's divergence from the very substance of classical utilitarianism (and here reference must be made to the importance that the evolutionary theory of his time came to have for Ehrenfels's work). For the uniqueness of his contribution to value theory and to social science is not so much to be seen in his formal introduction of economic analysis into the broader field of the empirical study of moral conduct but in his attempt at combining descriptive psychology, marginalist economics and evolutionary biology into a unified theory which purported to explain not only *why* particular valuations come about but also *how* these valuations change and develop over time.

Ehrenfels was a radical defender of evolutionary theory. Not merely did he use biological analogies, he thought that the very laws of evolution and selection as formulated by Darwin were at work in the development of individual and social valuations.[58] In this respect he went far beyond the current applications of evolutionary theory to the social sphere. Two kinds of evolution had to be distinguished: (i) *cultural* evolution, that is, the mere accumulation of material, social and psychic goods; and (ii) that kind of development which consists in the *constitutive* evolution of innate physical and psychic properties of individual organisms themselves. By reducing the severity of competition among people, social institutions and benefits favour cultural evolution at the cost of constitutive development. This insight was in fact at the root of Ehrenfels's objection to socialism. In the fashion of the social Darwinists he saw a great danger in any attempt artificially to steer the workings of a market whose laws he saw as being dependent on the very constitution of human nature.

Corresponding to these two kinds of evolution, Ehrenfels distinguished between two conceptions of morality. Where *humane* morality had postulated, as its supreme maxim, the utilitarian pursuit of the greatest welfare of the greatest number, the aim of *evolutionary* morality is the biological improvement of the human race.[59] These two requirements are often at odds with each other. It is, for instance, not certain that a change in the relative proportions of good and bad conduct presently existing is at all desirable in the interest of the whole. For the effort to produce more moral conduct might so impair the vitality of the human race as to result in an anaemic and nervously overwrought society wilting away from excess of sympathy and sense of duty, a society in a state of pessimism and moral hyperaesthesia.

Ehrenfels's rejection of the 'humane-liberal ideology'[60] is not only a repudiation of utilitarianism; it also betrays a strong scepticism about the classical liberal tradition. This becomes manifest in the modification which Ehrenfels proposed of Bentham's definition of society as a mere sum of individuals: 'By *society* we understand a sum of individuals which by the way of their symbiosis biologically benefit one from another.'[61] The individualism which had been the trademark of classical liberal thought is retained as a methodological principle; but in opposition to the assumption of the arbitrariness of human desires the preservation and constitutive progress of the species is postulated as the highest intrinsic value. It was on this idea that Ehrenfels based all his proposals in the fields of eugenics and sexual reform which made him indeed one of the most radical thinkers of his time.

In spite of its partly sketchy and inconclusive character, Ehrenfels's idea of applying marginal-utility analysis to the field of ethics was original enough to have inspired an entire group of value theorists.[62] Whilst agreeing with Ehrenfels on methodological grounds, they were, however, much more sceptical with regard to any premature extension of the model into the realms of evolutionary theory. With the exception of but a few, most authors working on the basis laid down by Ehrenfels did not follow him on those social and political lines which he had himself regarded as the true aim of his theoretical endeavours.

Some of the problems left open by Ehrenfels found a more coherent and conclusive treatment in the model of market morality developed by the Italian philosopher Mario Calderoni. Inspired by the writings of Pareto and the marginalist economists and — among the philosophers — by both utilitarians and pragmatists, but also by Brentano and almost certainly by Ehrenfels himself, Calderoni attempted to work out a theory justifying an explicit identification of the categories of ethics and marginalist economics.[63] In his doctoral thesis on the positive theory of criminal law he investigated the efficacy of fines or punishments as a deterrent against actions harmful to society. The upshot of his inquiries may be expressed in the claim that the marginal efficacy of a punishment decreases rapidly and tends to diminish in proportion with the degree of its severity. There is consequently always a level up to which a punishment fulfils the expected function as a deterrent; beyond this point, however, any more severe sentence may become counter-productive. It is the duty of judicious courts to pass that optimum sentence which suffices to keep prospective law-breakers from embarking on a criminal career and which makes offenders repent and expiate their offence without depriving them of the hope of starting a new life in conformity with the rules accepted in their society.[64]

Extending this conception to ethics at large, Calderoni came to regard moral life as a 'vast market where some people, or a majority of them, make determinate demands on other people who oppose such demands with more or less resistance and claim in their turn inducements, stimuli, rewards and compensations of a determinate kind'.[65] The moral market may therefore be seen as a system of distribution by the workings of which human actions receive rewards or sanctions as expressions of their appreciation or rejection by other individuals. Moral conduct is thus constantly guided by the positive or negative reinforcements which supply the acting person with valuable information about the social appreciation of his actions.

The basic idea underlying this conception may already be found in Ehrenfels's claim 'that the socially instrumental value of feeling-dispositions is causally related to their moral valuation'.[66] For Ehrenfels, too, the phenomena of moral approval and disapproval had been the pivot of every study of morality. But Calderoni went significantly beyond Ehrenfels on two counts: firstly, by making moral approval and disapproval not only apply to feeling-dispositions but directly to actions themselves; and secondly by establishing an even closer analogy between the workings of these phenomena and the mechanisms of commodity markets.

Marginalism, however, is not simply reducible to the claim that the utility of goods varies in proportion to their quantity. It also emphasises the fact that the significance of human actions does not derive from their 'total utility' but rather that actions are motivated 'by the *additional* advantage we can attain by way of our exchange operations'.[67] Against classical utilitarianism, Calderoni argues that the utility to be considered when judging the morality of a given action is not the total utility of all actions of the same kind, but rather the marginal utility corresponding to the desirability of a determinate increase or decrease of their number or frequency. Such change will be caused or favoured by incentives or encouragements (in whatever form) to those who carry out actions required by the social whole, or by discouragements or threats to those who abstain from such actions. Moral actions are then those actions which are *useful* for a given social whole in the sense that the individuals constituting the social whole have awarded them a positive moral valuation. And such a moral valuation is then exactly like a commodity price in that it is the resultant of a manifold of individual valuations. The moral valuation of an action is the higher the more this action turns out to be both useful for society and scarce with regard to the need for an increment of actions of the given kind.

The sense of the term 'virtue' is therefore of a thoroughly economic character: a virtuous act is one that needs some incentive, and some sort of public reward for it to be produced in the required quantity. Many attitudes (such as altruism and charity) will be held to be virtuous only so long as there is no threat that they may be practised excessively. Thus the value we are inclined to put on altruistic actions is strictly dependent on the presence of a surplus of egoists in our society. From the point where any further increase of such actions no longer promotes the needs of the social whole, these attitudes will no longer be regarded as virtues, and moral value will consequently rather be put on antithetical actions. Moral values, like all species of value, are characterised by the phenomenon of diminishing marginal utility. Morality can thus become incrementally counter-productive even where it has not yet reached levels that are categorically destructive of the whole society.[68]

The workings of the moral market have their built-in injustices or — as Calderoni expresses himself — their 'disharmonies'. These derive from what Jevons had called the 'law of indifference'. It asserts that 'in the same open market, at any one moment, there cannot be two prices for the same kind of article'.[69] The price is therefore the same for all producers, independently of the costs they have incurred in the production of the goods offered for valuation. It will always be just high enough to recompense the 'marginal producers' — those who will just be motivated to produce by the incentives they are offered, but who would no longer produce if these incentives were in any way diminished. Analogously, the appreciation which is attributed to a given kind of action depends strictly on the necessity of providing incentives sufficient to induce those who are least inclined to do so to act in accordance with the needs of the social whole. Those who are more inclined and more able will therefore enjoy a higher remuneration than would normally be necessary to induce them to perform the required action: they have incurred lower 'costs' in the production of the same action and will therefore profit from what, in Marshall's terms, may be called a 'producer's surplus'.

These economic 'disharmonies' have their repercussions also in the field of moral conduct. The moral valuations — in the form of rewards or sanctions — which are attributed to certain actions can only partly have regard to the extent and intensity of the costs which these actions involve for every individual agent. Just as the market price of a commodity results from its marginal costs, so the moral appreciation achieved by an action will depend on the magnitude of the incentive needed to motivate that agent who is least inclined to perform the required action. Agents who, by their natural propensity to act morally, incur lower costs in the production of moral conduct than those 'marginal producers', will therefore receive a surplus remuneration: one which exceeds the minimum amount needed to motivate those who are least inclined to act morally.

The mechanisms of the moral market are thus often in conflict with our intuitions about retributive justice. Even if all sanctions and precepts were tailor-made to induce everyone to act morally, there would still remain a great diversity in the individual conditions of agents, a diversity which cannot be abrogated without diminishing the efficacy of these very sanctions and precepts. These disharmonies 'cannot be diminished without causing, for the individuals considered, a concordant diminution in the stimuli to act morally.'[70] The inequality characterising our appraisal of human conduct and the 'psychic profit' which some agents reap is therefore implicit in every moral generalisation and represents, in fact, a necessary condition for the workings of any prescriptive system:

> Law and morality, though they be the most perfect systems we might imagine, must necessarily contain certain lacunae of injustice and

immorality without therefore failing to represent the *maximum* of justice and morality to which we may aspire in any given situation.[71]

It seems thus that Calderoni's model may be able to provide a decidedly liberal solution of Hobbes's dilemma of market morality: where for Hobbes it had been the task of the state to enforce the law so as to guarantee the necessary minimum of moral conduct, Calderoni sees this task as something that is achieved by the unfettered workings of the moral market itself. But his theory goes far beyond Ehrenfels's biological account not only in the technical aspects of the model proposed but also in its renunciation of any primary moral law. Where Ehrenfels had jeopardised liberal individualism by postulating the preservation and constitutive progress of the human species as the highest intrinsic value, Calderoni returned to a more consistent model of market morality. He does not give any normative account of *how to act*, but — in the spirit of descriptive ethics — attempts to explain *how* and *why* particular moral rules come to be *adopted* as a result of competing individual valuations. Given the considerable diversity of human abilities, needs, and aspirations, no stronger imperative may be assumed as a *general* ethical maxim than the Platonic $τὸ$ $τὰ$ $αὐτοῦ$ $πράττειν$ — that is, the injunction to do what every individual regards as 'his own', as the task proper to his own person.[72] Nothing less than this idea seems to have been intimated also by Otto Weininger in the quotation which serves as the epigraph of the present essay.

7. The Economic Approach to Human Behaviour

The market model of moral conduct as developed by Ehrenfels and Calderoni foreshadows in many respects some of the more recent work undertaken in the social sciences. It anticipates, in fact, all those approaches to social phenomena where 'the market itself, broadly conceived, is a mechanism for the development and not merely the reflection of value judgments'.[73]

Marginalist conceptions are at the basis of sociological *exchange theory* as developed by George C. Homans and Peter Blau. Elementary social behaviour is viewed as an exchange of intangible commodities such as esteem, assistance, and approval, the function of which can be described by theoretical terms borrowed from economic theory such as 'profit', 'cost', 'value', and 'investment'. Recompensations received are subject to the law of diminishing marginal utility: as persons receive added increments, each additional unit will be of less value to them.[74]

The interpretation of social behaviour as a competition for scarce rewards (in the form of material or psychic profit, power, prestige, privileges, and so on) and the workings of the 'social regulators' of praise and blame have, of course, already been anticipated in Ehrenfels's writings. And there is much which would seem to make the Austrian theory appear an even more promising approach to the explanatory theory of human behaviour in economic terms. It is free from the simplistic and empirically untenable assumptions of behaviourism and hedonism which constitute the psychological basis of exchange theory. Contrary to Homans and Blau, Ehrenfels is not bound to interpret man's actions as being exclusively guided by the stimuli which he receives from the praise or blame attributed to his actions by his competitors in the market; the Austrian theory allows for rational actors consciously appraising means and ends, having less than perfect knowledge, and being generally engaged in finding ways to attain what they regard as their own purposes. Moreover, the models of Ehrenfels and Calderoni have a more precise scope than those of exchange theory by virtue of their explicitly taking as their *explanandum* the field of moral valuation *sui generis*.

There are a number of more recent practitioners of what has come to be called an 'economic approach to human behaviour' who have tried to explain a wide range of social phenomena — including moral valuation — using microeconomic models based on marginalist principles.[75] As an extension of mainstream classical economics this approach is wedded to Robbins's definition of economic science as 'the science which studies human behaviour as a relation between ends and scarce means which have alternative uses'.[76] But the subject-matter of the 'new political economy' is no longer limited to the scarce material commodities and services of the neoclassicists. Rather, all human behaviour is viewed 'as involving participants who maximize their utility from a stable set of preferences and accumulate an optimal amount of information and other inputs in a variety of markets'.[77] Economic analysis has thus been applied to the study of crime, fertility, education, marriage, the incidence of suicide, altruism, voting behaviour, traditions and customs, and a host of other social institutions and phenomena. Econometric methods were employed to quantify (and thus render predictable) factors such as love, altruism, philanthropy, and religious faith, which would not, *prima facie*, seem to be magnitudes admitting of quantification.

Economic models have also been designed to apply explicitly to moral behaviour. The usual position is to interpret moral norms as the predominant social reaction to 'market failures', since the validity of moral norms can significantly reduce transaction costs in exchange processes on the market. Most of all, the size of the group within which an agent consciously interacts has been claimed to be a critical determinant of his choice among alternative moral rules.[78] The insignificance of the individual agent and the absence of private, internal benefits in large groups will generally make the adoption of a moral rule irrational in terms of the expected benefits. In small groups, on the other hand, the probability of an individual having a significant impact on the rest of the group is raised and the adoption of a moral rule is more likely; any increase in group size above some determinated level will, however, again cause the individual to modify (and perhaps abandon) the moral rule and become a private maximiser. In the wake of this argument, we can see why belief in God may be said to have a reinforcing influence on the viability of morality. In the context of some critical group size, because of the externalities involved, morality may have no force in the absence of a belief in a supra-personal legislator. The assumption of God's existence, and the knowledge that any values and norms of divine origin must be assumed as absolutes, effectively reduces, though it does not entirely eliminate, the negotiation costs which are otherwise incurred in establishing norms of behaviour.[79]

These modern approaches are, however, less revolutionary than one might think. In economics, they were clearly anticipated, for instance, by Philip Wicksteed, who continually insisted that the marginal principle could not be understood in all its generality and pervasiveness if it was not applied to every sort of resource allocation. The entire life, whether of an individual or of the community, was a constant problem in the allocation of the talents and the span of years granted to men. His analysis amounted to a refinement of Aristotle's doctrine of virtue as a *mean* into the doctrine that virtue lies in a nicely adjusted margin, or that virtue requires a conscientious balancing of one's duties at the margin:[80]

Virtue, wisdom, sagacity, prudence, success, imply different schemes of values, but they all submit to the law, formulated by Aristotle with reference to virtue . . ., for they all consist in combining factors $\kappa\alpha\tau$' $\dot{o}\rho\vartheta\grave{o}\nu$ $\lambda\acute{o}\gamma o\nu$, *in the right proportion*, as fixed by that distribution of resources which establishes the equilibrium of the differential significances in securing the object contemplated, whether that object be tranquility of mind, the indulgence of an overmastering passion or affection, the command of things and services in the circle of exchange, or a combination of all these, or of any other conceivable factor of life.[81]

In its picture of morality as a constant marginal adjustment of personal objectives, this conception is even closer to the ideas of Ehrenfels and Calderoni than to those of contemporary microeconomic theorists. But it shares with the economic approach to human behaviour the important insight that social values in general are incrementally variable: neither safety, diversity, rational articulation, democracy, nor morality is categorically a 'good thing' to have more of without limits. All are subject to diminishing returns, and ultimately negative returns. To have no morality at all, would imply an over-prevalence of force, whilst, on the other hand, unbounded morality would become irksome to individual autonomy. A modicum of decency and reserve greatly reduces the incessant costs accruing for individuals from the necessity of protecting life and belongings from every other human being.[82] The consequence of these ideas — the contingency of our moral rules — is aptly described in Calderoni's words:

> With the increment of 'virtuous' actions, they tend to diminish in value, as, analogously, the diminution of 'vicious' actions tends to make us less disposed to venture to diminish them any further; so that we shall always be able to conceive of a threshold, of course dependent on individual circumstances, beyond which a 'vice' becomes a 'virtue' and a 'virtue' turns into a 'vice'.[83]

Both Calderoni and the 'new economists' show that there is a marginal level up to which the maximisation of one's own personal utility may be productive, beyond which, however, any further purely egoistic acts would no longer increase but rather diminish the total welfare of the individual. This, then, is the point where it is rational — because in one's own interest — to adopt a moral rule.

Though there may be striking similarities in the technical aspects of their models and in some of their analyses — such as Ehrenfels's anticipation of many current attempts to discover economic analogies in the field of sociobiology[84] — the philosophical and psychological framework in which the Austrians move stands in marked opposition to that of the more recent economic approach to human behaviour. Most expositions of the latter are still beset with some of the same shortcomings that were characteristic of classical utilitarianism (compare section 2 above). And the arguments which present-day economists working in the Austrian tradition advance against the methodology of the 'new economists' — particularly against the Chicago and the Virginia schools — bear a remarkable resemblance to the standpoint from which members of the first Austrian school criticised the psychology and anthropology of Benthamite and Jevonsian hedonism.

Where Bentham had viewed man as a pleasure machine, neoclassical economists see him as a maximiser of his own utility, motivated by a stable set of preferences. The concept of choice or selection is not explicitly denied, of course, but it is usually seen merely as a 'softly' determined act of the human will; the will does act, but only as conditioned by its history. This theory excludes already at the outset the likelihood of any undesirable situations arising out of human errors of judgement and thereby also the very need for improvement or correction. It denies market participants the need as well as the scope for learning from experience. This not only deprives neoclassical microeconomic theory of much of its informative content; it also renders redundant the processes of competition, speculation and entrepreneurship commonly associated with human imperfections in an uncertain world. Humans are deprived of the capacity for spontaneous action and are made to appear, in Adam Smith's words, like 'pieces on a chessboard',[85] reacting creatures who are incapable of having independent aims, unable deliberately to scrutinise their positions and to alter their expectations and actions accordingly. And under these circumstances their relationships positively invite quantification and objectification in the same manner as do relationships in the physical world, while the market is made to assume the technical computational role of an allocative mechanism. Its efficient operation is then judged in terms of the optimality of its allocative pattern at a so-called equilibrium point.

The pivotal problem in this approach lies in the assumption of given wants or ends. The moral problem of how to live is then reduced to an economic one, and ethics is supplanted by a sort of 'higher economics'.[86] And the specific problem confronting the extension of economics into non-traditional areas (such as interpersonal relationships) is that human relationships are a web of interactive processes in which the 'goods' (or 'wants' or 'values') themselves are as much a part of the outcomes as the units consumed. More importantly, the 'goods' are never quite the same to different people, and much of our uniquely human existence would be lost if they were.

For the exponents of the economic approach to human behaviour, man is confronted with the ever-present conflict between ends and scarce means. For Robbins this constitutes the 'economic problem' which man must *overcome* and which has recognisable (calculable) *solutions*. To the Austrians, on the other hand, what we have here is not a problem with a calculable solution, but the very stuff of meaningful human existence. Seen from the Austrian perspective, pursuit of a 'less unsatisfactory' state of affairs is co-terminous with life itself.

Underlying the divergences between mainstream neoclassical economics — which finds one of its applications in the economic approach to human behaviour — and the Austrian tradition, is a different conception of the market. For Austrian economists, both of the first school and of today, man and his actions stand at the centre of economic theory. Markets are therefore not simply mechanisms which lead to equilibrium given an efficient allocation of resources. They are rather conceived of as a *spontaneous order* that emerges as people, attempting to pursue their own interests, adjust and readjust their own actions to the actions of others. Already Menger had interpreted price-formation as a struggle, a bargaining process between fairly wide limits within which any price is advantageous to both bargaining parties, bargaining power depending on the knowledge, skill, and insight of the parties involved.[87] The existence of a market is therefore — not only conceptually but also in real terms — dependent on the existence of competing entrepreneurs whose decision making and remaking determine the course of the movement of prices.[88]

Obviously, within the Austrian framework both market participants and the market which they actuate are placed within a perspective altogether different from that within orthodox neoclassical economics. Consequently, the roles assigned to them also differ. In the Austrian theory, human beings do not merely react to a given situation; they can and do act purposefully and they are capable of learning from experience, revising their plans accordingly. It is this continuous change in human entrepreneurial action which sets the market in motion, and yields the market process. Under these circumstances the market can no longer be viewed, as it is within the neoclassical framework, as a mechanical device acting in accordance with some automatic forces. It must be seen as a spontaneous system actuated by human valuations, knowledge and expectations as manifested in human actions. The role of the market here encompasses the gathering and transmitting of knowledge, the coordinating of disparate plans and the correcting of errors of judgement. And confidence in the market's ability to act as a self-regulating device implies confidence in people's abilities to learn from experience and to take advantage of opportunities for improvement whenever and wherever these happen to occur. It is this self-interest of market participants which makes markets self-regulating systems.[89]

It has sometimes been noticed by exponents of the economic approach to human behaviour that an explanatory theory of morality must in fact develop into a theory of moral entrepreneurship.[90] But the anthropology and the market theory presupposed by the neoclassicists would seem to vitiate any serious attempt to produce a comprehensive, consistent and explanatory theory of moral *agents*, that is, moral *entrepreneurs*. And on the basis of our previous discussion it should appear that the Austrian framework is much likelier to provide an adequate instrument for elaborating an economic theory of moral conduct.

8. Moral Entrepreneurship

Like market conceptions in general, market models of moral conduct admit of various interpretations. And just as the philosophical views of Ehrenfels and — to a lesser extent — of Calderoni are rooted in the Austrian philosophical tradition emanating from Brentano, so their conceptions of morality bear definite similarities to the Austrian economists' conception of the market as a *dynamic process*. It is Friedrich von Hayek — who in this respect deviates considerably from the mainstream neoclassical approach — who has done most to capture what is essential to this conception. The market, as Hayek conceives it, is a social institution that is remarkably effective in discovering economic error, that is, in discovering where existing resource allocation falls short of optimality. The true force of the invisible hand lies in the market's effectiveness not only in detecting error but also in creating inducements that will generate patterns of behaviour which are, relatively speaking, less erroneous. The market process is, in Hayek's words, a 'discovery procedure' through which the participants in the market acquire information.[91]

In a similar way, individuals, for Calderoni, acquire information about the social value attributed to their actions (i.e. the 'price' these actions achieve) only by offering these actions on the moral market. It is not that market prices (or, by analogy, moral rules) spontaneously offer already developed 'signals' which would suffice to coordinate a multitude of independent decisions; this fantastic state of affairs could occur only in a paradise world of realised equilibrium. It is, rather, in disequilibrium — when prices do *not* offer the correct signals — that agents are offered incentives, in the form of profits, to notice and correct the discrepancies which exist. As the Austrian economists claimed of asset markets, so the moral market, too, is an ongoing dynamic process. No two agents are likely to have the same preferences at the same time, nor the same knowledge about available possibilities, nor the same expectations about the future. Likewise, they are unlikely to have the same costs, even when producing the same outputs. It is the totality of such divergencies — economic and moral 'disharmonies' in Calderoni's sense — which constitutes a market, whether a market for commodities and assets or a market for moral rules and actions.

Moral rules, according to this conception, are totally dependent upon the coordination — or lack of coordination — of individual morally relevant decisions and actions. But this is not to say that the moral market, any more than an asset market, is an entirely random, anarchistic or arbitrary process. There are *laws* governing the changes of morality over time, laws which were in principle recognised by Ehrenfels ('*Gesetze der Wertveränderung*'), though in the context of a theory which was certainly distorted by evolutionistic and teleological assumptions. It is true that such laws are not natural phenomena, like the weather, but they are certainly not arbitrary. Hume described the rules of justice that authorise the possession and transfer of property as 'artificial', but he said that it would be perfectly correct to call them fundamental 'laws of nature' in that every society must have some rules of this type, rules which cannot be cast aside or substantially altered at will. And because there are also laws in the more general moral sphere we are not able — contrary to Bentham — to adopt any arbitrary moral rule *ad libitum*, even where the 'quantity of pleasure' would be equal. One important insight fundamental to the discovery of such laws is that the moral rules existing at any one period always reflect the needs and values of a time *prior* to that period.[92] Every action presently offered on the moral market changes the relation of supply and demand, and thereby both actuates the market and transforms it into something new.

The ethical problem of how to live, how to behave, may now come to be seen as primarily a problem of information. The moral market is an information-yielding system. Because every human individual, at any given time, has his own set of values, preferences and needs, the ends aimed at in the moral market cannot possibly be given in their totality to any one participant; they must necessarily be dispersed among all participants, as must also the means for their determination and coordination.[93] The harmony and order sought after in the moral sphere, which is too often conceived, for example by moral philosophers and welfare economists, as something absolute and extraneous, is thereby seen from the Austrian perspective as something determined *endogenously*, through the purposeful, spontaneous actions and interactions of innumerable individual decision-makers. The Austrians are in consequence better able to do justice to the empirical fact that there exist divergent patterns of moral rules. These divergent patterns are exactly analogous to divergent prices in a commodity or asset market. Both are indications of imperfect communication; both imply the existence of situations offering scope for profitable activities for the discerning entrepreneur.[94]

Every individual is in a certain sense a moral entrepreneur, is someone who manifests at least some degree of alertness in all his actions. The individual entrepreneur must offer actions on the moral market in order to discover how they are being valued by others. This is true not least in relation to the moral deviant, and above all in relation to the criminal. The latter has indeed an important role for the remaining market participants, since the way he is handled in the moral market is a particularly clear signal as to the value and (opportunity) costs of given types of actions. If there were no burglars, no murderers, and so on, in a given society, then the members of that society would not *know* certain rules (*thou shalt not steal*, *thou shalt not kill*). It seems, therefore, that a marginal supply of deviant behaviour tends to stabilise, rather than destabilise, the moral codes accepted by the larger group.

A special significance is awarded in a similar way to the phenomenon of experimentation with moral rules of the kind which is illustrated by the development of new life-styles amongst the fringes of society. Again, the role of such fringe groups as moral entrepreneurs is clear: some of them may thrive, and make a moral profit, some may dwindle and decay (make a moral loss). But whatever success on the market they turn out to have, their very introduction of a greater diversity would already seem to further the coherence of a group.

Liberals do not, of course, deny that a society's existence depends upon some agreement on moral rules. But they insist that this agreement is compatible with a plurality of moral ideals and that there is no evidence that a society will collapse or disintegrate if people experiment with different moral practices. It is the market that imparts to an aggregate of subjective, divergent valuations what we might call a measure of 'social objectivity' by striking a balance between them.

These remarks may show, perhaps, how the market model of morality on Austrian lines may solve some of the problems left open by classical and neoclassical 'utilitarian' market models. The Austrian approach is not based on any assumptions of hedonism, but only on assumptions about preference and choice. It seeks to explain how moral rules come about and why, in given conditions, particular actions are morally required or morally disparaged.

The theory is further a uniquely *human* theory: only human beings *act* and *choose*. It thus stands in marked contrast to those attempts which have been made to extend economic theory — and especially the ideas of marginal-utility theory — to organisms in general by pointing out analogies to the concept of scarcity in economics, for example in the availability of nutrients as a constraint affecting the growth and reproduction of plants, or to time and budget size constraints among animals.[95] Ethics has even been defined *tout court* as 'the study of the ways to allocate scarce resources', and this definition is supposed to 'serve equally well for economics and ecology — which indicates the essential identity of these two disciplines'.[96]

Such conceptions not only overlook the fact that morality as the object of ethics is not reducible to physical and inheritable properties of individuals but rather constitutes a complex social structure. They also eschew the entrepreneurial element, that is, precisely what is crucial to economic action in the Austrian view; the spontaneity of actions is filtered out by all such analogies, to the detriment of the understanding of 'economics' which results.

These are loose remarks only. Suffice it to say, in conclusion, that they hardly begin to do justice to the richness and diversity of implications of the Austrian view of morality as a self-regulating mechanism, as a *market* in precisely the Austrian sense, a view which captures the social nature of morality but which is yet perfectly consistent with the most fundamental tenets of individualism.

Notes

1. Weininger (1980, p. 57).
2. Hobbes (1968, p. 151).
3. Hobbes (1968, p. 208).

176 Markets and Morality

4. Hobbes (1968, p. 152).
5. See also Macpherson (1962, Chapter II; 1973, Chapters X, XIV).
6. Compare Bentham (1970, p. 11).
7. Halévy (1928, p. 478).
8. See Hayek (1976, pp. 17–23).
9. See Aiken (1948, pp. 42–69).
10. See Sweezy (1934).
11. See the essay by Fabian and Simons in this volume.
12. Compare Brentano (1969). On Brentano's value theory, see also Chisholm's chapter in this volume.
13. Compare Kauder (1962, p. 4; 1965, p. 89). See also section 6 of the paper by Fabian and Simons in this volume.
14. Compare Menger (1950, p. 115).
15. See Böhm-Bawerk (1959, vol. II, p. 432); Sax (1930, pp. 362ff); Engländer (1935, p. 515).
16. Compare Wieser (1927, p. 3).
17. On this controversy, see Mackenzie (1895); Orestano (1907, pp. 28–86); Laird (1929, pp. 136–40); Eaton (1930, Chapter VIII); and the Fabian and Simons paper in this volume.
18. Compare Meinong (1923, p. 162).
19. Ehrenfels (1893, p. 89).
20. Compare Ehrenfels (1897a, p. 65).
21. Ehrenfels (1897, p. 53). Compare also Laird (1929, pp. 122–5).
22. See Ribot (1905, p. 41): 'The value of things being their aptitude to produce a desire and this value being proportional to the strength of the desire, one has to admit that the concept of value is essentially, not absolutely, subjective.'
23. See Meinong (1894, p. 15; 1923, p. 41).
24. Meinong (1894, p. 97).
25. Compare also Sidgwick (1962, pp. 42–51).
26. Compare e.g., Rashdall (1907, pp. 15, 28, 40).
27. Ehrenfels (1897a, p. 2).
28. Hobbes (1968, p. 160).
29. Ehrenfels (1897a, p. 41). Compare the discussion in Smith (1985).
30. Compare Urban (1909, pp. 36, 85–9); Eaton (1930, pp. 131–4). For a more detailed account of Ehrenfels's position on hedonism, see Grassl (1982b, section II).
31. See Ehrenfels (1897a, pp. 24–35, 42); Kraus (1901, pp. 4, 18); Kreibig (1902, pp. 121–8; Meinong (1923, pp. 42ff, 96–103). Compare also Eaton (1930, Chapter X).
32. Böhm-Bawerk (1959, vol. II, p. 121).
33. See Menger (1950, pp. 55ff).
34. Menger (1950, p. 142).
35. On the anticipation of marginalist ideas in the works of Bentham, Bernoulli, and Gossen, see Kraus (1901, Chapter IV).
36. Böhm-Bawerk (1959, vol. II, p. 185; 1962, pp. 45ff).
37. Compare Böhm-Bawerk (1959, vol. II, p. 190).
38. Compare Böhm-Bawerk (1959, vol. III, pp. 135, 141). According to Kraus, his own correspondence with Menger had contributed to the position which the latter came to take on hedonism: see Kraus (1937, p. 383).
39. Böhm-Bawerk (1959, vol. III, p. 140).
40. The fact that the law of marginal utility had the same mathematical structure as the Weber–Fechner law in physiological psychology has led some economists to argue that the former was merely a special case of the latter. Against this assumption, see, e.g., Wieser (1927, p. 3).
41. See also Kraus (1901, Chapter IX); Ruppe-Streissler (1962, pp. 386–92).

42. Böhm-Bawerk (1959, vol. II, p. 188). See also Mises (1931).
43. Compare Böhm-Bawerk (1959, p. 424n.).
44. Wieser (1927, p. 3).
45. Böhm-Bawerk (1959, vol. II, p. 184). Compare also Wieser (1927, p. 3).
46. See also section 1 of the paper by Smith in this volume.
47. It is widely known that Meinong attended Menger's lectures on economics and that Ehrenfels was in close contact with Wieser during their time in Prague. On the importance which Brentanian philosophy (particularly through Marty) came to have for the Prague economist Oskar Engländer, see Kauder (1965, pp. 131ff). For a further exposition of the intellectual contacts between the first and the second Austrian school, see also Grassl (1982b).
48. On some of the parallels between praxeology and descriptive psychology, see the paper by Chisholm in this volume.
49. Compare Meinong (1894, pp. 9ff; 1923, pp. 20f).
50. Compare Meinong (1923, pp. 30ff).
51. Compare Meinong (1923, p. 4, n. 2); Ehrenfels (1893, p. 89; 1897a, pp. viii, 78 n.).
52. Meinong (1894, p. 5; 1923, p. 10).
53. A third volume of the *System der Werttheorie* was to have contained an account of the logical and psychological foundations of the theory of economic value, but it was never completed. See Ehrenfels (1897a, p. xiv).
54. Ehrenfels (1893, p. 95). With reference to this passage, Böhm-Bawerk made the distinction between intrinsic and instrumental value basic to his analysis of economic value, insisting that 'we do not prize and cherish goods for their own sake, but only because we expect them to promote our ends'. Böhm-Bawerk (1959, vol. II, p. 121).
55. Ehrenfels (1893, p. 99).
56. Ehrenfels (1897a, p. xiif).
57. See Ehrenfels (1897a, p. 36ff; 1897b). Compare also Eaton (1930, pp. 305ff).
58. See Ehrenfels (1903); compare also Grassl (1982b, section IV).
59. See Ehrenfels (1898, p. 80).
60. Ehrenfels (1903, p. 5).
61. Ehrenfels (1907, p. 15).
62. See, for example, Naumann (1893); Krüger (1898); Kreibig (1902); Orestano (1907); Urban (1909); Schwoner (1922); Perry (1926); Eaton (1930).
63. On Calderoni's use of the ideas of marginalist economics, see Grassl (1982a). On his ties with philosophers of the Brentano School, particularly on the possible influence of Ehrenfels' writings, see Grassl (forthcoming).
64. See Calderoni (1901).
65. Calderoni (1906, p. 294); see also Toraldo di Francia (1983, Chapter 3).
66. Ehrenfels (1894, p. 87).
67. Calderoni (1906, p. 299).
68. See also Sowell (1980, p. 108).
69. Jevons (1970, p. 137).
70. Calderoni (1906, p. 326).
71. Calderoni (1906, p. 322).
72. Compare Calderoni (1906).
73. Friedman (1967, p. 85).
74. See Homans (1961); Blau (1964); compare also the overview in Chadwick-Jones (1976, particularly chapters VII, VIII and XI).
75. See, e.g., Becker (1976); McKenzie and Tullock (1978); Radnitzky (1985).
76. Robbins (1932, p. 16).
77. Becker (1976, p. 14).
78. See Buchanan (1965).

178   *Markets and Morality*

79. See McKenzie (1977, section III).
80. For a marginalist interpretation of Aristotelian ethics, see Macfie (1936, p. 50).
81. Wicksteed (1933, vol. II, p. 776).
82. See also Sowell (1980, pp. 107ff).
83. Calderoni (1906, p. 316); see also Calderoni (1901, p. 138).
84. See Grassl (1982b, p. 19).
85. Smith (1959, p. 207).
86. See also Koslowski (1984, Chapter 4).
87. On the role of the entrepreneur in Menger's system, see Kirzner (1979, pp. 53–75).
88. On the nature of such real dependence relations, see the paper by Smith in this volume and the references there given.
89. See Mises (1949, pp. 258ff).
90. See McKenzie (1977, p. 221). In the sociology of deviant behaviour, initiation of novel patterns of rules has also been described as a case of 'moral entrepreneurship' (see Becker (1963, Chapter 8)). It is to be noted, however, that this sociological concept does not fully overlap with the economic concept of entrepreneurship and that the Austrian market theory of moral entrepreneurship furthermore seems to have a more profound explanatory power.
91. See Hayek (1937; 1978). Compare also Kirzner (1979, Chapter II).
92. See Ehrenfels (1898, p. 84).
93. Compare Hayek (1937).
94. Compare Kirzner (1973, pp.13ff).
95. See the papers collected in Staddon (1980).
96. Hardin (1980, p. 3).

Bibliography

Aiken, H.D. (1948). *Hume's Moral and Political Philosophy*, New York: Hafner.
Becker, G.S. (1976). *The Economic Approach to Human Behavior*, Chicago and London: University of Chicago Press.
Becker, H.S. (1963). *Outsiders: Studies in the Sociology of Deviance*, Glencoe: The Free Press.
Bentham, J. (1970). *An Introduction to the Principles of Morals and Legislation*, ed. by J.H. Burns and H.L.A. Hart, London: Athlone Press.
Blau, P. (1964). *Exchange and Power in Social Life*, New York: Wiley.
Böhm-Bawerk, E. von (1959). *Capital and Interest*, vol. II, *Positive Theory of Capital*; vol. III, *Further Essays on Capital and Interest*, South Holland: Libertarian Press.
Böhm-Bawerk, E. von (1962). 'Whether Legal Rights and Relationships are Economic Goods' in *Shorter Classics of Eugen von Böhm-Bawerk*, vol. 1, South Holland: Libertarian Press, 30-138.
Brentano, F. (1969). *The Origin of our Knowledge of Right and Wrong*, ed. O. Kraus, English translation by R.M. Chisholm and E.H. Schneewind, London: Routledge and Kegan Paul.
Buchanan, J.M. (1969). 'Ethical Rules, Expected Values, and Large Numbers', *Ethics*, 76, 1–13.
Calderoni, M. (1901). *I postulati della scienza positiva ed il diritto penale*, Florence: Ramella.
Calderoni, M. (1906). *Disarmonie economiche e disarmonie morali. Saggio di un'estensione della teoria Ricardiana della rendita*, Florence: Lumachi.

Chadwick-Jones, J.K. (1976). *Social Exchange Theory*, London and New York: Academic Press.

Eaton, H.O. (1930). *The Austrian Philosophy of Value*, Norman: University of Oklahoma Press.

Ehrenfels, C. von (1893–4). 'Werttheorie und Ethik', *Vierteljahrsschrift für wissenschaftliche Philosophie*, *17* (1893), 76–110, 200–266, 321–63, 413–75; *18* (1894), 77–97; repr. in Ehrenfels (1982).

Ehrenfels, C. von (1897a). *System der Werttheorie*, vol. I: *Allgemeine Werttheorie. Psychologie des Begehrens*, Leipzig: Reisland; repr. in Ehrenfels (1982).

Ehrenfels, C. von (1897b). 'Über ethische Wertgefühle', *Dritter Internationaler Kongress für Psychologie in München, 1896*, Munich: Lehmann, 231–4; repr. in Ehrenfels (1982).

Ehrenfels, C. von (1898). *System der Werttheorie*, vol. II: *Grundzüge einer Ethik*, Leipzig: Reisland; repr. in Ehrenfels (1982).

Ehrenfels, C. von (1903). 'Entwicklungsmoral', *Politisch-anthropologische Revue*, *2*, 214–26.

Ehrenfels, C. von (1907). *Grundbegriffe der Ethik*, Wiesbaden: Bergmann.

Ehrenfels, C. von (1982). *Philosophische Schriften*, vol. I: *Werttheorie*, ed. R. Fabian, Munich: Philosophia, 1982.

Engländer, O. (1935). 'Das Seelische und die Volkswirtschaftslehre', *Jahrbücher für Nationalökonomie*, *142*, 513–40.

Fabian, R. (ed.) (1985). *Christian von Ehrenfels. Leben und Werk*, Amsterdam: Rodopi.

Friedman, M. (1967). 'Value Judgments in Economics' in S. Hook (ed.), *Human Values and Economic Policy*, New York: New York University Press, 85–93.

Grassl, W. (1981). 'Grenznutzenlehre und Ethik' in E. Morscher and R. Stranzinger (eds), *Ethik. Grundlagen, Probleme und Anwendungen*, Akten des V. Internationalen Wittgenstein-Symposiums, Kirchberg/Wechsel, Vienna: Hölder-Pichler-Tempsky, 219–22.

Grassl, W. (1982a). 'La morale come mercato: utilitarismo e marginalismo nella filosofia morale di Mario Calderoni' in R. Faucci (ed.), *Gli italiani e Bentham. Dalla 'felicità pubblica' all'economia del benessere*, vol. 2, Rome: Franco Angeli, 29–41.

Grassl, W. (1982b). 'Christian von Ehrenfels als Werttheoretiker' in Ehrenfels (1982), 1–22.

Grassl, W. (forthcoming). 'Etica ed economia. La matrice austriaca del pensiero di Mario Calderoni'.

Halévy, E. (1928). *The Growth of Philosophic Radicalism*, London: Faber and Faber.

Hardin, B. (1980). *Promethean Ethics. Living with Death, Competition, and Triage*, Seattle and London: University of Washington Press.

Hayek F.A. von (1937). 'Economics and Knowledge', *Economica*, n. 5, 4, 33-54.

Hayek, F.A. von (1976). *Law, Legislation and Liberty*, vol. 2: *The Mirage of Social Justice*, London: Routledge & Kegan Paul.

Hayek, F.A. von (1978). 'Competition as a Discovery Procedure', as repr. in *New Studies in Philosophy, Politics, Economics and the History of Ideas*, London: Routledge & Kegan Paul, 179–90.

Hobbes, T. (1968). *Leviathan*, ed. C.B. Macpherson, Harmondsworth: Penguin.

Homans G.C. (1961). *Social Behaviour: Its Elementary Forms*, New York: Harcourt Brace and World.

Jevons, W.S. (1970). *The Theory of Political Economy*, 4th edn, Harmondsworth: Penguin.

Kauder, E. (1962). 'Aus Mengers nachgelassenen Papieren', *Weltwirtschaftliches Archiv*, *89*, 1–28.

Kauder, E. (1965). *A History of Marginal Utility Theory*, Princeton: Princeton

University Press.

Kirzner, I.M. (1973).   *Competition and Entrepreneurship*, Chicago: University of Chicago Press.

Kirzner, I.M. (1978).   *Perception, Opportunity and Profit: Studies in the Theory of Entrepreneurship*, Chicago: University of Chicago Press.

Koslowski, P. (1984).   *Ethik des Kapitalismus*, 2nd edn, Tübingen: Mohr.

Kraus, O. (1901).   *Zur Theorie des Wertes. Eine Bentham-Studie*, Halle: Niemeyer.

Kraus, O. (1937).   *Die Werttheorien. Geschichte und Kritik*, Brünn: Rohrer.

Kreibig, J.C. (1902).   *Psychologische Grundlegung eines Systems der Wert-Theorie*, Wien: Hölder.

Krüger, F. (1898).   *Der Begriff des absoluten Wertvollen als Grundbegriff der Moralphilosophie*, Leipzig: Teubner.

Laird, J. (1929).   *The Theory of Value*, Cambridge: Cambridge University Press.

Macfie, A.L. (1936).   *An Essay on Economy and Value*, London: Macmillan.

Mackenzie, J.S. (1895).   'Notes on the Theory of Value', *Mind*, new series, *4*, 425–49.

MacKenzie, R.B. and Tullock, G. (1978).   *The New World of Economics*, Homewood: Irwin.

Macpherson, C.B. (1962).   *The Political Theory of Possessive Individualism: Hobbes to Locke*, Oxford: Oxford University Press.

Macpherson, C.B. (1971).   'The Economic Dimensions of Ethical Behavior', *Ethics*, *87*, 208–21.

Meinong, A. von (1894).   *Psychologisch-ethische Untersuchungen zur Werth-Theorie*, Graz: Leuschner and Lubensky.

Meinong, A. von (1923).   *Zur Grundlegung der allgemeinen Werttheorie*, ed. E. Mally, Graz: Leuschner and Lubensky.

Menger, C. (1950).   *Principles of Economics*, Glencoe, Ill.: Free Press.

Mises, L. von (1931).   'Vom Weg der subjektivistischen Wertlehre' in L. von Mises and A. Spiethoff (eds), *Probleme der Wertlehre*, Part I, Munich and Leipzig: Duncker and Humblot, 73–93.

Mises, L. von (1949).   *Human Action. A Treatise on Economics*, New Haven: Yale University Press.

Naumann, M. (1893).   'Die Lehre vom Wert', dissertation, Heidelberg.

Orestano, F. (1907).   *I valori umani*, Turin: Bocca.

Perry, R.B. (1926).   *General Theory of Value: Its Meaning and Basic Principles Construed in Terms of Interest*, New York: Longmans.

Radnitzky, G. (ed.) (1985).   *General Economy: The Economic Approach Applied to Areas Outside the Traditional Areas of Economics*, New York: Paragon House.

Rashdall, H. (1907).   *The Theory of Good and Evil. A Treatise on Moral Philosophy*, vol. I, Oxford: Oxford University Press.

Ribot, T. (1905).   *La logique des sentiments*, Paris: Alcan.

Robbins, L. (1932).   *An Essay on the Nature and Significance of Economic Science*, London: Macmillan.

Ruppe-Streissler, M. (1962) 'Zum Begriff der Wertung in der älteren österreichischen Grenznutzenlehre', *Zeitschrift für Nationalökonomie, 22*, 377–419.

Sax, E. (1930).   'Bedürfnis, Wert und Vorzug', *Zeitschrift für Nationalökonomie, 1*, 256–67.

Schwoner, A. (1922).   *Wertphilosophie eines Outsiders*, Leipzig: Hirzel.

Sidgwick, H. (1962).   *The Methods of Ethics*, London: Macmillan.

Smith, A. (1959).   *The Theory of Moral Sentiments*, 6th ed., London: Branbury, Evans and Co.

Smith, B. (1985).   'The Theory of Value of Christian von Ehrenfels' in Fabian (1985, 150–71).

Sowell, T. (1980).   *Knowledge and Decisions*, New York: Basic Books.

Staddon, J.E.R. (ed.) (1980). *Limits to Action. The Allocation of Individual Behavior*, New York and London: Academic Press.

Sweezy, A.R. (1934). 'The Interpretation of Subjective Value Theory in the Writings of the Austrian Economists', *Review of Economic Studies, 1*, 176–85.

Toraldo di Francia, M. (1983). *Pragmatismo e disarmonie sociali. Il pensiero di Mario Calderoni*, Milan: Franco Angeli.

Urban, W.M. (1909). *Valuation. Its Nature and Laws*, London: Sonnenschein, New York: Macmillan.

Weininger, O. (1980). *Über die letzten Dinge*, Vienna: Braumüller, 1904, as repr. Munich: Matthes and Seitz.

Wieser, F. von (1927). *Social Economics*, New York: Adelphi.

Wicksteed, P.H. (1933). *The Common Sense of Political Economy*, 2 vols, London: Routledge & Kegan Paul.

5 BRENTANO ON PREFERENCE, DESIRE AND INTRINSIC VALUE

Roderick M. Chisholm

This essay will be divided into three parts. First I shall set forth certain general features of Brentano's theory of value. Secondly, I shall discuss one of these features in detail, namely, Brentano's theory of want and desire and his distinction between what he calls 'love' and 'hate'. Finally, I shall say something about the relation of Brentano's theory to present-day Austrian economics.[1]

1. General Features

What was Brentano's theory of value? We can describe it by reference to three assumptions.

First, Brentano assumes that there are two dimensions of emotion — which he calls 'love' and 'hate', respectively. Other possible pairs of terms are 'pro-emotion' and 'anti-emotion'; 'inclination' and 'disinclination'; and 'positive interest' and 'negative interest'. Wanting and desiring constitute one type of love, or pro-emotion.

Brentano assumes, secondly, that we can distinguish between desiring a thing 'for its own sake' ('in and for itself' or 'as an end in itself') and desiring it is a means to some other end.

Thirdly, he assumes that emotive phenomena, like intellectual phenomena, may be divided into those that are correct and those that are not correct. Thus if you desire someone's well-being as an end in itself, then your emotion is correct. But if you desire someone's pain as an end in itself, then your emotion is not correct. These points are as obvious to him as it is to us that, if you believe that seven and five are twelve, then your belief is correct, and that, if you believe that seven and five are thirteen, then your belief is incorrect.

Given these three assumptions he can now define *intrinsic good* and *intrinsic evil*. To say of a thing that it is intrinsically good is to say that it is correct to love that thing as an end — in and for itself. And to say of a thing that it is intrinsically bad is to say that it is correct to hate that thing as an end. And to say of one thing that it is *intrinsically better* than another thing is to say that it is correct to prefer the first thing as an end to the second thing as an end. Pleasure, knowledge and the exercise of virtue are examples of things that are intrinsically good. Pain and the exercise of vice are examples of things that are intrinsically bad. Some goods are intrinsically better than other goods, just as some evils are intrinsically better than other evils. For example, pleasure in the good is better than pleasure in the bad, and displeasure in the bad is better than displeasure in the good.

This theory of value provides the basis for Brentano's ethics. There are four marks that will serve to distinguish Brentano's theory of value. First of all, it is a theory of *intrinsic* value. Hence it is a theory about that which is 'good in itself' or 'good for its own sake', or 'good as an end', rather than a theory about that which is 'good as a means', or useful, or 'instrumentally good'. And analogously for that which is evil and that which is indifferent as well as for those things that are preferable to other things. Brentano's theory is not a theory about instrumental value, or about utility or market value. But, Brentano would insist, one of the axioms of 'praxeology' is this: if anything is valued as a *means* to some other thing, then something is valued *in itself* — that is to say, if there is something that is valued as a *means* to something else, then something is valued which is *not* valued merely as a means to some other thing.

Secondly, Brentano's theory is an *objective* theory. It presupposes that our evaluations are like our judgements or beliefs in being either *correct* or *incorrect*. Thus if I judge or believe with respect to a certain man that he is a thief and if you believe that he is not a thief, then at least one of us is wrong. At least one of us has made a judgement that is incorrect. Brentano would say, analogously, that if I value a certain thing in and for itself, and you take that same thing to be bad in itself, then, once again, at least one of us is wrong. (Brentano's *Vom Ursprung sittlicher Erkenntnis* was presented before the Wiener Juristische Gesellschaft in 1889. Baron von Hye, the *Obmann* of the society, had invited Brentano to defend a point of view that would contrast with the relativistic theory that had been presented earlier by R. von Ihering. He could not have found a better person for this than Brentano.)

One might ask whether *any* instance of love or hate could be said to be correct or incorrect. How could one *defend* the doctrine that there are correct emotions and incorrect emotions? Here is a fundamental point with respect to which the views of Brentano and his followers are to be distinguished from those that have been associated with the Vienna Circle and subsequent logical empiricism. To understand Brentano's attitude towards this question about emotive phenomena, we should consider its analogue in application to intellectual phenomena. What if one were to ask whether there are any *judgements* or *beliefs* that could be said to be correct or incorrect, to be true or false? It is not difficult to see that, if there is a procedure by means of which we can defend the doctrine that there are true or correct judgements and false or incorrect judgements, then there will be an analogous procedure by means of which we can defend the doctrine that there are correct emotions and incorrect emotions.[2]

Thirdly, Brentano's theory of intrinsic value is pluralistic. In this respect it distinguishes itself from the theories of Bentham, Mill and Sidgwick who had held that pleasure and pleasure alone is intrinsically valuable. Oskar Kraus summarises Brentano's general table of values in the following passage:

> . . . the following things are valuable or good considered in and for themselves; that is to say, they are such that they can be loved only correctly: every correct judgement and especially every judgement that is evident; every correct emotion and especially every emotion that presents itself as being correct; and also every enrichment of our presentational life.
>
> Every conscious act as something that is self-conscious contains inseparably some presentation. Therefore it is essential to all our mental activity that something valuable be given along with it. It follows that there is no evil that does not contain some trace of what is good.
>
> The following things, however, show themselves to be predominantly bad: every error; every sensible pain; every unjustified act of hate — especially every act of hate that is apprehended as being incorrect, thus primarily the hatred of that which is good. Naturally the love of that which is bad is also an evil — especially the love of that which is apprehended as bad. Sensible pleasure, on the other hand, is as such not only preferable to sensible pain but is also a state of consciousness which in and for itself is good. Like any other good or evil, it may be either a blessing or a disaster; this will depend on the circumstances.
>
> And so each of the three basic mental categories — presentation, judgement, and emotion — has its characteristic good. As we have already seen, the better is attained, not only by the summation of particular goods, but also by the ordering of these goods with respect to preferability — for such preferability is a function of qualitative as well as quantitative differences.[3]

Finally, Brentano's theory has a feature that may seem to conflict with what I have called its objectivity. This side of his view is usually put by saying that the terms 'good', 'bad', 'better', when used in connection with intrinsic value, are all 'syncategorematic'.[4] In holding this, Brentano is rejecting the simple theories of value predication that were presupposed by G.E. Moore and Max Scheler: the word 'good' they seemed to say, has as its intention a simple quality comparable to yellow or blue. But Brentano is also expressing his reism — and in particular his rejection of such entities as *Sachverhalte, Objektive* and propositions.

2. The Types of Love and Hate

Let us now note the various types of love and hate that Brentano recognises and the different way in which these types of love and hate are directed upon their objects.

First of all, sensuous pleasure and sensuous displeasure. Then there is non-sensuous enjoyment and what can be called non-sensuous 'disenjoyment'. Further, there is the distinction between the antecedent will and the consequent will. Then there is the endeavour to promote and the endeavour to obstruct. And, finally, there is desire and aversion.

Sensuous Pleasure and Sensuous Pain

We will begin with sensuous pleasure and sensuous pain — in the strict sense of the word 'pain'.

First, we must make two general points about Brentano's theory of sensation. It is essential to his conception to distinguish between the *act* and the *object* of sensation. Seeing is an example of the act of sensation. A patch of colour would be an object of sensation. Again, hearing is an example of an act of sensation; a sound is an example of an object of sensation. The objects of sensation are thus to be compared with what Russell and Moore had called 'sense-data' and with what earlier philosophers had called 'sense-impressions'. The words 'seeing' and 'hearing', therefore, are not to be taken in their ordinary senses.

A second feature of Brentano's theory is his doctrine that there are exactly *three* senses: sight, hearing, and what he sometimes calls the *Spürsinn* or 'the third sense'. Sense-objects of the third sense are exemplified by a bitter taste, a fragrant smell, a feel or a throb.

One of the basic philosophical questions about sensuous pain and sensuous pleasure is this: Are they to be classified as *acts* of sensation or are they to be classified as *objects* of sensation?

Stumpf had held that sensuous pleasure and pain are sense-objects — objects of what Brentano called the third sense. Stumpf's view may seem plausible in the case of sensuous pain. Brentano argued, however, that sensuous pleasure and sensuous pain are to be classified as intentional *acts* rather than as sensible *objects*. 'Sensuous pleasure is the agreeableness [*Angenehmsein*] of certain sensations of the third sense, and sensuous pain is the disagreeableness *[Unangenehmsein]* of certain sensations of the third sense.'⁵ The words 'agreeableness' and 'disagreeableness' are here to be taken as referring to mental acts — to pro-attitudes and anti-attitudes. Sensuous pleasure is the agreeableness of that sensation which has as its object what I shall call a certain kind of 'feel' — a feel that might be tactual, though it could also be gustatory or olfactory. This feel is a sense-datum — an object of a sensation of the third sense. And sensuous displeasure — sensuous pain — is the disagreeableness of that sensation which has as its object what I shall call a certain kind of 'throb'.

We may now see the danger of ambiguity and misunderstanding here. The words 'pleasure' and 'pain', in the present context, could be taken in one or the other of three quite different ways. Thus 'pleasure' could be taken to designate that sense-object I have called the feel. Or it could be taken to refer to that act of sensation which has the feel as *its* primary object. Or, again, it could be taken to refer to that emotion — that act of love — which has the act of sensation as its object. Brentano takes 'sensible pleasure' in the third way.

He interprets 'sensuous pain' analogously. He does not use it to designate that sense-object I have called the throb. Nor does he use it to refer to that act of sensation which has the throb as its primary object. Rather, he uses 'sensuous pain' to refer to that emotion — that act of hate — which has the act of sensation as its object.

This seems reasonable if we say, as Brentano does, that pleasure as such is good and that pain as such is bad. We should follow him in using 'pleasure' and 'pain' for the pro- and anti-attitudes, respectively. We should *not* use these words for the feel and the throb. After all, the feel, when it is too intense, is no longer agreeable. And the throb when it has a very low degree of intensity is no longer disagreeable and may even be agreeable.⁶ And what is good or bad is not the act of sensation; it is, rather, the agreeableness or disagreeableness of the act of sensation.

'But', a critic might object, 'there must be something in virtue of which the sensation is found to be agreeable or disagreeable. And this something — rather than the act of love or the act of hate — is what is good or bad.' Suppose we call this something X. If the objection is well taken, then we can also apply it to X itself ('there must be something Y in virtue of which X is agreeable or disagreeable') and we will find ourselves in a regress. The alternative is to say that some things may be agreeable or disagreeable without thereby having certain features *in virtue of which* they are agreeable or disagreeable. And this is what we may take Brentano to be saying of the acts of sensation in question.

Non-sensuous Pleasure and Displeasure

What now of non-sensuous pleasure and displeasure? Here, too, the distinction between act and object is central.

Consider the locution 'he is pleased that p' and the locution 'he is displeased that p'. The former might be illustrated by the sentence 'he is pleased that he won the election', said of a politician.

We should remind ourselves that, according to Brentano, every mental state presents itself with evidence. If I judge that so-and-so or if I have such-and-such a sensation, then it is directly evident to me that I judge that so-and-so or that I have such-and-such a sensation. And if there is a mental state which is being pleased that p, or being displeased that p, and if I am in such a state, then it should be directly evident to me that I am in that state.

Consider, then, our politician of whom we say 'he is pleased that he won the election'. What is the *object* of his pleasure? Our first response might be: the fact of the election turning out as it did. But if we say this, we are letting our ordinary language mislead us.

Let the politician in question be Charles Evans Hughes. He was the Republican candidate for the President of the United States in 1916, running against Woodrow Wilson. The election returns that were available on the evening following the voting convinced Hughes that he had won and he joyfully went to bed. It was not until the following morning that the returns from California made it clear that Wilson had won. What, then, had been the object of Hughes's enjoyment? If he actually *enjoyed* anything, it would seem strictly speaking what he enjoyed was, not the result of the election, but rather what he took to be his *learning* — *his coming to know* — the result of the election. And, indeed, instead of saying, 'He was pleased at the result of the election,' we may say instead 'he was pleased to learn — to hear — the result of the election'. It would be even more accurate to say: 'he was pleased to become assured about the result of the election'.

Hence pleasure and displeasure of this sort may be said to have a twofold intentional object. There is first the psychological state which is the direct object of the pleasure or displeasure. This would be, in our example, that psychological state which was Hughes's coming to be assured about the result of the election. And this, as we have said, was a state he could know directly and immediately to obtain. We may say that this state was the direct object of Hughes's enjoyment. The direct object of the pleasure is an intentional state of the subject, in our example, that intellectual attitude which is his coming to believe that he won the election. And the indirect object of the pleasure may be equated with the intentional *object* of that psychological act which is the direct object of the pleasure. In our example this was the state of affairs which was Hughes's winning the election.

If we ask, as Brentano does, whether 'pleasure in the bad' is good and whether 'displeasure in the bad' is bad, we should, presumably, assume that 'the good' and 'the bad' are intended to refer to the intentional object of that psychological state which is the primary object of the pleasure or displeasure, respectively.

There is, therefore, the danger of a serious ambiguity in the use of the expression 'object of pleasure'. Thus Leonard Nelson, in the following passage, uses the expression 'pleasure in' in a way that is quite different from Brentano's use:

> But pleasure in contemplating the beautiful is not pleasure in the beautiful itself, and displeasure in contemplating what is ugly is not displeasure at what is ugly; rather, this pleasure or displeasure relates to our own state of feeling. This is made particularly apparent by the fact that such pleasure or displeasure is altogether independent of the existence of the object, namely the beautiful or the ugly.[7]

Brentano himself has a rather strange view of non-sensuous pleasure and displeasure. His studies in the intensity of sensation led him to the view that the intensity of a psychological *act* — say, the intensity of a liking or a disliking — is always a function of the intensity of the *object* of that act. The intensity of the liking or disliking of a throb or a feel is a direct function of the intensity of the throb or the feel. He then goes on to say that the intensity of *non-sensuous* pleasure or displeasure is a function of the intensity of some object of *sensuous* pleasure or displeasure. Thus whenever we experience intense joy or grief, then, according to Brentano, there is an intense sensuous pleasure or displeasure that accompanies ('redounds upon') that joy or grief. I cannot help but feel that, in saying this, Brentano was trying to round out his theory and was not speaking as a descriptive psychologist.

Desire and Aversion

Desire and aversion constitute a third type of love and hate. I here intend the words 'desire' and 'aversion' to refer to states that are essentially unpleasant. The man who craves a drink may be said to be experiencing sensations which he 'disenjoys'. Indeed, his state is one of *aversion toward* those sensations. And it may be that he desires the drink as a means to removing them. So in this case the object of desire is merely a means; and the end is the removal of that state which is the object of the aversion.

There is also a *pleasant* experience that is sometimes described as a 'desire'. This is the experience of phantasy wherein one dreams of fulfilment. Hence it would seem to be essentially a matter of enjoying the thought of fulfilment.

3. Antecedent Will and Consequent Will

Other types of love and hate may be explicated by reference to the traditional distinction between *antecedent will* and *consequent will*. This distinction presupposes that your attitude toward a certain compound state of affairs is a consequence of the attitudes you may have toward the various components of that state of affairs.[8] Your attitude toward each of the various components of the compound state will be your antecedent will; the resulting attitude toward the wider state of affairs will be your consequent will.

Leibniz says that

this consequent will, final and decisive, results from the conflict of all the antecedent wills, of those which tend towards good, even as of those which repel evil; and from the concurrence of all these particular wills comes the total will. So in mechanics compound movement results from all the tendencies that concur in one and the same moving body, and satisfies each one equally, in so far as it is possible to do all at one time.[9]

Leibniz refers to the view of certain Christians, according to which 'God wills to save all men according to his antecedent will, but not according to his consequent will.'[10] The distinction enables him to say that evil is never the object of God's antecendent will; it is, rather, part of the object of his consequent will.

Actually, as Leibniz notes, the distinction would seem to presuppose a primitive antecedent will, a final consequent will, and various intermediate wills. Thus he writes:

> The *primitive antecedent will* has as its object each good and each evil in itself, detached from all combination, and tends to advance the good and prevent the evil. The *mediate will* relates to combinations, as when one attaches a good to an evil: then the will will have some tendency towards this combination when the good exceeds the evil therein. But the *final and decisive will* results from consideration of all the goods and all the evils that enter into our deliberations, it results from a total combination. This shows that a mediate will, although it may in a sense pass as consequent in relation to a pure and primitive antecedent will, must be considered antecedent in relation to the final and decretory will.[11]

St Thomas, in making a similar distinction, distinguishes between the object *per se* of an emotion and the object *per accidens*.[12] The object *per se* would be the object of the consequent will; an object *per accidens* would be whatever is entailed by the object of the consequent will. Hence St Thomas's distinction is not the same as that between antecedent and consequent will. For both antecedent and consequent will may have an object *per se* and various objects *per accidens*.

Brentano wrote to Kraus in 1908 that one respect in which the *Ursprung sittlicher Erkenntnis* required emendation or perhaps even correction had to do with this distinction between antecedent and consequent will. He noted that the two types of will may be distinguished in the following way. There is no irrationality or inconsistency in making incompatible objects of one's antecedent will. I can look favourably toward my staying home this evening and reading, and I can also look favourably toward my going out this evening and hearing some music. There can be many such objects of the antecedent will. But there can be only one object of the consequent will.[13]

In developing his theory of the consequent will, Brentano first distinguishes an act of *love, simpliciter*, from an act of *love that involves a preference*. Of two situations, *each* of which, taken as such and as if alone, is an object of my love, I may yet *prefer* one to the other. Each of these occurrences, considered in itself and apart from its consequences, is an object of my favourable inclination. But of these two things that I thus love, I may yet *prefer* one to the other.

Brentano next distinguishes a *wish that involves a decision* from an act of *love that involves a preference*. Though my antecedent preferences may point one way, I may decide that, when all other relevant things are considered, I would prefer to have it the other way around. In such a case, I will have considered the two situations in the context of what I take to be their total consequences and then I will have arrived at a preference with respect to these two larger situations.[14]

With this concept of a wish that involves a decision, Brentano goes on to define what he calls an *act of will*. What distinguishes an act of will from what is merely a wish that involves a decison is

> always something we ourselves have to bring about. We can will only those things that fall within our power, or, at any rate, those things that we earnestly believe to be within our power. . . . Thus we can define an act of will as a wish or a want that involves a decision and which has as its object something that we are to bring about ourselves and that we confidently expect will result from the desires that we then have. Hence one might say that an act of will is a want or a wish such that we have arrived at it by coming to a decision and such that we believe it can be realised by our own endeavours.[15]

The complex concept of an act of will thus contains a multiplicity of elements: love, conviction, preference, decision, and causation. The first four elements are psychological, and the fifth — that of causation — occurs only as part of the intentional object of the second. Here we have a paradigm case of what Brentano called 'descriptive psychology'.

4. Subjectivity and *Wertfreiheit*

We are now in a position to make certain general points about the relation between Brentano's point of view and that of subsequent Austrian economics.

The distinction that Ludwig von Mises was to draw between 'praxeology' and 'catallactics' would certainly have been congenial to Brentano.[16] Praxeology — or the theory of human action — is an a priori discipline; its axioms can be determined by reflecting upon the nature of what it is to act and to choose. It would be, indeed, a part of what Brentano calls 'descriptive psychology'. 'Catallactics', on the other hand, is an a posteriori discipline which presupposes praxeology and applies it to actions that involve market exchange and monetary calculation. Brentano would certainly have accepted this distinction. But whether he would have accepted the application of the method of *Verstehen* to this economic application of praxeology, I cannot say. It is not the sort of question to which he addressed himself as a philosopher, although there is reason to believe that Brentano was not impressed by Dilthey's views about the *Geisteswissenschaften*.

Brentano also would have been quite ready to characterise praxeology as a 'subjective' or 'psychological' discipline. Lachmann has argued that Austrian economics is essentially subjectivistic.[17] It has been said that 'what distinguishes Lachmann from other economists is his total devotion to subjectivism in economics. ... Economic phenomena cannot be explained unless they are related, either directly or indirectly, to subjective states of valuation.'[18] Essentially the same thing may be said of the theory of intrinsic value as Brentano conceived it. It cannot be studied without reference to those intentional states that Brentano had called 'love' and 'hate'. The theory of value is a part of what Brentano called 'descriptive psychology'. And descriptive psychology, according to him, is an a priori discipline to be compared with Leibniz's *characteristica universalis*.[19] 'Subjective', therefore, does not mean the same as 'capricious' or 'arbitrary'. The judgements of descriptive psychology — and therefore of praxeology — are necessary and true. But Brentano would have said 'apodictic' and 'correct'. Hence the theory of value is in one sense *subjective* and, as we have noted, in another sense *objective*. There is no contradiction, therefore, in saying that the theory of value is *both* subjective and objective. It is *subjective* in that it is concerned with certain psychological or intentional attitudes. It is *objective* in recognising that these attitudes may be distinguished as being correct or incorrect.

Kirzner has said that one of the basic insights of Austrian economics is the thesis according to which 'there is an indeterminacy and unpredictability inherent in human preferences, human expectations, and human knowledge'.[20] What would Brentano have said about this? He thought he could prove that *determinism* is true — and so if we take Kirzner's statement one way, then we must say that Brentano would have rejected it. That is to say, he would have rejected the theory that human preferences are causally undetermined. But there is another way of taking it which, I think, would have been endorsed by Brentano: the factors governing human preferences, expectations, and knowledge are so vast and so complex, that it is next to impossible for one human being to predict with any degree of accuracy all the actions of another.

In the lectures on 'Descriptive Psychologie' that Brentano gave at the University of Vienna in 1890–1 he expressed a general scepticism about the possibility of discovering psychophysical laws.

Finally a word about *Wertfreiheit*. There can be confusion in philosophy — and in economic theory — because of the failure to distinguish between praxeology and catallactics; there can also be confusion because of the failure to distinguish between intrinsic and instrumental value. Both Menger and Brentano are clear about this point. Yet I wonder whether there may not be some confusion in the controversies about what Max Weber called the *'Wertfreiheit'* of the social sciences.[21]

Judgements of intrinsic value, according to Brentano, are apodictic and correct. I am sure that he would regard them as an essential part of praxeology. Now economics — or catallactics — presupposes praxeology. And therefore economics presupposes those truths which constitute the theory of intrinsic value. How could one say, then, that economics and the other social sciences should be 'value-free'?

The answer can only be that economics and social science more generally should not presuppose the truth of judgements of *instrumental* value. These judgements are generalisations about what types of means tend to produce those ends that are instrumentally good, and those that are instrumentally bad. I say economics should not *presuppose* these judgements of instrumental value. But this is not to say that the economist should not *make* such judgements. Such judgements should occur, however, not at the beginning, but at the end of an adequate science of economics.

Ludwig von Mises spoke of ethical judgements as being 'arbitrary' and as having no place in economics.[22] Presumably he would have made the same point about judgements of intrinsic value. Brentano would have pointed out to him that whatever can be said, *pro* and *con*, with respect to the principles of praxeology can also be said, *mutatis mutandis*, with respect to the principles of the theory of intrinsic value. If the principles of praxeology are axiomatic, so, too, are the principles of the theory of intrinsic value. The latter principles may not be a *part* of the science of economics; this is a matter of definition. But the economist is in no position to *deny* these principles — any more than he is a position to deny the principles of logic and mathematics. And Brentano would have said these judgements — unlike judgements of instrumental value — *should* be presupposed by any adequate social science.[23]

Notes

1. Brentano's principal writings on this topic are: *Vom Ursprung sittlicher Erkenntnis*, Leipzig: Felix Meiner, 1922, and *Grundlegung und Aufbau der Ethik*, Berne: Francke, 1952. These have been translated into English as: *The Origin of Our Knowledge of Right and Wrong*, London: Routledge & Kegan Paul, 1969, and *The Foundation and Construction of Ethics*, London: Routledge & Kegan Paul, 1973.

2. It is significant to note that, in his lecture 'On the Concept of Truth' (1889), Brentano appeals to the concept of the correctness of *emotion* in order to illuminate the concept of the correctness of judgement, rather than conversely. See *Wahrheit und Evidenz*, Hamburg: Felix Meiner, 1974, p. 25; *The True and the Evident*, London: Routledge & Kegan Paul, 1966, p. 21.

3. Oskar Kraus, 'Die Grundlagen der Werttheorie', *Jahrbücher der Philosophie, 2*, (1914), pp. 27–8.

4. See Oskar Kraus: *Die Werttheorien*, Brünn: Rohrer, 1937, pp. 51, 171–2, 178, 213; Anton Marty, *Untersuchungen zur Grundlegung der allgemeinen Grammatik und Sprachphilosophie*, Halle: Max Niemeyer, 1908, 429–30.

5. See Brentano, *Untersuchungen zur Sinnespsychologie*, second edition, Hamburg: Felix Meiner Verlag, 1979, 235–40.

6. But it may be questioned whether Brentano would agree with this last point. He *seems* to hold that emotional qualities are intrinsic to certain objects of the third sense.

7. Leonard Nelson, *Critique of Practical Reason*, Scarsdale: Leonard Nelson Foundation, Inc., 1957, p. 340. Compare the German edition, *Kritik der praktischen Vernunft*, Hamburg: Felix Meiner Verlag, 1972: 'Die Lust an der Betrachtung des Schönen ist aber nicht eine Lust am Schönen selbst . . . ' (p. 390).

8. The 'components' of a given state of affairs should be thought of as states of affairs that are *entailed* by the given state of affairs. Hence what is logically implied, but not entailed, will not be a 'component' in the present sense of the term.

9. G.W. Leibniz, *Theodicy: Essays on the Goodness of God, the Freedom of Man, and the Origin of Evil*, London: Routledge and Kegan Paul, 1951, p. 137.

10. Ibid, p. 166.

11. Ibid. pp. 189–90.

12. Compare *Summa Theologica*, Supplement, Q. 94 ('Of the Relations of the Saints toward the Damned'), reply to the second objection.

13. Brentano, *Ursprung*, p. 112 (*Origin*, p. 114). For a study of the relevance of Brentano's theory of value to theodicy, see Georg Katkov, *Untersuchungen zur Werttheorie und Theodizee*, Brünn: Rohrer, 1937.

14. Compare Brentano, *Grundlegung und Aufbau der Ethik*, p. 218ff. (English edition, p. 200ff); Brentano, *Ursprung*, pp. 112–5, 156–8 (English edition, pp. 113–6, 150–2).

15. 'Wir können das Wollen also definieren als ein entscheidendes Wünschen, das etwas von uns selbst zu Verwirklichendes zum Gegenstand hat und von uns als Wirkung unseres Begehrens überzeugt erwartet wird. Es ist m. a. W. ein Wunsch, für den wir uns entschieden haben und an dessen Realisierbarkeit durch unser Eingreifen wir glauben' (*Grundlegung und Aufbau der Ethik*, p. 219 (English edition, p. 200)).

16. See Ludwig von Mises, *Human Action: A Treatise on Economics*, New Haven: Yale University Press, 1949, pp. 32, 233–5.

17. Ludwig M. Lachmann: *The Legacy of Max Weber*, London: Heinemann, 1970.

18. From p. 3 of W.E. Grinder's Introduction to Ludwig M. Lachmann, *Capital, Expectations, and the Market Process*, Kansas City: Sheed, Andrews and McMeel, 1977.

19. See Brentano's *Meine letzten Wünsche fur Österreich*, Stuttgart: J.G. Cotton, 1895, pp. 84-5, and his *Deskriptive Psychologie*, Hamburg: Meiner, 1982.

20. Israel M. Kirzner, 'On the Method of Austrian Economics' in Edwin G. Dolan (ed.) *The Foundations of Modern Austrian Economics*, Kansas City: Sheed and Ward, 1976, pp. 40–51; see p. 42.

21. See Israel M. Kirzner, 'Philosophical and Ethical Implications of Austrian Economics' in Dolan, *Modern Austrian Economics*, pp. 75–88.

22. Quoted in Murray N. Rothbard, 'Praxeology, Value Judgments, and Public Policy,' in Dolan, *Modern Austrian Economics*, 89–111; compare p. 108.

23. Compare Oskar Kraus's discussion of *Wertfreiheit* in *Die Werttheorien*, pp. 450–4.

6

EMANUEL HERRMANN: ON AN ALMOST
FORGOTTEN CHAPTER OF AUSTRIAN
INTELLECTUAL HISTORY

Rudolf Haller

1. The Rise of the Evolutionary Idea

Bearing in mind the limitations to which all historical generalisations
are subject, one can characterise the nineteenth century as the century
of the rise of evolution. This is true first of all in the trivial sense that,
with the publication of Darwin's *Origin of Species* in 1859, the
Aristotelian dogma of the unchangeability of biological species was
finally and irrevocably confounded. But it is true also in a deeper sense.
For, as has been variously remarked, the idea of development was
applied to the totality of history — in a much wider sense than was the
case among the Darwinians — already by the German speculative
idealists Schelling and Hegel, and by the early positivists, above all
Comte. Reason and consciousness in general are seen from this
perspective as being determined in their nature by the passage of time
and by the development which takes place in time; and indeed the
totality of existence is seen in a Heraclitean perspective as a *becoming*,
as something that gradually, through determinate phases and levels,
approaches some goal, whether this be — as in Hegel's case — the
absolute consciousness of God, or — as in the case of Comte — the
final culmination of all science. F.A. von Hayek has of course correctly
pointed out that amongst the most important ideas shared by Hegel and
Comte there belongs also the idea of 'a universal history of all mankind,
understood as a scheme of the necessary development of humanity
according to recognisable laws'.[1] Certainly the nature of these laws is
understood completely differently by the speculative idealists and by
the positivists. But even if it were to be agreed that Comte derived his
conception of the stages in the evolution of the mind from empirical
observation, he seems nevertheless to breathe the same speculative
atmosphere as Hegel in his conception of the stages of the self-realising
spirit:

For both, society appears as an organism in a fairly literal sense.
Both compare the stages through which social evolution must pass

with different ages through which individual man passes in his natural growth. And for both, the growth of the conscious control of his destiny by man is the main content of history.[2]

2. The Nature of Economic Science

It was without doubt this enthusiasm for the guiding idea of evolution which facilitated the penetration of the historical method into the science of economics, predominating in the works of, for example, Friedrich List and Wilhelm Roscher.[3] Emanuel Herrmann's *Prinzipien der Wirtschaft*, which appeared three years after his *Leitfaden der Wirtschaftslehre*, are dedicated to Roscher, as is also Carl Menger's *Principles of Economics*. And Herrmann's works seek superficially to share the two characteristic features of Roscher's approach: the demand that economics accede to the status of an exact science, and the claim to autonomy of its principles.

But however much Herrmann feels himself indebted to Roscher, his innermost intentions seem in the end to diverge from those of his master. For Herrmann, what is at issue is not so much the application to economic phenomena of a historical method, as the discovery and the making precise of the guiding principles of economics itself, as a discipline in the process of realising its autonomy. In his *Allgemeine Wirtschaftslehre* — a general theory of economics 'systematically set forth via easily understood sketches' — published in Graz in 1868, Herrmann presents the basic principles of this self-autonomising process. The theory of economics should free itself from all limitations which ensue (or would threaten to ensue) from its association with or dependence on other disciplines. Above all the conception of economics as a branch of political science should be abandoned, as, equally, should any conception of economics as a part or appendage of sociology. Economic theory should also cease to be confused with technological disciplines of any kind. For this theory was indeed still, in the middle of the nineteenth century, characterised by the fact that it conceived and understood itself either as political science or as social theory. Clearly, however, if this principle is to be put into effect, then a criterion of independence has first of all to be set out; only then can the question be decided as to the precise nature of the economic science which would thereby result. Thus, for example, there is no way in which economics should conceive itself as relating to a unified field of objects after the fashion of the sciences of, say, mineralogy or zoology, since the field of economic action in regard to both its objects and its modes of appearance, lacks any determinate boundaries.

There remains as a positive criterion of demarcation only the supreme principle of *economising*, a fundamental idea which is understood by Herrmann in so wide a sense as to apply not only to productive activities in general but to all phenomena of nature and of the human mind. If it could once be established that in the end all objects are or can be made subject to the principle of economising, then, Herrmann argues, a systematic framework for political economy would follow almost as a matter of course. The resulting discipline would be, first of all, a *morphology* of the changes and transformations of an entire economy; and then also it would be an *aetiology* and *pathology* of specific economic phenomena, which are assumed to be effects which give rise to endogenously and exogenously determined states of health or illness. The fundamental stages in the application of the method of investigation of such phenomena Herrmann lists as 'location of the object, decomposition, observation, description and comparison'. And he immediately formulates a rule, which might be called the 'Principle of Non-Suppression', to the effect that 'there is no fact, not even the most insignificant . . . which may be overlooked or set to one side as being without influence'.[4] This systematic framework of morphology, aetiology and pathology characterises all of Herrmann's later writings, to which the remainder of this paper is devoted.

It would be mistaken to suppose that, in the then just beginning *Methodenstreit* in the theory of political economy — a precursor of the so-called *'Positivismusstreit'* in twentieth-century German sociology — Herrmann were simply to be aligned with the historicists. Just as Menger, in his 'methodological catechism',[5] the *Untersuchungen über die Methode der Sozialwissenschaften und der politischen Ökonomie insbesondere*,[6] does not reject the adoption of the methods of the natural sciences in the field of political economy, but rather precisely demands it, so too does Herrmann make this demand, as is shown by his programmatic writings. Thus it is without doubt that he holds to the postulate that *the methods of research in political economy can be none other than those of the natural sciences.*

This demand is clearly expressed even in the *Leitfaden der Wirthschaftslehre*, where we find set out for economic theory precisely that programme which Franz Brentano, in his fourth habilitation thesis, projected for philosophy: 'Vera philosophiae methodus nulla alia nisi scientiae naturalis est.'[7] Herrmann compares this new attitude with the transformation of alchemy into the new theory of chemical combinations. In short, he seeks a renewal of traditional economic theory in all essential respects. And in the interpretation of his own postulate he manifests a conception of the sovereign independence of economics which is comparable to that of Menger. The method of the natural sciences should not be applied in any slavish fashion; but neither should the field of economic research be limited in such a way that it would lie outside the realm of nature. Herrmann remarks that the avoidance of any anthropomorphising teleology in economics does not imply the affirmation for economic phenomena of that planlessness or purposelessness which has been seen as being characteristic of natural events. And this is surely correct, not least in virtue of the fact that the causal connection between events is itself capable of being conceived in analogy with the relation between an intention and its realisation, that is, under the aspect of a possible action.[8] Here, too, the fundamental idea of economising serves as a crucial guiding principle, and Herrmann takes this to imply that a limitation of political economy to objects and events exclusively within the sphere of human action would signify a too narrow interpretation of this fundamental idea. It is rather, 'mere heresy and superstition' to wish to establish any kind of frontier between man and the remaining totality of existing things. On the contrary: 'It is precisely the economy of nature (in the old, atrophied sense of extra-human reality) which constitutes the most beautiful and most magnificent part of the theory of economy.'[9] And the argument which is brought forward in support of this conception naturally employs once more the fundamental idea of economising in its comparison between human achievements and the achievements of nature:

> What is the economising of human work, of our own constructions, of our machines, when set against that economising in accordance with which the secreting organs of plants and the organs of sensation and volition of animals function and create![10]

3. The Principle of Economising

The fundamental idea of economising, conceived by Herrmann as an organic principle, he now sees as underlying both the dynamics of the economy and society in general. Even if it is true that the total or world economy does not achieve the same level of perfection as, say, an animal organism, it is nevertheless, according to the organicistic conception, an organic totality — nourished, renewed, further developed and extended by the operations of a multiplicity of constituent organs which influence each other reciprocally. Certainly one cannot conceive these organs as in any sense perfect. Many have indeed advanced no further than the embryonic state (banks, for example); others have reached a state of maturity; yet others (leech handlers) have already withered away.

Herrmann sees the building block of the entire economy as consisting in the household, 'the most individual and at the same time most universal enterprise', whose end is in general that of 'supplying for a personal entity (an individual man, a married couple, a family, a social grouping) the means required for sustenance and growth of its bodily and spiritual existence in the most economic fashion'.[11]

It is ultimately, therefore, individual needs and desires which steer the total organism of the economy, and the question arises how, given all the specific interests, individual needs and goals, it can come about that the total organism not only exists, but develops and grows. The key to this 'miracle' — as Herrmann describes it — lies in a harmony of the totality of interests. This conception is unquestionably obscure, since both the underlying concept of a natural distribution of interests and the concept of the healthy economic body are themselves defined within the framework of Herrmann's very system. Each separate will can deviate from the interest of the totality only to the extent that the possibility of this deviation lies in the interest of the individual as much as in that of the totality. Otherwise the disadvantages will outweigh the advantages, which would already signify a state of ill-health, either of the individual or of the total body.

Without going into the details of the separate 'organs' and of the symptoms and causes of health and disease, it is by now surely manifest that the economic system has hereby come to be conceived as something both dynamic and goal-directed, the investigation of which results in an autonomous discipline conceived after the model of the natural sciences.

In order to bring into light the specific constraints to which individual drives, wishes, needs, concerns and provisions are subject, Herrmann adopts as the starting point of his theory 'circumspection and calculation' [*Umsicht und Berechnung*]. In order to grasp completely the mode of operation of the economic organism, he conceives the acting entity as a *rational agent*, who would establish and take account of all economically relevant circumstances, measure the extent of their influence and thereupon set in motion that economic calculation whose central motivating principle is that of economising. The goal of economic calculation is in every case the same: the most economical selection of ways and means of arriving at a determined goal. The 'alpha and omega of all economy' — as Hermann calls his formula of economising — should not, however, be understood in its most literal interpretation, according to which the economising character of an action would lie in our aiming, in the selection of means, at a surplus of advantage over disadvantage. It is to be understood rather as signifying that the projected surplus in the means to be selected should be greater 'than the respective surpluses of all those means which might have been selected in its place'.[12] It is of course evident, both to the acting economiser and to the economic theorist, that it is impossible to calculate the sum of all consequences of the employment even of already existing means, leaving aside any consideration of those means which have yet to appear. Herrmann therefore underlines his conviction that 'all economic observation and calculation is a matter of guesswork . . . is not a matter of knowledge, but of conjecture'.[13]

It is clear that the above-mentioned economising principle is nothing other than a principle of the rationality of action of the type which has been further developed by contemporary decision theory. The principle affirms that a person who is subject to risk in virtue of his lack of knowledge of the circumstance to which his actions will give rise (or of the relevant probability distributions), will act in such a manner that the expected utility of his action is not equalled or exceeded by the expected utility of any alternative action. It is of course not always very clear what is to be counted amongst the consequences of a given decision, and it is for this reason that Hermann speaks of guesswork and conjecture — in a way which was anticipated by Whewell in the first half of the nineteenth century and has since been reiterated by Popper — except that Popper holds the view that, in the sphere of human action, because of the instability of the basis of action, prognoses are not possible at all, a view which stands in conflict with the practice of the more developed part of the social sciences, that is, precisely political economy, which has not adopted a sceptical attitude of this kind; and it is surely evident that one is better able to judge the status of a scientific discipline by examining its most developed branches, rather than those of its constituent disciplines which have been left behind in the race.[14]

That calculation which lies at the core of Herrmann's economising formula is of course no more than a rudimentary prototype of the principle of maximisation of expected utility. It points, nevertheless, in the right direction, in so far as the value of a given economising $EV = (A—D)—(A_i—D_i)$ represents a calculation of the difference between the total advantage $(A—D)$ deriving from the provision, maintenance, application and eventual elimination of the valued good, and the corresponding surplus of advantage over disadvantage for alternative means of provision. Herrmann seems to be unclear about which consequences of application should be taken account of in such calculation. But he nevertheless demands that this method approximate in its exactitude to chemical calculation.[15] The wealth of examples which Herrmann brings forward in illustration of his formula is impressive, but it is the underlying idea — in certain respects as much a heuristic device as a principle of explanation — which is of primary interest.

It deserves pointing out here also that his conception — developed in the halcyon days of the industrial period — is suffused with an enthusiasm for technology, although the inventor of the postcard — equally a product of his economising formula — did not close his eyes to the drawbacks of the development of an industrial society. He points repeatedly to the possible social, ecological and psychological injury which it might bring in its wake, the taking account of which he saw as being required by any just and rational evaluation. And he underlines repeatedly the fact that a correct calculation should be carried out within a total framework of *competition* between all forms of advantage and disadvantage. It is only the 'absolutely greatest surplus of advantage over disadvantage which decides the selection'.[16] Thus it is only where a species of competition arises that the law attains its force that, in our calculations, the surplus can be entered as a profit. The original formula must therefore be made more precise, in such a way that in the resultant economising, $E = (A—D) - \max_{i=1,\dots,n}(A_i—D_i)$, the best

of all the individual competing surpluses is subtracted from the surplus of the actually selected means.

4. Herrmann and Mach

It has of course been acknowledged (though it is also still in many cases too readily overlooked) that Ernst Mach, in his formulation of his law of the economy of thought as an explanatory principle of science in general, was influenced by his reading of Herrmann and by his contact with this many-sided thinker whom he had come to know during their days in Graz.[17] Mach developed a systematic conception of the idea of economy as an economising of experience in general, that is, as the unification of those rules which make experience possible. Natural laws are in this precise sense nothing other than unified descriptions of facts which could be accumulated in an ununified state only in the mind of an individual whose memory was infinite. Language itself appears as the prototype of the economy of thought. It involves, certainly, a 'sacrifice in exactitude', but has the powerful advantage that, in economising on repetition, it unifies our pictures of a continuously changing world in such a way that that which is more significant is brought into prominence, that which is irrelevant is overlooked. Physics refines those concepts which have their origin and their foundation in those parts of our common language which relate to material things. Herrmann, too, sees the laws of economics as unifications of experiences. But he does not wish to subjugate their investigation to any practical goal. If political economy is to be a science — and not merely the political art of wealth-creation or 'science of wealth' as Adam Smith describes it — then it must be practised as a branch of the natural sciences. Only when men become so firmly conversant with the basic laws of physics — as, for example, in earlier times they were familiar with biblical history — will a true culture arise. But Herrmann advances a mechanistic theory as little as did Mach. On the contrary, he embraces, like Mach, the idea of evolution, with which he associates the idea of the systematisation of the structure of the economic system. Thus we see an evolutionary dynamics bound up with a holistic statics, even if Herrmann can complain that a 'Darwin of the science of economics' has perhaps not even yet been born.[18] The extent to which Herrmann himself employs the Darwinian explanatory framework is exhibited in his sketch of an explanation of innovation. The *ars inveniendi* has, familiarly, always presented great difficulties to the logician and the philosopher of science. What explanation can be provided of the phenomenon of a new invention's being somehow *in the air*? The answer to this question that is provided by those theories which view the individual as a representative of an entire culture, is just as unsatisfactory as the answer of the exponent of chance, who adopts a *generatio aequivoca*. An adequate answer must surely recognise that the preconditions of an innovation may be somehow materially present in such a way that they are bound up causally with the new idea, so that the latter is, as it were, produced through analogising processes of thought — as the idea *postcard* is merely 'a slight mutation of the idea-species *letter*'.[19]

5. Herrmann and Menger

In its ascription of a law-like character even to the processes of innovation, Herrmann's methodological approach is in certain crucial respects similar to that of Carl Menger, although in other respects it would receive his disapproval. What carries us forward, and thereby works counter to the awful lack of memory exhibited by science, is the looking back from the presently achieved state to that point in which it has its origins.

Once the object-domain investigated by a given discipline has been determined, there may remain a multiplicity of ways and means of exploring it, of clarifying the relations which obtain within it, and so on. But what is thereby forgotten is that it is also possible to infer from the method of inquiry, i.e. from the investigations themselves, to that which is inquired about; and this need not be identical to the object-domain initially delineated. Thus it may be the case that the application of quantitative concepts and methods is demanded by the first, because these are admitted by its objects, but excluded by the second, because they fail to give expression to the intensions of those predicates the investigation of which is comprehended by the method chosen.

And one can clearly recognise that these problems are not themselves problems of a specifically economic theory. For whether, for example, there exist essential laws, and what character these laws might have, are problems which lie at the root of *every* science and which concern the philosophy of science in general.

In this respect the great methodological treatise of Carl Menger[20] is a work which affects the philosopher and the theorist of science no less than the political economist. There has been a great deal of deliberation as to the intellectual background of Menger's work. It is not, in my judgement, capable of being simply usurped as the catechism of an antipositivistic methodology divorced from that of the natural sciences. For it appears at least open to question whether one can justifiably see the emphasis on *Verstehen* as the methodological tool of the social sciences — something which is certainly characteristic of the neo-Austrian school — as having been anticipated already by its founder.[21]

It can, however, be affirmed without restriction already of Menger himself — and this holds even more of his successors — that his theory grants a predominant place to the individual actions of the human subject, to his needs, desires and hopes; and it is on this basis that the theory claims to answer the crucial question of how, given the existence of individual acts and of mutually contradictory intentions and actions, the totality of the social process or of the economy may become explicable. This is precisely the question which was raised by Emanuel Herrmann, who at the very same time was defending in Austria the organicist-evolutionary economic model: how is it possible that, by a causal process whose outcome is unforeseen, economic and social institutions representing also the interests of separate individuals should not merely arise but, indeed, be furthered and promoted. But whilst Herrmann advances a never more closely defined 'total interest of society' as being responsible for the harmony of these separate interests, Menger employs the line of argument of methodological individualism.

Menger's constantly reiterated argument against the historical school rests centrally upon an affirmation of the affinity both of the *objects* of political economy and the natural sciences and of their respective *principles of investigation*. But he sees this affinity as residing first and foremost in the phenomenon of idealisation or conceptual abstraction as this is exhibited in the theory-formation of all the natural sciences. Scientific method in general directs itself exclusively to the task of comprehending and describing the relevant phenomena from one or more perspectives.

> Every theory, of whatever kind it may be and whatever degree of strictness of knowledge it may strive for, has primarily the task of teaching us to understand the concrete phenomena of the real world as exemplifications of a certain regularity in the succession of the phenomena, i.e. genetically.[22]

But even if it is true that a certain similarity obtains in this respect between the two standpoints of methodological individualism and holistic evolutionism, we shall nevertheless not be able to overlook the fact that Menger's objections to the so-called 'organic method of inquiry' apply also to the work of Herrmann. Menger's discriminating position certainly does not reject entirely the organicistic interpretation of social phenomena or of the economy. His arguments are directed only against the exaggerated extrapolation of an analogy. If it is (also) the task of science to investigate real unities, that is to say, integral wholes, then this cannot of course stand in conflict with the idea of an exact and rigorous method of inquiry.

But by the latter Menger always understands an atomistic or individualistic mode of consideration of the phenomena, one which would explain the coming into being of organic formations as the not always foreseen consequences of the actions of economic subjects following their specific individual interests. And one of the principal arguments which Menger brings forward against an anatomical or physiological interprettation of economic or, more generally, social formations, consists in pointing to the undeniable fact that a whole series of social phenomena arise as the result of conscious shaping of the will and of deliberately established conventions. An organic interpretation is, he holds, inappropriate to such phenomena, it being, rather, a *pragmatic* interpretation which is required, one which would take account of the intentions, motives and beliefs of individuals. Phenomena are interpreted 'pragmatically' in Menger's sense, when the concrete goals, means and circumstances which are decisive to a particular action or network of actions are taken into account. It would be to assert nothing new to remark that one's understanding of the goal of knowledge also determines the manner in which it is to be attained, just as, conversely, it is possible to infer the goal from the nature of the path which is chosen. To make a mistake about either will normally bring with it a corresponding mistake about its correlate. and whilst Menger conceives the grasping of a general essence and of a general interrelatedness of the phenomena through the setting forth of exact laws as the central principle of his epistemological foundation of the social sciences in general, Herrmann (and, subsequently, Mach) believes that he can see in the principle of economising the basis of the formation of all knowledge. But because, according to Herrmann's conceptions, the evolution of human society, as of human knowledge, represents merely one further stage in the evolution of nature, the principle of economy will constitute a unifying bond between nature and mind: it is not merely a *ratio cognoscendi*, but also a *ratio essendi.*

Biographical Note

Since it cannot be assumed that the reader will be familiar with the details of Herrmann's life, the following brief summary has been provided. There is almost no literature on this many-sided thinker, author and inventor, and if his name is encountered at all, other than in connection with the study of Ernst Mach, then it will almost certainly be as the inventor of the postcard. In the twenty-seventh edition of Othmar Spann's *Die Haupttheorien der Volkswirtschaftslehre auf lehrgeschichtlicher Grundlage* (the last edition of which appeared as vol. II of Spann's *Gesamtausgabe* (Graz: Akademische Druck- und Verlagsanstalt, 1967)), Herrmann's name is not even mentioned. The Austrian Post Office produced in 1977 an edition of 1,900,000 stamps dedicated to Herrmann, but unfortunately philately does not yet signify any serious concern with things or persons represented on the faces of stamps.

Emanuel Alexander Herrmann, inventor of the postcard and responsible also for a series of other patented devices, was born in Klagenfurt on 24 June, 1839, the oldest of four sons of Alexander Herrmann, later head of the regional civil service, and of his wife Elisabeth (*née* Steiner von Steinberg). Between 1848 and 1856 he attended the local *Gymnasium*, going on from there to read law at the universities of Vienna, Prague and Graz. He began his professional career as an official in the office of the procurator fiscal in Klagenfurt, and this led him immediately back to Graz, where he habilitated in 1863 as *Privatdozent* in political economy. His acquaintance with Mach, who served as professor of mathematics in the University of Graz between 1864 and 1867, falls into this period. In 1865 Herrmann married Maria Grundmann, and in 1868 he was called to the Theresian Military Academy in Wiener Neustadt as professor of political economy and general legal sciences *('Enzyklopädie der Rechtswissenschaften')*. During all this time he retained an involvement in the affairs of the town of his birth, and was active between 1870 and 1877 as member of the Carinthian State Parliament in Klagenfurt. In 1869 he edited with his friend Valentin Pogatschnigg a collection *(Deutsche Volkslieder aus Kärnten)* of Carinthian folk songs. In the year before he had published his work on the economics of insurance *(Theorie der Versicherung vom wirthschaftlichen Standpunkt)* and had invented the postcard, which was immediately brought into use in Austria-Hungary, from where it spread throughout the world. Ten years later he published a collection of historical novellas *(Hexameron. Geschichten aus der Geschichte)*. From Wiener Neustadt he moved to Vienna to become professor in the new Vienna Trade Academy. In 1872 he was appointed departmental head in the Ministry of Trade, and — in connection with his work on the reorganisation of technical education in Austrian schools — moved on from there in 1874 to become permanent secretary in the Ministry of Culture and Education. Finally in 1882 he was made *Ordinarius* in political economy in the Vienna *Technische Hochschule*. After teaching there for almost 20 years he died in Vienna on 15 July 1902, and was buried in the cemetery at Meidling.

Notes

1. F.A. von Hayek, *The Counter-Revolution of Science*, Glencoe: Free Press, 1952, p. 96f. Compare R. Haller, 'Phasen der Wissenschaft', in K. Salamun, ed., *Sozialphilosophie als Aufklärung. Festschrift für Ernst Topitsch*, Tübingen: Mohr, 1979, pp. 247–60.

2. Hayek, *The Counter-Revolution of Science*, p. 198.

3. See W. Roscher, *Grundriss zu Vorlesungen über die Staatswirtschaft nach historischer Methode*, Göttingen, 1843; *System der Volkswirtschaft*, 5 vols, Leipzig, 1854ff.; K.G. Knies, *Die politische Ökonomie vom geschichtlichen Standpunkte*, 2 vols, 2nd ed., Braunschweig, 1881–83; Friedrich List, *The National System of Political Economy* (English translation), London, 1904, and also the works of the later historical school: G. Schmoller, L. Brentano, G.F. Knapp, etc.

4. Herrmann, *Allgemeine Wirthschaftslehre*, p. 18f.

5. L.M. Lachmann, 'The Significance of the Austrian School of Economics in the History of Science' in Lachmann, *Capital, Expectations, and the Market Process*, Kansas City: Sheed Andrews and McMeel, 1977.

6. First published Leipzig: Duncker and Humblot, 1883; repr. in vol. II of Menger's *Gesammelte Werke*, ed. F.A. von Hayek, Tübingen: Mohr, 1969; English translation as *Problems of Economics and Sociology*, Urbana: University of Illinois Press, 1963.

7. Compare also R. Haller, *Studien zur österreichischen Philosophie*, Amsterdam: Rodopi, 1979, p. 166f., and 'Wittgenstein and Austrian Philosophy' in J.C. Nyíri, ed., *Austrian Philosophy: Studies and Texts*, Munich: Philosophia, 1981, pp. 91–113, esp. p. 92ff.

8. Compare G.H. von Wright, *Explanation and Understanding*, London: Routledge and Kegan Paul, 1971, ch. 2.

9. Herrmann, *Allgemeine Wirthschaftslehre*, p. 20.

10. Ibid.

11. Herrmann, *Leitfaden der Wirthschaftslehre*, p. 174f.

12. *Allgemeine Wirthschaftslehre*, p. 31; compare also *Leitfaden*, pp. 45–76.

13. *Leitfaden*, p. 48.

14. Compare Ludwig von Mises's famous essay, 'Soziologie und Geschichte. Epilog zum Methodenstreit in der Nationalökonomie', *Archiv für Sozialwissenschaft und Sozialpolitik*, 61, 1929, 465–512, p. 467; English translation in von Mises, *Epistemological Problems of Economics*, Princeton: Van Nostrand, 1960.

15. Herrmann, *Prinzipien*, p. 243.

16. Herrmann, *Leitfaden*, p. 89f.

17. Compare E. Mach, 'Die Leitgedanken meiner naturwissenschaftlichen Erkenntnislehre und ihre Aufnahme durch die Zietgenossen', *Scientia*, 7, 1910, p. 225; see also R. Haller, 'Poetic Imagination and Economy' in J. Agassi and R.S. Cohen, eds, *Scientific Philosophy Today. Essays in Honor of Mario Bunge*, Dordrecht: Reidel, 1981.

18. Herrmann, *Miniaturbilder aus dem Gebiete der Wirthschaft*, p. 62.

19. Ibid., p. 101.

20. Menger, *Untersuchungen über die Methode der Sozialwissenschaften*.

21. Lachmann, 'Significance of the Austrian School', pp. 153ff.

22. Menger, *Untersuchungen*, p. 88; English translation, p. 94.

Selected Bibliography of Emanuel Herrmann's Writings

Allgemeine Wirthschaftslehre systematisch in leichtfasslichen Studien dargestellt. Vol. 1: *Das Gesetz der Arbeitstheilung als Grundlage der Technik und Ökonomik*, Graz: Verlag Josef Pock, 1868.

Theorie der Versicherung vom wirthschaftlichen Standpunkte, Graz: Verlag Josef Pock, 1868 (third enlarged edition, Vienna: Donegen, 1897).

Deutsche Volks-Lieder aus Kärnten, edited and selected by E. Herrmann, Graz: Leykam, 1869 (later edition edited with V. Pogatschnigg, Graz: Leykam, 1884).

Leitfaden der Wirthschaftslehre, Graz: Verlag Josef Pock, 1870.

Miniaturbilder aus dem Gebiete der Wirthschaft, Halle: Louis Nebert, 1872.

Prinzipien der Wirthschaft, Vienna: Lehmann und Wetzel, 1873.

Naturgeschichte der Kleidung, Vienna: v. Waldheim, 1878.

Hexameron. Geschichten aus der Geschichte, Vienna: v. Waldheim, 1879.

Cultur und Natur. Studien im Gebiete der Wirthschaft, Berlin: Allgemeiner Verein für Deutsche Literatur, Serie XII, 1887.

'Volkswirthschaft und Unterricht. Ein Beitrag zur Schulreform vom volkswirthschaftlichen Standpunkte', *Volkswirthschaftliche Zeitfragen*, vol. 9, no. 71/2 (1888).

'Die Familie vom Standpunkte der Gesammtwirthschaft', *Volkswirthschaftliche Zeitfragen*, vol. 10, no. 80 (1888).

Sein und Werden in Raum und Zeit. Wirtschaftliche Studien, 2nd edn, Berlin: Allgemeiner Verein für Deutsche Literatur, 1889.

Technische Fragen und Probleme der modernen Volkswirthschaft, Leipzig: 1891.

Wirtschaftliche Fragen und Probleme der Gegenwart. Studien zu einem Systeme der reinen und technischen Ökonomie, Leipzig: 1893.

Das Geheimniss der Macht. Originalstudien, 2nd edn, Berlin: Allgemeiner Verein für Deutsche Literatur, 1896.

7

THE AUSTRIAN CONNECTION: HAYEK'S LIBERALISM AND THE THOUGHT OF CARL MENGER[1]

Jeremy Shearmur

1. Introduction

Despite his Austrian origins, Hayek is often regarded as the latter-day spokesman of a largely British liberal tradition. This tradition — ranging through Mandeville, Hume, the Scottish Enlightenment, Burke and bits of J.S. Mill — is, however, in some ways Hayek's own creation. For it was he who grouped these people together and attributed to them a common position, which he then developed in his own writings (Hayek 1967, 1978). This he contrasted with another more rationalistic strand in liberalism, which he denounced as 'false individualism', for example in his 'Individualism: True and False' of 1945.[2]

Hayek's readers in the English-speaking world have had some difficulty in placing his views. There have been some attempts to assimilate them to conservatism (e.g. Letwin 1976). But Hayek is an enthusiast for change,[3] and is single-minded in his attachment to the market. He has, for example, written of his

> faith in the spontaneous forces of adjustment which makes the liberal accept changes without apprehension, even though he does not know how the necessary adaptations will be brought about. ... It is, indeed, part of the liberal attitude to assume that, especially in the economic field, the self-regulating forces of the market will somehow bring about the required adjustments to new conditions, although no one can foretell how they will do this in a particular instance (Hayek 1961, p. 400).

He has advocated radical moves in the field of economic policy,[4] and his writings also contain almost utopian proposals for constitutional reform (Hayek 1973–8, vol. 3). All this makes it difficult to present Hayek as a conservative, and he has also explicitly dissociated himself from a conservative reading of his work in his 'Why I am not a

Conservative' (Hayek 1961, Postscript).

At the same time, some of Hayek's contemporaries who would naturally be considered among the leading representatives of the British liberal tradition have found Hayek's views uncongenial. For example his fellow liberal and one-time colleague at the London School of Economics, Lionel Robbins, said that he 'always found the greatest difficulty in accepting . . . Hayek's disposition to classify the nineteenth century English Utilitarians with his "false" continental Rationalists'. He described this as a 'fundamental' point of disagreement between them (Robbins 1961). And he expressed the feeling that 'this is apt to lend support to illiberal uses of . . . Hayek's main position'. Roy Harrod (1946), the distinguished liberal economist and biographer of Keynes, also expressed grave reservations about the combination of traditionalistic and radical elements in Hayek's work:

> The attempt to link Smithian economics to Burke's conservatism is not a happy one. It is true that they are both inimical to centralist planning and rely on the unfettered working of existing institutions. But whereas Burke was anxious to make us look to the hidden virtue in established things, Smith's system was fully rationalist. Professor Hayek is right in urging that this does not imply that *each* individual is fully rational; but the *raison d'être* of the system as a whole and its parts can be demonstrated by argument. This is quite in contrast to the emotional foundations of loyalty on which Burke builds.

I suggest in the present essay that we may be helped in the identification and understanding of Hayek's views if we note an 'Austrian connection' in his work. Hayek (1961, Preface) has told us that his mind 'has been shaped by a youth spent in [his] native Austria and by two decades of middle life in Great Britain'. I believe that many features of Hayek's work are clarified if he is placed in an Austrian context, and that we are assisted in understanding his liberalism if it is related to some themes in the work of Carl Menger, the founder of the Austrian school of economics.[5] The connection with Menger is important not only in the general area of social theory, but also in the formation of Hayek's views on the character of economic knowledge, as set out by Hayek in his inaugural address at the London School of Economics. That view of economics (which he subsequently elaborated) does much to explain why there is not the clear-cut division that Harrod discerns between Hayek's 'Burkean' and 'Smithian' concerns.

2. Carl Menger and the Organic Character of Law

The suggestion that there is a parallel between the work of Hayek and of Carl Menger is, prima facie, not startling. Hayek's own economic and methodological ideas are very much in the tradition of the Austrian school of economics. Hayek was himself the editor of a collected edition of Menger's works (Menger 1933–6); and in addition to writing a biographical introduction to that collection,[6] he has written a substantial essay on 'The Place of Menger's *Grundsatze* in the History of Economic Thought'.[7] Hayek has referred to Menger in many places in his other works, and although (as far as I have been able to discover) he has not himself explicitly discussed the particular ideas to which I wish to draw attention, he has listed Menger as one of his 'main intellectual forebears' in respect of his social philosophy (Hayek 1967, p. 84).

However, Professor T.W. Hutchison, when reviewing the first volume of Hayek's *Law, Legislation and Liberty*, dissented strongly from Hayek's association of his views with those of Menger. Hutchison noted the presence, in this volume, 'of a number of well-known Hayekian themes', mentioning 'the distinction between individualism true and false' and 'the Burkean predilection for spontaneous, unplanned institutions, as against those shaped by conscious "constructivist" reason', and then wrote:

> Here, as before, Professor Hayek cites Carl Menger without making it clear that his own views on this subject differ, apparently very markedly, from Menger's, who complained of 'that one-sidedness which we have seen as characterising Burke's and Savigny's opposition to the rationalism and pragmatism of the French Age of Enlightenment.[8]

Hayek is thus seen by Hutchison as holding views that differ markedly from those of Menger, and also as being less sympathetic to rationalism. I would like to suggest that, although there is something in what Hutchison says, Menger's writings — especially those on law — contain an approach to social philosophy which is both distinctive and very close to some aspects of Hayek's work.[9] Let us look, briefly, at Menger's views.

In Book 4, Chapter 2, of Menger's *Untersuchungen über die Methode der Sozialwissenschaften*,[10] Menger takes some time off from his critical discussion of the historical school of economics, to discuss the historical school of jurisprudence (of Savigny *et al.*)[11] and to contrast its work with what he calls a 'pragmatic' understanding of the law and the economy, which he attributes to Adam Smith and his school. The contrast with which Menger is concerned is between the view that social institutions 'are always the intended product of the common will of society as such, results of expressed agreement by members of society or of positive legislation' (1963, pp. 174–5), and the view which he attributes to Burke, and singles out for emphasis in the writings of Savigny and Niebuhr, that

> law, like language, is at least originally not the product of an activity of public authorities aimed at producing it, nor in particular is it the product of positive legislation. It is, instead, the unintended result of a higher wisdom, of the historical development of nations (1963, p. 175).

Menger criticises the 'pragmatic' approach as having 'in the main . . . only an understanding for *positive* creations of public authority', claiming also that '[i]t therefore did not know how to value the significance of "organic" social structures for society in general and economy in particular and therefore was nowhere concerned to *preserve* them'. He continues by suggesting that:

> What characterises the theories of A. Smith and his followers is [a] one-sided rationalistic liberalism, the not infrequently impetuous effort to do away with what exists, with what is not always sufficiently understood, [and] the just as impetuous urge to create something new in the realm of political institutions, often without sufficient knowledge and experience (1963, p. 171).

This is close to the terms in which Hayek criticises the rationalistic strand of the individualist tradition.[12] The parallel with Hayek's ideas (notably his criticism of legal positivism)[13] is further extended by what Menger later says in an Appendix. For Menger contrasts law of an 'organic' character with law that has its source in authority (Menger 1963, p. 229), where 'the victor can set certain limits for the vanquished', and so on.

Menger explains that his reason for making this point against the views of 'the Smithian School' is not simply to maintain

> what had organically developed as unassailable, as if it were the higher wisdom in human affairs as opposed to the intended ordering of social conditions. The aim ... [is], on the contrary, the full understanding of existing social institutions in general and of organically created institutions in particular, the retention of what had proved its worth against the one-sidedly rationalistic mania for innovation in the field of economy. The object was to prevent the dissolution of the organically developed economy by means of a partially superficial pragmatism, a pragmatism that, contrary to the intention of its representatives, inexorably leads to socialism.[14]

It is important to note that Menger's remark about 'not simply maintaining what had organically developed as unassailable' was not just a matter of words. In his Appendix VIII, Menger (1963) offers a 'conjectural history' of law (in the style of his better-known sketch of the origin of money[15]). In this, he tries to show how this 'organic' development can, in principle, be understood individualistically, as an alternative to the explanatory idea of a *Volksgeist* found in the work of the historical legal theorists. He also dissociates himself from some of their more conservative views (as he does in the passage cited in the quotation from Hutchison above).

In this latter connection, he criticises the assertion

> that common law, in spite of its not turning out to be the result of a social will aimed consciously at the common good, benefits the latter nonetheless to a higher degree than ... corresponding positive legislation could (1963, p. 233).

For, he continues,

> common law has also proved harmful to the common good often enough, and on the contrary, legislation has just as often changed common law in a way benefitting the common good.

The general view at which Menger arrives may be summed up as follows. He insists on the importance of common law, and, more generally, of institutions which have not been deliberately designed. But he takes issue with the historical jurists for uncritically proclaiming the superiority of common law and other undesigned institutions. Menger suggests that those involved in positive legislation should learn from common law. But, at the same time, he insists that common law and inherited institutions must be critically examined as to their suitability, and, where necessary, improved. All this, for example, is to be found in the following passage, with which Menger concludes his Appendix:

> If individual eras have failed to recognise the peculiar worth of common law and changed the law by immature or hasty reforms, instead of bettering it, it was the duty of the historical school of jurists to avoid a similar procedure for the future — not by proclaiming the higher wisdom of common law, but by teaching the proper evaluation of the insight they had gained in legislation. The fruit of their view was not to be the avoidance in principle of positive law development, however well stipulated. It had to be the purification of the latter by new insight gained from the thoughtful consideration of common law ... [The] historical school of jurists had to make us understand the previously uncomprehended advantages of common law ... but never ... may science dispense with testing for their suitability these institutions which have come about 'organically'. It must, when careful investigation so requires, change and better them according to the measure of scientific insight and the practical experience at hand. No era [he concludes with an allusion to Savigny's *Vom Berufe unserer Zeit* ...] may renounce this 'calling'.

Menger's views are thus not the same as those of Burke or of Savigny — and Hutchison was right to emphasise this. But they are far from those of Bentham and other 'rationalistic' liberals. I wish to suggest here that they provide at least in part a model for Hayek's own approach. For that, also, includes a recognition of the importance of 'undesigned' institutions, but also a recognition of the importance of their being scrutinised critically (consider, in this connection, Hayek's frequent approving references to Popper's 'critical rationalism'[16]). In Hayek's work there is also the suggestion that one should attempt to extract the principles that lie behind successful 'organic' institutions, and make use of them when designing positive legislation (Hayek 1978, 'The Confusion of Language in Political Thought').

To substantiate all this as an interpretation of Hayek's social and political philosophy would require more space than is available to me here. I also have insufficient space to discuss the respects in which Hayek's views differ from those of Menger.[17] I will, however, give an indication of the presence of these Mengerian themes in Hayek's work. To this end, I will briefly discuss Hayek's inaugural address at the London School of Economics. For in this piece (to which, in my view, not enough attention has been given by those interested in Hayek's work) not only is a view close to that of Menger developed, but it is developed in the form of reflections on the discipline of theoretical economics. In this way, we can see how, for Hayek, the gap that Harrod discerned as existing between Smith and Burke is closed. For Hayek would seem to offer a single theoretical approach to the concerns of each theorist.

3. Economics and the Understanding of Organic Institutions

In his inaugural address at the LSE in 1933, 'The Trend of Economic Thinking',[18] Hayek offered a number of general reflections on theoretical economics. (This lecture is also remarkable for containing — in the form of reflections on economics — many themes that come to characterise Hayek's later writings on social philosophy.) He initially suggests that what led to the development of economic theory (both through the history of the discipline, and in his own career as an economist) is 'an intense desire to reconstruct a world which gives rise to profound dissatisfaction' (1933, p. 122). For, he explained:

> It was only when, because the economic system did not accomplish all we wanted, we prevented it from doing what it had been accomplishing, in an attempt to make it obey us in an arbitrary way, that we realised that there was anything to be understood. It was only incidentally, as a by-product of the study of such isolated phenomena, that it was gradually realised that many things which had been taken for granted were, in fact, the product of a highly complicated organism which we could only hope to understand by the intense mental effort of systematic enquiry (1933, p. 123).

Later in his lecture, Hayek characterises the aim of the economist as being gradually to construct a 'model which aims at reproducing the working of the economic system as a whole' (1933, p. 129). In this connection, he claims that the effect of theoretical analysis since the time of Hume and Smith

> has been to show that, in the large part, the coordination of individual efforts in society is not the product of planning, but has been brought about, by means which nobody wanted or understood, and which in isolation might be regarded by some as the most objectionable features of the system.

He later adds, with a reference to Mises,[19] that we still

> refuse to recognise that the spontaneous interplay of the actions of individuals may produce something which is not the deliberate object of their actions, but an organism in which every part performs a necessary function for the continuance of the whole, without any human mind having devised it ... that we are part of a 'higher' organised system which, without our knowledge, and long before we tried to understand it, solved problems the existence of which we did not even recognise ... The recognition of the existence of this organism is the recognition that there exists a subject-matter for economics.

Lest, however, all this might seem to be an expression of a Panglossian conservative functionalism (similar, say, to that which Menger had criticised in the German historical school of jurisprudence), it is perhaps worth mentioning that Hayek also stresses, later in his lecture (and elsewhere, especially in his earlier writings[20]) that '[t]his does not by any means imply that the economist will arrive at a purely negative attitude towards any kind of deliberate interference with the working of the system' (1933, p. 133). (Although Hayek does say that he is opposed to 'those proposals for interference which are not based upon an understanding of the system'.)

There are, in all this, obvious parallels with the views of Menger which we have examined above. There is perhaps a difference in tone, for Hayek sounds less radical. Hayek seems less willing to make fundamental changes in the economic system than is Menger in the institutions with which he is concerned. But I think that this can be accounted for by the influence on Hayek of Mises's argument that it is *only* through the (inherited, but improvable) market order that effective coordination of economic activity can be achieved in a large-scale industrial society.[21]

An approach similar to Menger's also runs through much of Hayek's later work. For example, Hayek has tried to develop theories as to the character of the valuable 'organic' institutions that we have inherited. He has been concerned, particularly, with forms of organisation which allow for the possibility of the utilisation of socially divided knowledge, and for individuals to learn by trial and error. In this connection, he has offered not only ideas about specific instances of such institutions, such as the market and a liberal system of law, but also ideas about the kind of understanding that we can achieve of the workings of such institutions.[22] In particular, he has claimed (for example, in his Nobel prize lecture, 'The Pretence of Knowledge' in Hayek (1978)) that we cannot have the detailed knowledge which many economists had hoped for, under the influence of models drawn from certain areas in the natural sciences. It is in such ways that the difference between Hayek's views on economics and those of Harrod and certain other British liberals ('Smith's system was fully rationalist') becomes clear.

There is also Hayek's criticism of 'constructivist' approaches to problems of social policy. This amounts to a plea that we should not overlook the existence, the importance, and the often useful functions performed by undesigned institutions. Hayek has also argued that we should attempt to deal with social problems in a manner that does not disrupt the working of such institutions (compare, here, Hayek's discussion of various practical policy problems at the end of his *Constitution of Liberty*). In addition, there has been the attempt, culminating in his *Law, Legislation and Liberty*, to extract the principles that underlie such institutions, in such a way that they might be used in the construction of new social institutions which, he hopes, will enable us to return to something closer to a liberal social and political order (Hayek 1973–8, vol. 3; 1976–8).

Thus, I would suggest, we have in Hayek's inaugural address at the LSE an approach which is close to that of Carl Menger, and which treats the *economic* system, and our knowledge of it, in terms that are similar to those in which Hayek later treats of other social institutions. There is, as a result, a single approach to all these phenomena in Hayek's work. It is neither that of the rationalistic liberal, nor that of the conservative — which explains the problems that conservatives and liberals in the English-speaking world have had in the comprehension of Hayek's views. And it is in the identification of Hayek's views that, I believe, attention to 'The Austrian connection' is important.

4. Concluding Remarks

My aim, in this brief essay, has been to contribute to the identification of Hayek's views, as a prologomenon to their evaluation. This evaluation must wait for a future occasion. But if my account of Hayek's views is even part of the truth, then the following issues seem to me pressing.

First, has Hayek *succeeded* in producing a single theoretical approach to the set of problems raised by Burke and by Smith? In this connection, one may ask what *positive* claims Hayek is making about institutions that we inherit from the past, and on what basis. For as soon as we perceive that there are alternative ways open to us of conducting our affairs, we would seem to require a positive (theoretical) rationale for continuing to behave as we did before, rather than for adopting some newly perceived alternative. Hayek here seems to vacillate.[23] Sometimes he appears to be offering a conservative functionalism, backed up by a none-too-convincing account of the emergence of beneficent social institutions through a process of group selection (Hayek 1973–8, vol. 3, Postscript; Watkins 1976b; Gray 1980). At other times, he makes an identification between what is a positive heritage from the past and the principles of a *Rechtsstaat* liberalism and a market-based social order, for the desirability of which he offers arguments of a more rationalistic character, and to which he also suggests possible improvements.

This latter approach seems to me clearly superior; but it also faces certain problems. First, there are problems resulting from Hayek's view of economics and its methodology. Hayek has placed great emphasis on the role of the market in coordinating the plans of individuals, and as allowing for the utilisation of knowledge that is dispersed in society and held by individuals in perhaps only a tacit form. He has also stressed the importance of the market as a forum within which learning may take place by trial and error. In the course of his arguments, he has placed emphasis on the importance of the utilisation, in the methodology of economics, of methodological individualism, and of 'subjectivism', in the sense of starting from the agent's perspective.[24] However, all this may lead to a difficulty for his political philosophy. For, on the basis of such ideas, it may be difficult to demonstrate anything very specific about what we can expect from the performance of a market system. In particular, those who favour such an approach should, I think, be given pause by the fact that Lachmann, who has taken such ideas furthest, has been led to views that have been described as 'nihilistic' by their critics.[25] Such conclusions would, however, seem a disaster for Hayek, given the role that positive claims about a market order play in his political thought.[26]

Second, there are difficulties about Hayek's identification of our positive heritage from the past with a liberal economic and social order.[27] Hayek, I would suggest, does not distinguish sufficiently clearly three rather different theses: (i) that there are certain forms of social organisation which permit the use of individual initiative, the use of socially distributed knowledge, etc. (and which, as Hayek has argued, may have various other distinctive properties); (ii) that we may have stumbled across institutions of such a kind, without having set out to achieve them; (iii) that there has been some general process of group selection at work in the past, which has been responsible for inherited institutions having such a character. The third thesis seems to me both implausible and unnecessary — though, of course, environments that give such results may have existed at certain times in the past, and there is nothing to stop us trying deliberately to create such environments, if we so desire.

But suppose that Hayek's views were recast, so as to emphasise points (i) and (ii), together with the idea that we can set out to improve our institutions so as to make them better serve the functions that Hayek considers so important. If this were the case, and if one were even able to show that such a Hayekian liberalism represented the best attainable social order, there would still be problems concerning its acceptability to those who actually live within it. For it may not be possible to make its advantages clear to them, and such a society may appear to lack moral legitimacy. At the very same time, the freedom, mobility and material well-being that such a society offers to its citizens would seem, of itself, to weaken some of the informal mechanisms which in earlier forms of social organisation had kept people complying with inherited social institutions, or institutions favoured by those in privileged social positions (Shearmur 1979; 1985).

As a result, those who favour a liberalism such as Hayek's have, I believe, not only to show the advantages of such an approach, but also to show how liberalism can be self-sustaining as a form of social organisation. Such a task would involve problems of a wider character than are today usually tackled by normative social theory (at least in its liberal forms[28]). But in undertaking such a task one could follow Hayek's lead in looking back for inspiration to the work of theorists of the eighteenth century. For one has only to look at the work of Rousseau or of Adam Smith with such problems in mind to see, as a major theme in their work, a concern both with normative social theory and with theories about how to bring about (and maintain) the social conditions under which their ideals can be realised. In this way, the liberal theorist pursuing Hayek's concerns may be led from the Austrian connection back to the problematic of the Scottish Enlightenment.[29]

Notes

1. Based in part on a paper, 'Hayek and the Invisible Hand', delivered to a joint meeting of the Carl Menger Society and the Seminar for Austro-German Philosophy, London, April 1980. I would like to thank Barry Smith for suggestions and comments on an earlier version of the paper.

2. Subsequently reprinted in Hayek (1948).

3. See, notably, Hayek (1961, p. 41): 'progress is movement for movement's sake'.

4. For example, his ideas about the denationalisation of money, and his proposals for dramatic action to combat inflation.

5. I am not wishing here to claim that there is a liberal tradition in Austria of longer standing that is important in helping us to understand Hayek's work. J.C. Nyíri, in his paper in this volume on liberalism in the Austro-Hungarian empire, has uncovered a number of interesting figures who combine liberal and conservative views; but none of them seems to hold those views that I discern in Menger and, subsequently, in Hayek.

6. Also published as Hayek (1934).

7. In Hicks and Weber (1973).

8. See Hutchison (1974, p. 451). Hutchison's quotation is from Menger (1963, p. 181). In the light of my thesis in the present paper, I find Hutchison's criticism of Hayek somewhat ironic, as it does not seem to me that Hayek, in that particular volume, does identify his views strongly with those of Menger, other than in the context of the methodology of social science.

9. See also, on Menger and Hayek, L. Schneider's 'Introduction' to Menger (1963); and for a brief but illuminating comment on Menger's views about law, see Hutchison (1973, p. 26ff).

10. In what follows, I will cite the translation, *Problems of Economics and Sociology*.

11. A useful introduction to this historical school is provided by Small (1924).

12. Compare Hayek (1973–9, vol. 1, p. 10 and n. 5). It is somewhat ironic that Menger (for understandable enough reasons) takes Smith as the figure-head of the movement that he criticises, while Smith is better regarded as one of the key theorists of a liberalism close in some ways to that of Hayek himself. On Smith, see Haakonssen (1976, 1981); Stein (1980); Hont and Ignatieff (1983); Winch (1978); Shearmur (1985); and the brief discussion of the issue of Menger's interpretation of Smith in Hutchison (1973).

13. Compare Hayek (1961, 1973–8).

14. See Menger (1963, p. 177). Compare also with the concluding remark here, Hayek (1944; 1973–8, vol. 1, p. 57).

15. See Menger (1963, Book 3, Chapter 2, Section 4; 1981, Chapter 7, Section 4), and, for discussion, Watkins (1976a).

16. Although their views are by no means identical: compare, in this connection, Shearmur (forthcoming). As Larry Briskman has emphasised to me, however, there are strong resemblances between Menger's views as I have sketched them in this paper and Popper (1963, 'Towards a Rational Theory of Tradition').

17. One important difference relates to a point noted by Miller (1976): Hayek's

scepticism about the powers of reason. This relates to the Burkean and traditionalistic aspects of Hayek's work, to the theme of evolutionary group selection (which looms increasingly large in Hayek's later work) and, as John Gray has emphasised, to Hayek's more general philosophical and psychological ideas; for example the themes of his *Sensory Order* (1952a). (See John Gray, 'Hayek on Liberty and Tradition' (1980), and his *Hayek on Liberty*.) See also the text to note 22 in this paper.

18. Hayek (1933); this lecture has not been reprinted in any collection of Hayek's writings to date.

19. Mises played a most important role in turning Hayek from his initial Fabian views to classical liberalism. See Hayek (1981).

20. See, especially, his writings up to and including *The Road to Serfdom* (1944). In some of his later work there is more emphasis on existing institutions as the product of group selection.

21. See Hayek's (1948) discussion of the problem of socialist calculation.

22. For example, in his writings about 'explanation of the principle': see Hayek (1952a; 1967).

23. Compare Hamowy (1971) and Gray (1980). Related issues were also discussed in Shearmur (1976).

24. Hayek's work is important in that it does not stop at that point (as, say, might be claimed of Winch (1958)), but instead argues that the social scientist should go on to explain how actions undertaken by such agents may have unintended consequences which those very agents may not themselves understand. See Hayek (1952b, 'Scientism and the Study of Society'); also Shearmur (1983).

25. See, for example, Lachmann (1977 and 1978).

26. Compare, here, the way in which the long-run advantages of a market system must be invoked against particular claims for 'social justice'. On this whole argument, compare the related argument within the natural law tradition in Locke and Adam Smith, discussed in Hont and Ignatieff (1983, 'Introduction').

27. Note in this connection the historical opposition between Hegel (1942) — who in his discussion of law in the 'civil society' section of his *Philosophy of Right* represents the *Rechtsstaat* tradition — and the historical jurist Savigny (1831).

28. Such an approach is almost a commonplace among the critics of liberalism.

29. Thus my own research includes both work on Hayek and a treatment of the social philosophy of Adam Smith and of the development of the problematic of classical liberalism.

Bibliography

An extensive bibliography of Hayek's works and of secondary literature on Hayek is to be found in Gray (1980).

Barry, N. (1979). *Hayek's Social and Economic Philosophy*, London: Macmillan.

Barry, N. (1982). 'The Tradition of Spontaneous Order', *Literature of Liberty*, 5, pp. 7–58.

Berghel, H. *et al.* (eds) (1979). *Wittgenstein, the Vienna Circle and Critical Rationalism*, Dordrecht/Boston: Reidel; Vienna: Hölder-Pichler-Tempsky.

Cohen, R.S., Feyerabend, P., & Wartofsky, M.W. (eds) (1976). *Essays in Memory of Imre Lakatos*, Dordrecht/Boston: Reidel.

Gray, J. (1980). 'Hayek on Liberty and Tradition', *Journal of Libertarian Studies, 4*, 119–37.

Gray, J. (1984). *Hayek on Liberty*, Oxford: Blackwell.

Haakonssen, K. (1976). 'Natural Justices', dissertation, University of Edinburgh.
Haakonssen, K. (1981). *The Science of a Legislator*, Cambridge: Cambridge University Press.
Hamowy, R. (1971). 'Freedom and the Rule of Law in F.A. Hayek', *Il Politico, 36*, pp. 349–71.
Harrod, R. (1946). 'Review of Hayek, *Individualism: True and False*', *Economic Journal, 1*, p. 439.
Hayek, F.A. von (1933). 'The Trend of Economic Thinking', *Economica, 13*, pp. 121–37.
Hayek, F.A. von (1934). 'Carl Menger', *Economica*, new series *1*, pp. 393–420.
Hayek, F.A. von (1944). *The Road to Serfdom*, London: George Routledge.
Hayek, F.A. von (1946). *Individualism: True and False* (Pamphlet), Dublin: Hodges, Finnis.
Hayek, F.A. von (1948). *Individualism and Economic Order*, London: George Routledge.
Hayek, F.A. von (1952a). *The Sensory Order*, London: Routledge & Kegan Paul.
Hayek, F.A. von (1952b). *The Counter-Revolution of Science*, Glencoe, Illinois: The Free Press.
Hayek, F.A. von (1961). *The Constitution of Liberty*, London: Routledge & Kegan Paul.
Hayek, F.A. von (1967). *Studies in Philosophy, Politics and Economics*, London: Routledge & Kegan Paul.
Hayek, F.A. von (1973–8). *Law, Legislation and Liberty*, London: Routledge & Kegan Paul, vol. 1, 1973; vol. 2, 1976; vol. 3, 1978.
Hayek, F.A. von (1976–8). *The Denationalisation of Money*, London: Institute of Economic Affairs.
Hayek, F.A. von (1978). *New Studies in Philosophy, Politics, Economics and the History of Ideas* London Routledge & Kegan Paul.
Hayek, F.A. von (1981). 'Foreword', to L. von Mises, *Socialism*.
Hegel, G.W.F. (1942). *Hegel's Philosophy of Right*, translated by T.M .Knox, Oxford: Clarendon Press.
Hicks, J.R. & Weber, W. (eds) (1973). *Carl Menger and the Austrian School of Economics*, Oxford: Clarendon Press.
Hont, I. & Ignatieff, M. (eds) (1983). *Wealth and Virtue*, Cambridge: Cambridge University Press.
Hutchison, T.W. (1973). 'Some Themes from *Investigations into Method*', in Hicks and Weber (1973), pp. 15–47.
Hutchison, T.W. (1974). 'Review of Hayek: *Law, Legislation and Liberty*, vol. 1', *Economica*, p. 451.
Hutchison, T.W. (1981). *The Politics and Philosophy of Economics*, Oxford: Blackwell.
Lachmann, L. (1977). *Capital, Expectations, and the Market Process*, ed. W. Grinder, Kansas City: Sheed, Andrews & McMeel.
Lachmann, L. (1978). 'An Austrian Stocktaking: Unsettled Questions and Tentative Answers' in Spadaro (1978), pp. 1–18.
Letwin, S. (1976). 'The Achievement of Hayek' in F. Machlup (1976), pp. 147–62.
Machlup, F. (ed.) (1976). *Essays on Hayek*, New York: New York University Press.
Menger, C. (1871). *Grundsätze der Volkswirthschaftslehre*, Vienna: Braumüller.
Menger, C. (1883). *Untersuchungen ueber die Methode der Sozialwissenschaften und der politischen Oekonomie insbesondere*, Leipzig: Duncker and Humblot.
Menger, C. (1933–6). *The Collected Works of Carl Menger*, ed. F.A. von Hayek, London: London School of Economics.
Menger, C. (1963). *Problems of Economics and Sociology*, Urbana: University of Illinois Press.

224   *Hayek's Liberalism and the Thought of Carl Menger*

Menger, C. (1981). *Principles of Economics*, New York/London: New York University Press.
Miller, E. (1976). 'Hayek's Critique of Reason', *Modern Age*, Fall, pp. 383–93.
Mises, L. von (1981). *Socialism*, Indianapolis: Liberty Press.
Popper, K.R. (1963). *Conjectures and Refutations*, London: Routledge & Kegan Paul.
Robbins, L. (1961). 'Hayek on Liberty', *Economica*, pp. 66–81.
Savigny, F.C. von (1831). *Of the Vocation of our Age for Legislation and Jurisprudence*, translated by Hayward, London.
Shearmur, J.F.G. (1976). 'Libertarianism and Conservatism in the Work of F.A. von Hayek', talk given to Carl Menger Society, London.
Shearmur, J.F.G. (1979). 'Abstract Institutions in an Open Society' in Berghel *et al.* (1979), pp. 349–54.
Shearmur, J.F.G. (1982). 'Norman Barry: The Tradition of Spontaneous Order', *Literature of Liberty*, Winter, pp. 13–16.
Shearmur, J.F.G. (1983). 'Subjectivism, Falsification and Positive Economics' in J. Wiseman (1983), pp. 65–86.
Shearmur, J.F.G. (1985). *Adam Smith's Second Thoughts* (pamphlet), London: Adam Smith Club.
Shearmur, J.F.G. (forthcoming). 'Popper, Liberalism and Social Democracy' (in French) in R. Bouveresse (ed.), *Karl Popper et la science d'aujourd'hui*.
Small, A. (1924). *The Origins of Sociology*, Chicago: Univesity of Chicago Press.
Spadaro, L. (ed.) (1978). *New Directions in Austrian Economics*, Kansas City: Sheed, Andrews and McMeel.
Stein, P. (1980). *Legal Evolution*, Cambridge: Cambridge University Press.
Watkins, J.W.N. (1976a). 'Two Criticisms of Hobbes' in Cohen *et al.* (1976), pp. 691–716.
Watkins, J.W.N. (1976b). 'Review of Hayek: *Law, Legislation and Liberty*, vol. 1', *Philosophy of the Social Sciences*, 6, pp. 369–72.
Winch, D. (1978). *Adam Smith's Second Thoughts*, Cambridge: Cambridge University Press.
Winch, P. (1958). *The Idea of a Social Science*, London: Routledge and Kegan Paul.
Wiseman, J. (ed.) (1983). *Beyond Positive Economics?*, London: Macmillan.

8 AUSTRIAN ECONOMICS UNDER FIRE: THE HAYEK-SRAFFA DUEL IN RETROSPECT

Ludwig M. Lachmann

1. Introduction

When the history of economic thought in the twentieth century comes to be written, there is no doubt that the decade of the 1930s will occupy a very special place in it. The 'Keynesian revolution', the rise of new theories of competition such as those of Chamberlin and Joan Robinson, the beginnings of growth theory in Harrod's work, all belong to this decade. Prominent thinkers of the century, such as Hicks and Shackle, published their first writings during it. The 1930s were indeed 'years of high theory'.

For Austrian economics, however, this was a tragic decade. Owing to the political circumstances of the time many Austrian philosophers and economists were compelled to leave Austria. Some of the emigrants were successful in the countries of their adoption, others were not. Professor Hayek, having made a triumphal entry into the University of London in 1931 as Tooke Professor of Economics and Statistics, had become a rather lonely figure by 1939, when the London School of Economics was evacuated from its London premises for the duration of the Second World War. The decline in the fortunes of Austrian economics is usually attributed to the Keynesian revolution and the success of the full employment policy in Nazi Germany, its historical background, which made even liberal economists cast furtive glances at what they otherwise professed to abhor.

In 1967, in *The Hayek Story*, Sir John Hicks wrote:

> When the definitive history of economic analysis during the nineteen-thirties comes to be written, a leading character in the drama (it was quite a drama) will be Professor Hayek. Hayek's economic writings . . . are almost unknown to the modern student, it is hardly remembered that there was a time when the new theories of Hayek were the principal rival to the new theories of Keynes (Hicks, 1967, p. 203).

The Keynesian revolution is usually dated to 1936 as 'the new theories of Keynes' took shape in the *General Theory of Employment, Interest and Money* published in February 1936. In this paper we shall be concerned with an episode four years earlier, in 1932, when the new Austrian theories to which Hayek gave provisional shape in *Prices and Production* (1931) incurred the wrath of Mr Piero Sraffa, who reviewed the book in an article 'Dr. Hayek on Money and Capital' in the *Economic Journal* of March 1932. In the June issue Hayek wrote ('Money and Capital: a Reply'). His reply drew a brief two-page rejoinder from his opponent.

Sraffa's review was an onslaught conducted with unusual ferocity, somewhat out of keeping with the tone ordinarily adopted by book reviewers in the *Economic Journal*. It is significant that the altercation took place less than a year after Hayek's arrival in London. The new Austrian ideas had barely been presented by him when they were challenged by a scholar with an international reputation for incisive analysis, who, supposedly engaged in other fields, had gone out of his way to deliver the onslaught.

What was the ordinary economist of 1932 to make of all this? The feeling prevailing in London and other British universities was one of utter bewilderment. Hayek's ideas had been difficult to grasp. In Hicks' words, '*Prices and Production* was in English, but it was not English economics. It needed further translation before it could be properly assessed' (Hicks 1967, p. 204). Sraffa's review, however, was evidently not designed to provide such a translation. It appeared to proceed from assumptions no more familiar than were Hayek's. The more perceptive sensed that they were witnessing a clash of two irreconcilable views of the economic world. The less perceptive were just puzzled by what the two contestants were after. But nobody liked what he saw.

Here we have to remember that the possibility that these were the opening shots in a battle between two rival schools of economic thought was not one that would readily occur to the average Anglo-Saxon economist of the 1930s. The *Methodenstreit* was happily a matter of the past. The conviction of the unity of economic thought was a major article of the creed of the graduate schools. School rivalries belonged to an unenlightened past one had fortunately left behind. When Keynes, in the *General Theory*, began to talk about 'classical economists', to denote his own thought by contrast to theirs, even some of his closest friends began to feel uneasy. This was to them a new and unfamiliar mode of discourse.

With the Austrian emigrés the conviction of the unity of economic thought was strong, and in the circumstances of their emigration naturally became stronger.[1] For Hayek Paretian general equilibrium was the pivot of economic theory, the centre of gravity towards which all major economic forces tended.[2] For him the task of trade cycle theory was to show how it came about that these major forces were temporarily impeded and their effects delayed, and since the cycle was supposed to start with a boom and end with a depression, he saw in the depression the ultimate triumph of the equilibrating forces.

His opponent took a very different view of the modern market economy. Equilibrium meant to him something quite different.

2. The Background to Sraffa's Attack

Mr Sraffa's review of Hayek's book was his only publication in 25 years, from *The Laws of Returns under Competitive Conditions* (Sraffa, 1926) to his Introduction to the Ricardo edition of the Royal Economic Society in 1951.[3] This fact in itself indicates the significance its author attributed to his review. In 1932 most contemporary economists missed this significance and, as we saw, were baffled by Sraffa's piece and Hayek's reply to it. Fortunately, in the 1980s we are in an altogether different position.

With the benefit of hindsight we are now able to understand that Sraffa's critique of Hayek's book marked the start of the neo-Ricardian counter-revolution. This is usually dated to 1960, the year in which Sraffa published his famous book *Production of Commodities by Means of Commodities* which bore the subtitle *Prelude to a Critique of Economic Theory*. We can now see that Sraffa's paper in 1932 was, as it were, a prelude to this *Prelude*. The aim of the neo-Ricardian counter-revolution is to undo the subjectivist revolution in economic thought which took place in the 1870s, led by Jevons, Menger, and Walras, in which it was shown that the value of economic goods depends on the (subjective) utility they have to different individuals, and not on their (objective) cost of production. And since Menger and his Austrian successors were, among the assailants of the classical citadel in the 1870s, the most consistent subjectivists, while in the School of Lausanne the original Walrasian subjectivism of utility was soon sterilised in the shape of Paretian indifference curves, it is perhaps not surprising that a prominent Austrian economist became the first target of the new counter-revolution.

Seen from the perspective of today, it is not at all hard to understand why the readers of 1932 were so puzzled by this attack on Hayek: they never were told from what kind of a position it was made. For in this encounter Mr Sraffa wore a strange mask. He never informed his readers that the presuppositions of the views he presented to them, since they reflected an analytical creed which had fallen into oblivion 60 years earlier and was therefore bound to be unfamiliar to them, were, to them at least, 'new'. The reason for the disguise he chose to wear is obvious. Had he told the readers of the *Economic Journal* plainly that his criticism of the book under review proceeded from a Ricardian view of the nature of the economic system, he could not have hoped to carry many of his readers with him. The neo-Ricardian counter-revolution, in the circumstances of 1932, could not be expected to win adherents before its main articles of faith had been espoused in public, and this could hardly be done in a review article. As Sraffa's main aim evidently was to discredit Hayek in the eyes of the readers of the *Economic Journal*, who were brought up on a Marshallian view of the economic system, he had better not let them know how different were his views from theirs. For his polemical purpose it was better that they should be puzzled than that they might become suspicious.

Contemporary readers, by contrast, know the history of the counter-revolution and can turn their historical knowledge to good account. Moreover, they are enjoying the benefit of the writings of the post-Sraffa generation, such as those of Professor Garegnani (e.g. 1976), Dr Levine (1980) and Dr Milgate (1979). Having lived through 20 years of the 'revival of Classical Political Economy', whether or not impressed by the sheer verve and mental vigour of its proponents, if not by their achievements, we have learnt a good deal we did not know in 1932.

In only two brief passages of Sraffa's article do we catch a glimpse of his anti-subjectivist aim and Ricardian purpose. A footnote on p. 47 ends with the words 'Dr. Hayek, who extols the imaginary achievements of the "subjective method" in economics, often succeeds in making patent nonsense of it'. On p. 50, in discussing disequilibrium in the cotton market, he is compelled to define what he means by equilibrium. So we read: 'But if, for any reason, the supply and the demand for a commodity are not in equilibrium (i.e. its market price exceeds or falls short of its cost of production), its spot and forward prices diverge.' Here it becomes quite clear that to Sraffa equilibrium means 'classical' long-run cost-of-production equilibrium (that is, price equals cost of production), a norm from which market prices always diverge, while to Hayek equilibrium is 'neoclassical' market-clearing equilibrium in all markets (what neo-Ricardians nowadays call 'supply-and-demand equilibrium') with no particular regard being paid to the difference between the long and short run. And here, then, we have got to the bottom of our dispute and are provided with a clue to most of the other points at issue between the two contestants.

Hayek clearly perceived that the attack on him was conducted from (what in 1932 was) a somewhat unorthodox position and, we may guess, sensed that his opponent had something of substance to hide. So he issued a challenge to him. 'I should also like to ask him to define his own attitude to these problems more clearly than he has yet done. From his article one gains the impression that his attitude is a curious mixture of, on the one hand, an extreme theoretical nihilism which denies that existing theories of equilibrium provide any useful description of the non-monetary forces at work and, on the other hand, of an ultra-conservatism which resents any attempt to show that the differences between a monetary and a non-monetary economy are not only, and not even mainly, "those characteristics which are set forth at the beginning of every textbook on money"' (Hayek, 1932, p. 238).

But he met with a flat refusal. Sraffa (1932b, p. 250) declined to say where he stood, for the less than cogent reason that Hayek's assumptions were altogether too fanciful to be taken seriously. 'After this Dr. Hayek will allow me not to take seriously his questions as to what I "really believe". Nobody could believe that anything that logically follows from such fantastic assumptions is true in reality.' Today we can appreciate the real reasons for his refusal to be drawn.

3. Sraffa's Review

Sraffa starts his review with an attack on Hayek's monetary assumptions. While giving his blessing to an inquiry which 'would resolve itself into a comparison between the conditions of a specified non-monetary economy and those of various monetary systems', he feels that Hayek has failed to conduct it properly.

'But the reader soon realises that Dr Hayek completely forgets to deal with the task which he has set himself, and that he is only concerned with the wholly different problem of proving that only one particular banking policy (that which maintains constant under all circumstances the quantity of money multiplied by its velocity of circulation) succeeds in giving full effect to the "voluntary decisions of individuals", especially in regard to saving, whilst under any other policy these decisions are "distorted" by the "artificial" interference of banks. Being entirely unaware that it may be doubted whether under a system of barter the decisions of individuals would have their full effects, once he has satisfied himself that a policy of constant money would achieve this result, he identifies it with "neutral money"; and finally, feeling entitled to describe that policy as "natural", he takes it for granted that it will be found desirable by every right-thinking person' (Sraffa, 1932a, p. 43).

On the next page the attack is pressed while, suddenly, we become award of how far away we are from the world of Ricardo and the classical quantity theory. Of Hayek we are told:

> The money which he contemplates is in effect used purely and simply as a medium of exchange. There are no debts, no money-contracts, no wage-agreements, no sticky prices in his suppositions. Thus he is able to neglect altogether the most obvious effects of a general fall, or rise, of prices. (p. 44.)

While we cannot but admire the adroitness of a pose that enables Sraffa to stand with one leg in Ricardo's world and with the other in our world of industrial fix-prices, we cannot but reflect that in the latter world expectations, a manifestation of subjectivism, must surely carry some weight. On the same page we actually find a few words of praise for Hayek:

> Such a theory, according to him, ought simply to consider the influence of money on the relative prices of commodities — which is excellent, provided that money itself is one of the commodities under consideration; but Dr. Hayek goes further and rejects not only the notion of general price-level but every notion of the value of money in any sense whatever.

The conclusion of this part of the review is severe:

> The reader is forced to conclude that these alleged differences can only arise, either from an error of reasoning, or from the unwitting introduction, in working out the effects of one of the two systems compared, of some irrelevant non-monetary consideration, which produces the difference, attributed to the properties of the system itself. The task of the critic, therefore, is the somewhat monotonous

one of discovering for each step of Dr. Hayek's parallel analysis, which is the error or irrelevancy which causes the difference (pp. 44–5).

We learn with some surprise that Sraffa, a prominent neo-Ricardian, regards those parts of Hayek's book devoted to Austrian capital theory as largely a waste of time. As the time dimension of production is a Ricardian theme its dismissal is rather unexpected.

Dr. Hayek as it were builds up a terrific steam-hammer in order to crack a nut — and then he does not crack it. Since we are primarily concerned in this review with the nut that is not cracked, we need not spend time criticising the hammer. The part which its description plays in the book is little more than that of obscuring the main issue; a maze of contradictions makes the reader so completely dizzy, that when he reaches the discussion of money he may out of despair be prepared to believe anything (p. 45).

Thus, in 1932 we did not learn what Sraffa thought of the Austrian theory of capital.[4]

After this, in the second part of the article, we encounter three issues which turn out to be major areas of contention between our Austrian author and his critic. These are: saving and investment; the problem of malinvestment; and the meaning to be attributed to the notion of the natural rate of interest'.

With the first of these we can deal fairly briefly here because it did not remain for long an issue between neo-Ricardians and Austrians, but after 1936 turned into one between Keynesians and their opponents. We have to remember that we are in 1932, half-way between *Treatise* and *General Theory*, and before the Myrdalian distinction between magnitudes *ex ante* and *ex post* became known outside Sweden. Keynesians, using the terminology of the *Treatise*, spoke of the divergence between savings and investment (meaning *ex ante*) caused by the fact that in our society savers and investment decision-makers are typically different classes of people. Austrians like Mises and Hayek, by contrast, subscribed to the view, which at that time was a tenet of all mainstream economics, and nothing particularly Austrian, that saving determines investment through the interest mechanism.

Sraffa, adopting the Keynesian view,[5] in a footnote attacks Hayek, who in his book had assumed that when banks grant increased credits all these are granted to producers (no consumer credit in the world of 1930).

The essential contradiction is that Dr. Hayek must both assume that the 'consumers' are the same individuals as the 'entrepreneurs', and that they are distinct. For only if they are identical can the consumers' decisions to save take the form of a decision to alter the 'proportions' in which the total gross receipts are divided between the purchase of consumers' goods and the purchase of producers' goods; and only if they are distinct has the contrast between 'credits to producers', which are used to buy producers' goods, and 'credits to consumers', which are used to buy consumers' goods, any definite meaning (Straffa, 1932a, p. 45n).

Hayek's reply shows how unfamiliar he still is, in 1932, with Keynesian ways of thought.

I do not understand why Mr. Sraffa should suggest that a consumer who is not an entrepreneur will not affect the proportion between the demand for consumers' goods and the demand for producers' goods by his decision to save. It is certain that when he invests his savings by lending them out at interest he is instrumental in directing part of his money income to the purchase of producers' goods, without himself becoming an entrepreneur (Hayek, 1932, p. 241n).

Would anybody be so 'certain' about it today? We also must note that Hayek here uses the verb 'to invest' in its ordinary financial meaning which, since Keynes, is not the meaning in which economists use it today.

Today there appears to be fairly wide agreement that, in modern industrial society at least, we had better refrain from saying either that savings determine investment or that investment determines savings. In the first place, there is no such thing as *a* rate of interest, there is a structure of interest rates on a wide variety of financial assets in a complex network of asset markets iinked by intermediation. The elements of this structure respond to a large variety of influences prompted in part by divergent expectations about the magnitudes of rates of interest in the future. Put briefly, it is impossible to say that the rate of interest brings savings and investment into equality as such a statement would imply that its function is confined to the market for new capital, while in reality it extends to the markets for all existing assets on each of which the rate of yield has to equate supply and demand. On the other hand, as Hicks showed in *The Crisis in Keynesian Economics* (Hicks, 1974, pp. 9–30), the Keynesian teaching that investment determines savings via the multiplier process is also untenable, at least without considerable qualification.

4. The Complementarity of Capital

We next have to turn to the problem of malinvestment which, in the context of the controversy we are discussing, arises in connection with Hayek's assertion that capital resources brought into existence in response to a money rate of interest below the level of the natural rate cannot be maintained once credit inflation has been stopped and monetary equilibrium is restored. Their owners and their creditors suffer capital loss.

Sraffa demurs:

> As a moment's reflection will show, 'there can be no doubt' that nothing of the sort will happen. One class has, for a time, robbed another class of a part of their incomes; and has saved the plunder. When the robbery comes to an end, it is clear that the victims cannot possibly consume the capital which is now well out of their reach. If they are wage-earners, who have all the time consumed every penny of their income, they have no wherewithal to expand consumption. And if they are capitalists, who have not shared in the plunder, they may indeed be induced to consume now a part of their capital by the fall in the rate of interest; but no more so than if the rate had been lowered by the 'voluntary savings' of other people (Sraffa, 1932a, p. 48).

Hayek provides an effective retort.

> That the physical quantity of these capital goods will, for some time, continue to exist unchanged does not mean that their owners have not lost the greater part, or all, of their capital. It is of very little use for the machine manufacturer to hold on tight to his capital goods when the producer who used to buy the machines is either unable, or finds it unprofitable at the higher rate of interest, to do so now. Whether he likes it or not, the actions of other people have destroyed his capital (Hayek, 1932, p. 243).

Having described Sraffa's objecton as 'surprisingly superficial' Hayek proceeds to ask him a couple of pointed questions.

Is Mr. Sraffa really unfamiliar with the fact that capital sometimes falls in value because the running costs of the plant have risen; or does he belong to the sect which believes in curing such a situation by stimulating consumption? And would he really deny that, by a sudden relative increase in the demand for consumers' goods capital may be destroyed against the will of its owners? (p. 244).

The thought expressed in these two passages remains as significant today as it was in 1932. Nothing we have witnessed in 20 years of the 'revival of Classical Political Economy' is likely to still our misgivings. Neo-Ricardian thought appears to be unable to cope with the problem of capital resources which can undergo considerable changes in value while retaining their physical form.

Neo-Ricardians stand in need of a theory of capital, as without one they can have nothing to say about capitalism and its markets. In reality capital is concrete and heterogeneous, not abstract and homogeneous. Only certain forms of capital combinations, certain modes of capital complementarity, produce productive results, others do not. Hence there is always the danger that a capital resource may lose some of its complements. Moreover, capital values depend on future, not present, earnings. A theory of capital which takes no account of expectations can tell us little about the real world. The theory of capital, then, offers no promising ground for a return to classical objectivism in the theory of value.

In the face of these facts supporters of the 'classical revival' are unable to claim that all they are interested in is the process of reproduction of the economic system as a whole, and that they are entitled to abstract from such details as we have mentioned. For the maintenance of capital is a human art and a problematic endeavour, not an automatic occurrence, and he who chooses a level of abstraction too high to notice this fact can learn but little about our world.

5. Interest and Equilibrium

We now come to the third of our contentious issues, the problem of the meaning of the Wicksellian 'natural rate of interest'. It gained some importance a few years later when Sraffa's argument on this issue provided the inspiration for the notion of 'own-rates of interest' in Chapter 17 of Keynes's *General Theory* (see Keynes, 1936, p. 223n).

In *Prices and Production* Hayek stated the problem in these words:

> In a money economy, the actual or money rate of interest may differ
> from the equilibrium or natural rate, because the demand for and the
> supply of capital do not meet in their natural form but in the form of
> money, the quantity of which available for capital purposes may be
> arbitrarily changed by the banks (Hayek, 1935, p. 23).

Sraffa objects. 'An essential confusion, which appears clearly from
this statement, is the belief that the divergence of rates is a characteristic
of a money economy.' He continues:

> If money did not exist, and loans were made in terms of all sorts of
> commodities, there would be a single rate which satisfies the
> conditions of equilibrium, but there might be at any one moment as
> many natural rates of interest as there are commodities, though they
> would not be equilibrium rates. The arbitrary action of the banks is
> by no means a necessary condition for the divergence; if loans were
> made in wheat and farmers (or for that matter the weather)
> 'arbitrarily changed' the quantity of wheat produced, the actual rate
> of interest on loans in terms of wheat would diverge from the rate on
> other commodities and there would be no single equilibrium rate
> (Sraffa, 1932a, p. 49).

On the next page he argues that on any forward market the ratio
between forward and spot price implies a rate of interest. He goes
on:

> In equilibrium the spot and forward price coincide, for cotton as for
> any other commodity, and all the 'natural' or commodity rates are
> equal to one another, and to the money rate. But if, for any reason,
> the supply and the demand for a commodity are not in equilibrium
> (i.e. its market price exceeds or falls short of its cost of production),
> its spot and forward prices diverge, and the 'natural' rate of interest
> on that commodity diverges from the 'natural' rates on other
> commodities. Suppose there is a change in the distribution of
> demand between various commodities; immediately some will rise
> in price, and others will fall, the market will expect that, after a
> certain time, the supply of the former will increase, and the supply of
> the latter fall, and accordingly the forward price, for the date on
> which equilibrium is expected to be restored, will be below the spot

price in the case of the former and above it in the case of the latter; in other words, the rate of interest in the former will be higher than on the latter. It is only one step to pass from this to the case of a non-money economy (p. 50).

Sraffa then shows the relevance of this argument to industrial fluctuations of any kind.

It will be noticed that, under free competiton, this divergence of rates is as essential to the effecting of the transition as is the divergence of prices from the costs of production; it is, in fact, another aspect of the same thing.

He concludes: 'This applies as much to an increase of saving, which Dr. Hayek regards as equivalent to a shift in demand from consumers' to producers' goods, as to changes in the demand for or the supply of any other commodities' (ibid.).

In this argument four points call for our special attention. Firstly, we have here, in a few lines, a succinct sketch of the whole of classical theory and its *modus operandi*, with particular regard to the relationship between long-run equilibrium price, determined by cost of production, and market prices determined by supply and demand.

Secondly, this complex of relationships is given expression in a context of spot and forward markets. Forward prices, while evidently determined by expectations, are always nearer to equilibrium prices than are spot prices, though it is not suggested that they ever coincide. As forward markets without expectations are hardly conceivable, expectations are introduced, albeit in somewhat attenuated form: they are always orientated to equilibrium price. This raises a number of questions we shall have to return to later on.

Thirdly, the role of demand in classical theory is made articulate in a manner that serves the clarification of some baffling questions. Changes in demand affect market prices immediately, but they affect output quantities, and not equilibrium prices, in the long run.

Fourthly, the discussion explicitly concerns the relations between market prices and equilibrium price in the market for one commodity. Relationships between markets for different commodities are not discussed. This also is a matter requiring further discussion.

Hayek feels that in replying to Sraffa on this point (the natural rate of interest) he can deal with it much more briefly than on malinvestment 'since his confusion here must have been obvious to most readers. Mr.

Sraffa denies that the possibility of a divergence between the equilibrium rate of interest and the actual rate is a peculiar characteristic of a money economy' (Hayek, 1932, p. 245).

To Sraffa's passage, quoted above, on what would happen if money did not exist and loans were made in terms of commodities, Hayek's reply is

> I think it would be truer to say that, in this situation, there would be *no single rate* which, applied to all commodities, would satisfy the conditions of equilibrium rates, but there might, at any moment, be as many 'natural' rates of interest as there are commodities, *all* of which would be *equilibrium rates*; and which would all be the combined result of the factors affecting the present and future supply of the individual commodities, and of the factors usually regarded as determining the rate of interest (ibid.) (emphasis in original).

Hayek continues: 'The inter-relation between these different rates of interest is far too complicated to allow of detailed discussion within the compass of this reply.'

One thing is clear: when Hayek and Sraffa use the word 'equilibrium' they use it to denote quite different things. For Hayek it means market-clearing demand-and-supply equilibrium, for Sraffa long-run cost-of-production equilibrium. Neither is ready to consider other kinds of equilibrium, for example, an inter-market equilibrium involving equality of interest rates in various commodity markets.

What is much less clear to us is to what extent Hayek was aware that by admitting that there might be *no single rate* he was making a fatal concession to his opponent. If there is a multitude of commodity rates, it is evidently possible for the money rate of interest to be lower than some but higher than others. What, then, becomes of monetary equilibrium?

Perhaps all Hayek meant to say was that no pattern of divergence of interest rates, whatever it be, would ever last long enough for it to have any permanent effect on capital investment. Perhaps this is what the emphasis on 'the factors usually regarded as determining the rate of interest' is meant to imply. As it was, Sraffa was able to end his *Rejoinder* to Hayek's *Reply* with a scoffing phrase:

> Dr. Hayek now acknowledges the multiplicity of the 'natural' rates, but he has nothing more to say on this specific point than that they 'all would be equilibrium rates'. The only meaning (if it be a meaning) I

can attach to this is that his maxim of policy now requires that the money rate should be equal to all these divergent natural rates (Sraffa, 1932b, p. 257).

It is not difficult, however to, close this particular breach in the Austrian rampart. In a barter economy with free competiton commodity arbitrage would tend to establish an overall equilibrium rate of interest. Otherwise, if the wheat rate were the highest and the barley rate the lowest of interest rates, it would become profitable to borrow in barley and lend in wheat. Inter-market arbitrage will tend to establish an overall equilibrium in the loan market such that, in terms of a third commodity serving as *numéraire*, say steel, it is no more profitable to lend in wheat than in barley. This does not mean that actual own-rates must all be equal, but that their disparities are exactly offset by disparities between forward prices. The case is exactly parallel to the way in which international arbitrage produces equilibrium in the international money market, where differences in local interest rates are offset by disparities in forward rates. In overall equilibrium it must be as impossible to make gains by 'switching' commodities as currencies.[6]

This overall equilibrium of interest rates constitutes a third type of equilibrium which is neither Sraffa's nor Hayek's. It need have nothing to do with costs of production, but neither is it entailed by the equality of demand and supply in commodity markets. It requires a vigilant and efficient arbitrage acting between markets, a special type of entrepreneurial action and institutions appropriate to it. What Hayek should have said is not that there might be as many rates of interest as there are commodities *all* of which would be equilibrium rates, but that only *some of them* would be. While overall equilibrium requires equality of demand and supply in each single market, the latter is not a sufficient condition of the former.

6. Expectations Emasculated

At the beginning of this paper we said that in 1932 only the more perceptive sensed that they were witnessing a clash of irreconcilable views of the world. Half a century later, we know much more and can assign to this dispute its place in the history of economic ideas.

These, then, were the opening shots of the neo-Ricardian counter-revolution of our days. Its aim, as we said, is to undo the work of the subjective revolution of the 1870s. Austrian economics is the most consistent form of subjectivism among the schools of economic thought today. So, naturally, Austrian economics is under fire.

We learnt that our two authors have entirely different notions of equilibrium. These are naturally related to their attitudes to subjectivism. For Hayek equilibrium is an ever-present force. Equilibrium prices are primarily governed by demand. The proportions of capital and consumer goods in the gross national product are determined by the relative preferences of saver-consumers. It takes the arbitrary action of the banks to tamper with an otherwise firmly entrenched equilibrium.

For Sraffa real-world market prices are determined by supply and demand. But behind them, as a centre of gravity, there lies the equilibrium position. Equilibrium prices are determined by the objective, partly technical, conditions of production and distribution, while demand determines equilibrium quantities of goods produced. Sraffa has no need to assume interference by banks in order to explain disequilibria. To him they are an everyday occurrence.

Every counter-revolution has to incorporate a few of the achievements of the revolution it is directed against, but then must neutralise them in order to prevent them from affecting vital organs of the body politic. The same is the case with the neo-Ricardian counter-revolution. It has found a new role for demand, which once had a place of pre-eminence in the subjective revolution, in the determination of market price and equilibrium output. But its exponents resolutely refuse to ask any questions about what lies behind demand. The acts of human minds, the delineation of purpose, the making and carrying out of plans, which shape and impart meaning to demand, are all completely ignored. So the counter-revolutionaries have contrived to incorporate in their doctrine one of the achievements of subjectivism, albeit in a suitably emasculated form. It can do them no harm.

It seems that Sraffa is making an attempt to deal in somewhat similar fashion with expectations, the introduction of which into economic theory was another great achievement of subjectivism. In the passage quoted above from Sraffa (1932a, p. 50) we are told that in the case of a shift in demand among commodities 'immediately some will rise in price, and others will fall; the market will expect that, after a certain time, the supply of the former will increase, and the supply of the latter fall, and accordingly the forward price, for the date on which equilibrium is expected to be restored, will be below the spot price in the case of the former and above it in the case of the latter'. What is

240   *Austrian Economics under Fire*

introduced here is a 'market expectation' orientated to an equilibrium price known presumably to at least a majority of traders. What lies behind it, the configuration of divergent expectations of bulls and bears, without which trade in forward markets cannot exist, is ignored. By giving exclusive emphasis to expectations 'for the date on which equilibrium is expected to be restored' expectations are introduced into the argument in emasculated form. In an uncertain world no equilibrium position can be known with certainty.

This attenuation of expectations is a great pity. For Sraffa's argument, when slightly redesigned, lends itself to a subjectivist reinterpretation of the setting in which interest rates are determined.

A rate of interest requires a loan contract. A loan contract involves a combination of a spot and a forward transaction: A lends to B, B promises to return the amount lent at a later date to A. Such transactions become explicit in spot and forward markets. No forward market can operate without the divergent expectations of bulls and bears which every day give it its concrete shape. The forward price reflects a balance of bullish and bearish expectations. Daily fluctuations in it primarily reflect changes in the strength and determination of the two market parties. Hence changing expectations must affect interest rates via forward prices. In this way a gun originally designed to fire on the citadel of Austrian economics may be turned into a weapon in its defence. Why it was not done in the 1930s is a tale to be told another day.

The duel we have described did the reputation of Austrian economics a good deal of harm. Hayek's authority as an economic thinker of the first rank had been challenged with some vehemence in the august pages of the *Economic Journal*. Nobody knew what to make of it. Some of Hayek's recently gained supporters began to hesitate. When, four years later, the Keynesian revolution broke out, its assault forces encountered not a phalanx, but divided ranks.

Notes

1. At home, in Vienna, Illy and Mayer meanwhile emphasised what separated Austrian economic thought from that of the School of Lausanne, from Walras and Pareto. Their thesis that equilibrium theory, since it is unable to explain how prices are actually formed in markets, can tell us nothing about economic processes, has today a strikingly modern ring. It is to be hoped that in the Austrian revival of our days their work, today almost forgotten, will find the attention it deserves. See Illy (1948), and Mayer (1932) and also now the reprint of Schönfeld-Illy (1924).

2. In his *Reply*, Hayek wrote: 'I have been assuming that the body of existing pure

economic theory demonstrates that, so long as we neglect monetary factors, there is an inherent tendency towards an equilibrium of the economic system' (1932, p. 238).

As Hicks says of Hayek, 'He took his model very "pure": much purer than Wicksell himself had been accustomed to take it. Prices (all prices) are perfectly flexible, adjusting instantaneously, or as nearly as matters' (Hicks, 1967, p. 205–6).

3. We ignore here a couple of pages contributing to a symposium on 'Increasing Returns and the Representative Firm', in *Economic Journal, 40*, pp. 89–92 (March 1930).

4. For his later view see Sraffa (1960, p. 38).

5. Sraffa never was a Keynesian, nor could he be. We now have Professor Joan Robinson's testimony: 'Looking back now, I see that in the tumultuous years when Keynes' *General Theory* was being written, Piero never really quite knew what it was that we were going on about' (Robinson, 1979, p. 1).

One may regard long-run equilibrium as the centre of the economic system. Or one may hold that 'in the long run we are all dead'. One cannot hold both views simultaneously.

One of several misfortunes suffered by Austrian economics in the 1930s was that it came under fire from both sides at about the same time.

6. See also Lachmann (1956, pp. 75–6) and Lerner (1953, pp. 361–78).

Bibliography

Garegnani, P. (1976). 'On a Change in the Notion of Equilibrium in Recent Work on Value and Distribution' in Murray Brown *et al.* (eds), *Essays in Modern Capital Theory*, Amsterdam: North-Hollange.

Hayek F.A. von (1932). 'Money and Capital: A Reply to Mr. Sraffa', *Economic Journal, 42*, pp. 237–49.

Hayek, F.A. von (1935). *Prices and Production*, 2nd edn, London: Routledge.

Hicks, J. (1967). *Critical Essays in Monetary Theory*, Oxford: Oxford University Press.

Hicks, J. (1974). *The Crisis in Keynesian Economics*, Oxford: Blackwell.

Illy, L. (1948). *Das Gesetz des Grenznutzens*, Vienna: Springer. See also Schönfeld-Illy.

Keynes, J.M. (1930). *A Treatise on Money*, 2 vols, London: Macmillan.

Keynes, J.M. (1935). *The General Theory of Employment, Interest and Money*, London: Macmillan.

Lachmann, L.M. (1956). *Capital and its Structure*, London: London School of Economics, 2nd ed., Kansas City: Sheed Andrews and McMeel, 1977.

Lerner, A.P. (1953). *Essays in Economic Analysis*, London: Macmillan.

Levine, D.P. (1980). 'Aspects of the Classical Theory of Markets', *Australian Economic Papers*, June.

Mayer, H. (1932). *Der Erkenntniswert der funktionellen Preistheorien*, Vienna: Springer.

Milgate, M. (1979). 'On the Origin of the Notion of "Intertemporal Equilibrium" ', *Economica*, February, *46*.

Robinson, J. (1979). 'Misunderstandings in the Theory of Production', *Greek Economic Review*, August.

Schönfeld-Illy, L. (1924). *Grenznutzen und Wirtschaftsrechnung*, Vienna, repr. Munich: Philosophia, 1983.

Sraffa, P. (1926). 'The Laws of Returns under Competitive Conditions', *Economic Journal, 36*, pp. 535–50.

Sraffa, P. (1932a). 'Dr. Hayek on Money and Capital', *Economic Journal, 42*, pp. 42–53.

Sraffa, P. (1932b). 'A Rejoinder', *Economic Journal, 42*, pp. 249–51.
Sraffa, P. (1960).   *Production of Commodities by Means of Commodities. Prelude to a Critique of Economic Theory*, Cambridge: Cambridge University Press.

NOTES ON CONTRIBUTORS

Dr Barry Smith is a lecturer in the Department of Philosophy at the University of Manchester.

Dr Wolfgang Grassl is Secretary-General of the Austrian Association of Hoteliers, Vienna.

Dr Peter M. Simons is a lecturer in the Institut für Philosophie of the Universität Salzburg.

Dr Reinhard Fabian is a research fellow at the Forschungsstelle und Dokumentationszentrum für österreichische Philosophie, Graz.

Professor J.C. Nyíri is head of the Department of the History of Philosophy at the University of Budapest.

Professor Roderick M. Chisholm is a professor in the Department of Philosophy at Brown University, Providence, Rhode Island and also in the University of Graz.

Professor Rudolf Haller is head of the Department of Philosophy and director of the Forschungsstelle und Dokumentationszentrum für österreichische Philosophie, Graz.

Jeremy Shearmur is Director of Studies in the Centre for Policy Studies, London.

Ludwig M. Lachmann is a professor emeritus at the University of the Witwatersrand and a visiting professor at New York University.

INDEX

244